Tuned Out

Tuned Out

Why Americans Under 40 Don't Follow the News

DAVID T. Z. MINDICH

New York   Oxford
OXFORD UNIVERSITY PRESS
2005

Oxford University Press

Oxford   New York
Auckland   Bangkok   Buenos Aires   Cape Town   Chennai
Dar es Salaam   Delhi   Hong Kong   Istanbul   Karachi   Kolkata
Kuala Lumpur   Madrid   Melbourne   Mexico City   Mumbai   Nairobi
São Paulo   Shanghai   Taipei   Tokyo   Toronto

Copyright © 2005 by Oxford University Press, Inc.

Published by Oxford University Press, Inc.
198 Madison Avenue, New York, New York, 10016
www.oup.com

Oxford is a registered trademark of Oxford University Press

Library of Congress Cataloging-in-Publication Data
Mindich, David T. Z., 1963–
    Tuned out : why Americans under 40 don't follow the news / David T. Z. Mindich
        p. cm.
    Includes bibliographical references and index.
    ISBN-13 978-0-19-516141-0
    ISBN-10 0-19-516140-8 / 0-19-516141-6 (pbk)
    1. Press—Influence. 2. Newspaper reading. 3. Broadcast journalism. 4. Television and
reading—United States. 5. Mass media and youth. 6. Youth—Books and reading. I. Title.

PN4731.M49 2004
302.23'083—dc22   2004046938

Printing number: 9 8 7 6 5 4 3 2

Printed in the United States of America
on acid-free paper

To my parents, Leonard Mindich and Margot Zucker Mindich,
who followed the news and walked in the 1965 Selma-to-Montgomery protest.
And to my brothers, Jeremy Mindich and Dan Mindich,
who attended in utero but would have also walked willingly.

Contents

Preface   ix

1. A Generational Shift   1

2. How Tuned Out Are They?   18

3. Talking with Young People I: Striptease News and the Shifting Balance Between Need and Want   34

4. Talking with Young People II: Who Follows the News and Why   60

5. Television, the Internet, and the Eclipse of the Local   77

6. The Decline of General News and the Deliberative Body   95

7. Conclusion: How to Tune Back In   112

Appendix A: People Surveyed or Interviewed for This Project, 2001–2003   128

Appendix B: Format of the Standard Interview   130

Appendix C: Responses to Questions 11–21   132

Bibliography   134
Notes   143
Index   163

Preface

The thesis of this book, that young people have largely abandoned traditional news, was not one that I pursued. Instead, it came to me, like a news flash, as I was teaching a class one afternoon in January 2001. On that day, the first of the semester in Media Law and Ethics, I distributed an informal quiz to test students' background knowledge of the law. I had reason for optimism. These particular students were among the best and brightest in a top department in a selective college. And it was an excellent time to ask students about politics and the law: The Supreme Court had just halted the 2000 presidential election and the hearings to confirm John Ashcroft as attorney general were well underway.

The results were startling. Of 23 students, 18 could not identify even one Supreme Court justice. Only one could name the attorney general nominee. Most revealing of all, four wrote that the attorney general nominee was Colin Powell; it is likely they homed in on the word "general," reflecting a total ignorance of what an attorney general is or does. Later, as I conducted interviews with young people across the country—from New Orleans to Boston to Kansas City to Los Angeles to Burlington—I discovered that this first group of students was not less informed than their peers; in fact, they were more tuned in than most.

Young people have always had a lot on their mind that has nothing to do with news. But in the 1950s and 1960s, young people were *nearly* as informed about news and politics as their elders were. This has changed dramatically. This book will show that the average 20-something is getting far less news from newspapers, television, radio, and, yes, even the Internet, than you could ever imagine. In addition, more 30-somethings are getting less news than ever before, too. The decline in news consumption, which has taken place over the past four decades, has produced two generations of young adults who, for the most part, have barely an outline of what they need to make an informed decision in the voting booth.

The decline in news consumption begs a number of interesting questions. What makes some young people tune out and some tune in? How has the balance between entertainment and news shifted over time? What are young people consuming instead of news and what drives their decisions about what to consume? What does the decline do to our local communities? And what does it do to democracy itself? Finally, when faced with this great stampede away from an informed citizenry, what do we do about it? The book offers real answers to these questions and ends with real solutions to these problems.

I started the research for this book completely unaware of the problem's complexity, causes, and consequences. But as I traveled the country interviewing young people, I made two great discoveries along the way. First, that most of the people I met were just as curious (and puzzled) as I was about why their peers don't follow the news. Many believed (erroneously, you will see) that young people were always as averse to news as they are now. Many also believed that somehow young people were consuming lots of news via television (actually, the average viewer age at CNN is around 60).[1] And many believed that young people were gobbling up Internet news (in a recent poll, only 11% of young people cite the Internet as a major source of news).[2] The second thing I learned was that, despite their disengagement with news, young people are as thoughtful and passionate and self-reflective as they have ever been, ready to interact with news if we just provide the right conditions for them to do so. This is very important to know. After all, there is no democracy without an informed citizenry, and the future of our democracy depends on young people tuning back in.

I could not have written this book without the help and guidance of friends and strangers. It was Dianne Lynch, an extraordinary professor and scholar at Saint Michael's College, who convinced me that I should write a book about the topic I could not stop talking about—why young people were not following the news. Other colleagues, Traci Griffith, Jon Hyde, Kimberly Sultze, Paul Beique, Kevin Kelley, and Mike Donoghue offered advice and help, too. I am indebted to Saint Michael's College, especially Marc vanderHeyden, Jan Sheeran, and John Kenney, for institutional support, including travel grants and a yearlong sabbatical. And thanks to the Saint Michael's College library staff.

A number of students read sections of the manuscript, including Alison Lima, Jessica M. McEachern, Adrienne Lanchantin, Gerd Stodiek, Matt Leon, and Matthew Powers. Jennifer Plebani Lussier, a graduate student, checked (and augmented) my statistical analysis.

I am also grateful to the editors and reviewers at Oxford University Press: Peter Labella and Sean Mahoney, whose enthusiasm, superb editing, and focusing deadlines brought the project to fruition; Niko Pfund, who handled the initial proposal; and the anonymous reviewers, who offered support and advice.

Talking to young people was a central part of the book. A number of people helped me set up the interviews, including Carrie Towns, Jim Rowland, George McCleary, Carol Holstead, and Kanon Cozad in Kansas and Missouri; Michael Socolow and Kristine Asselin in Massachusetts; Jon Donley and John Fitzmorris in Louisiana; Anne Judson Yeager, Joanna Colbert, and Adam Lapidus in California; and Anne Judson, Joel Senesac, Robert LaRoche, Mike Long, and Jim Price in Vermont.

Scholars and friends from around the country helped along the way, including David Abrahamson, Dane S. Claussen, Beth Mintz, Nick Danigelis, Carolyn Kitch, Mitchell Stephens, and Carl Prince. Thank you, too, to fellow alumni from Cable News Network (CNN), especially Don Ennis and Kate Skattebol. Friends also helped me develop ideas, including Joe Mardin, Marco Joachim, Saul Kravec, Marc Lazar, Michael Gottesegen, Vicki Brower, Milton Moses Ginsberg, George Kirschner, and Gerald Orange.

Family members gave me feedback on my writing and ideas: Jeanne Richmond, Margot Zucker Mindich, Leonard Mindich, Jeremy Mindich, and Dan Mindich. I also got a lot of help from my wife, Barbara Richmond, and our children, Talia and Isaiah. But really what I need to thank them for goes way beyond this book.

Tuned Out

CHAPTER 1

A Generational Shift

It was a great national contest that will be immediately recognizable to you. Two men were vying for one prize. Although tens of millions of ballots were cast, the margin separating the two was less than 1 percent of the total. The announcer ticked off the state-by-state tallies as the two candidates, both Southerners, watched closely. One candidate had won Ohio and New York. The other had won a great bounty: Florida. As the night wore on, reporters came to us live from massive placard-waving rallies in the candidates' hometowns. Minutes later, the network was ready to make its announcement, one that would answer the question on the minds of millions.

Let's keep the announcement on hold for a few seconds. Although no one should be reduced to a demographic, if you are above the age of 40, chances are excellent that you recognize the above scenario as belonging to the contest between George W. Bush and Al Gore. If you are younger than 40, however, you might very well be thinking about an entirely different contest. For you, the denouement of the above contest may have come in the form of an announcement by the Fox network's Ryan Seacrest: "The winner of American Idol 2003 is Ruben Studdard."[1]

The similarities between *American Idol*, a "reality" talent show in which audience members vote for the best singers, and the contest involving Bush and Gore are fun to note: the close vote, the state-by-state tallies, the rallies in Southern hometowns, and even a vote tally dispute about the margin of victory.[2] We Americans have always been good at entertaining ourselves and

1

if the numbers are to be believed, up to 40 million people tuned in to watch the *American Idol* finale in May 2003.[3] There's nothing wrong with a little low-calorie escapism.

But if we go further in the comparison between *American Idol* and Bush-Gore, the picture is less amusing. Forty million people watched *American Idol*'s conclusion, but only 37 million watched the second debate between Bush and Gore. When we consider young people separately, this gap is widened. The debates drew a much older crowd, with a lot of young Americans tuning out.[4] America's younger citizens were far less invested in the presidential debates and far more invested in *American Idol*. Twenty-four million votes were cast, mainly by young people, for contestants Ruben Studdard or Clay Aiken. Although some of these votes were by minors, somewhat limiting a comparison here—it is nevertheless sobering to remember that only 4 million (16.6%) of 18 to 24-year-olds voted in the 1998 midterm elections. The placard-waving rallies of the *American Idol* show were filled with exuberant young people, clapping and yelling enthusiastically. Even civic groups came out: "YMCA for Clay," read one sign in a rally for Clay Aiken in Raleigh, North Carolina. The "reporter" for Fox said there were "8,700 screaming fans" at the rally. This show of civic pride and organization is in direct contrast to the national trend, especially among young people, of declining civic involvement and declining political enthusiasm.

And then there was the general knowledge about the "candidates." While many *American Idol* fans could name all of the top ten contestants, few young people even knew the names of more than one or two of the presidential primary candidates in 2000 and fewer still knew the issues. In 2000, one poll asked which presidential primary candidate was the sponsor of campaign finance reform in congress. Only 4 percent of 18- to 24-year-olds knew it was John McCain.[5] And while most young people seemed to know the names of the judges of *American Idol*—Simon Cowell, Paula Abdul, and Randy Jackson—few knew the names of any of the Supreme Court justices who decided the election for Bush in 2000.*

This brings us to the thesis of this book, that across America, young people have abandoned traditional news. By "traditional" I mean the general interest and political news you get from newspapers, magazines, television, and

---

*A poll found that three times as many Americans could name three of the Three Stooges (59%) as could name three of the nine Supreme Court justices (17%). As you will see, the rate among young people who knew Supreme Court justices may be substantially lower. Joan Biskupic, "Has the Court Lost Its Appeal? In Poll, 59% Can Name 3 'Stooges,' 17% Can Name 3 Justices," *Washington Post*, 12 October 1995.

A hometown rally for American Idol *"candidate" Clay Aiken, May 21, 2003.*   Reproduced by permission of Fremantle Media North America/19 Television.

the Web. Older Americans are still reading newspapers and have been doing it all their lives. But the generational shift is severe: While more than 70 percent of older Americans read a newspaper every day, a habit they picked up in their youth, less than 20 percent of young Americans do so now.[6] Further, data show that the newspaper habit is not one that increases much with age. That is, you typically pick up the habit in your twenties, or you never do. It used to be that most 25-year-olds, and certainly 35-year-olds, followed the news. But for the past few decades, most have not. Eighty percent of young people don't read the newspaper today, and there is no evidence that they will read 20 years from now, either.

It would be less troubling if the 80 percent of young people who do not read newspapers every day watched TV news or logged on to news Web sites. Most don't. The average viewer age of prime-time entertainment is 42-years-old, which is, as one would expect, roughly the median age of the population as a whole. At CNN, which recently changed its format to attract younger viewers, the average age ranges from 59 to 64.[7] At the broadcast networks, the median viewer age for the evening news has been climbing steadily—from the low 50s in 1991 to 60 today.[8] As Dan Rather ages, so do his viewers; the ads during his show hawk denture cleaners, arthritis medicine, Viagra, and Depends. And because young people are not watching, they are not courted. As MTV's Tabitha Soren once said, "It's a Catch-22. Why cover them if they don't watch you? But why should they watch you if you don't cover them?"[9] Unless something breaks this cycle, the death of aging news consumers will mark a profound change in the social and political landscape of America's future.

It would be easy to dismiss the decline in newspaper readership and television news viewership among young people by saying that they get their news, somehow, via the Internet and other sources. As I will show later, however, most young people use the Internet for everything *but* news. That the Internet has not closed the news gap between young and old is apparent: While young Americans in past decades knew as much as their elders on a range of topics, this is no longer the case.[10] Studies over the last decade have found that Americans over 50 are nearly twice as likely to follow particular domestic and political news stories as those under 30.[11]

Across the news industry, executives fret over the future of news and its declining audience. But the United States is facing a crisis that extends far beyond the news industry. While math and reading skills of young Americans remain relatively stable, their average political awareness has become remarkably shallow. While the Internet has allowed many to develop expertise in their own narrow interests, fewer are willing or able to develop a generalist's gaze. Knowledge of sports and celebrities continues to rise, but local and national political literacy has plummeted.

What are the political, journalistic, and social consequences of a new generation of young Americans with little interest in traditional news? The existing answers have been less than revealing. The newspaper industry sees the problem in terms of consumers, not citizens, and is at sea as to how to recapture market share.[12] Some conservative critics of education point to the failures of liberal education, particularly multiculturalism.[13] But these conservatives, led by William Bennett, offer little beyond "values," cultural literacy, and other generalities.[14] No one has clarified the crisis, much less proposed solutions to it. Through research, analysis, and interviews with journalists and young adults, this book charts the consequences of and proposes solutions to the decline of news in America.

A recent poll showed that 75 percent of young people trusted that the U.S. military would do "the right thing," up from around 20 percent in 1975. At the same time, trust in the media has declined to 36 percent from a high of 54 percent in 1989.[15] While trust in the government has its place—and a certain amount is necessary—how can we hold our leaders accountable when we don't trust the watchdogs? We can accept faith when it is informed by facts. We can accept *American Idol* if it doesn't totally eclipse news knowledge. But America is facing the greatest exodus of informed citizenship in its history.

Not the Sole Fault of "Media" or Young People

Although I will outline how the rise of certain media, especially entertainment on television, correlates with a decline in news consumption, this book is not a diatribe against the media, in part because history tells us that those who have attacked the media have often been wrong. For example, Socrates said that introducing writing into the academy would allow students to "merely appear to be wise instead of really being so."[16] Socrates advocated for a purely oral culture, even as Plato set down Socrates' words for eternity. But the otherwise great Socrates failed to understand the many benefits of writing to the arts and sciences and he was plainly wrong; this book tries to avoid similar statements about other media systems.

Nor does this book blame young people for the problems outlined herein. As I will show, the decline in news consumption began in the 1960s as the first generation born with television was coming of age. In other words, the 20-year-olds of today are not the first to abandon the news; it was their parents. Nor does this book wax nostalgic for a rosy and informed past: In the 1950s and 1960s, at the height of the Cold War, a poll revealed that only 55 percent of Americans knew that East Germany was a communist country. Less than half knew that the Soviet Union was not part of NATO.[17] I do not find students to be less thoughtful or literate than they have ever been. When I told a senior professor at a large university about this project, he said the decline in news consumption was because the kids of today are illiterate and in a near-vegetative state. "I'm tired of watering the vegetables every day," he told me as he was getting ready to retire. This view couldn't be farther from my own. I am constantly impressed with the thoughtfulness and intelligence of young people. And while SAT scores have declined a bit in the last 40 years, elements of literacy are most certainly on an upswing as more young Americans begin to replace televisions and telephones with reading and typing on the Internet.[18]

Why

Why have most younger Americans stopped following the news? This, and what to do about the problem, are the central issues of the book. As in any good murder mystery, there are many shady and questionable suspects, each with leaky alibis that may or may not add up.

Complacency

On September 11, 2001, planes struck the World Trade Center and the Pentagon. Within minutes, millions of Americans were watching television, listening to the radio, and logging on to the Internet for news. I went to a classroom and watched with 30 college students as the Pentagon was struck and each Trade Center tower collapsed. The day certainly made clear that young people (and old people, too) will care deeply about some forms of news. Every student in that classroom confronted a grim spectacle: a horrific loss of life; an unfolding national disaster of unknown proportions; the destruction, in real time, of two of the world's tallest buildings; and an attack on the greatest symbol of American military power. After watching the news unfold, hour after hour, I started to question the thesis of this book. Almost on cue, however, a female student leaned over to me and asked, "Who is this Osama bin Laden they keep talking about?" During a news report about the president's movements, she asked, "If something happens to Bush, who becomes president?" Within a month after the terror attacks, radio stations that cater to younger listeners were reporting that ratings had returned to normal. And the gains for broadcast and cable news were short-lived and modest.[19]

E. J. Dionne, Jr., in *Why Americans Hate Politics*, lamented the lack of intelligent political conversation among politicians and among the public. Viewing the debate over the 1991 Gulf War as a rare exception, Dionne asked, "Does it take a war to make us take politics seriously?"[20] Do Americans avoid the news because they feel it doesn't matter? Are we complacent, because as Jefferson said, we are blessed with a large and fertile land, separated by two great oceans, insulated from Europe's "exterminating havoc"?[21] Is it because we are suffering from, in the words of one writer, "hapathy," a combination of happiness and apathy?[22] That would certainly explain why, despite having one of the freest presses in the world, that most Americans cannot name their own congressional representative.[23] The problem with this theory is that the people who have the most reason to be complacent—wealthy, white, educated older men—are the very people who generally consume the most news.[24] In other words, if the comfort that America provides makes people turn off news, why do those who are the most comfortable in America consume the most news?

Perhaps the answer is not complacency but a perceived isolation from the political process. Many of the young nonreaders of news I have spoken with believe that the political process is both morally bankrupt and completely insulated from public pressure. Perhaps political news is only relevant to people who still believe that the political structure is responsive. Thus it may be less the complacency of affluence than the doldrums of despondency that cause citizens to abandon news.

Trust

There has been a steady decline in the public's trust of the media. And there is evidence that this distrust extends to both entertainment and news. Can you blame Americans for not appreciating a distinction? When Disney acquires ABC News and then tells it that bad reports about the parent company are off-limits, when CBS News kills a solid story about big tobacco only days before its own corporate merger, when the *Los Angeles Times* breaks down the inviolate wall between business and editorial, Americans are right to lose respect for the journalistic enterprise. A student of mine once began a sentence: "Journalists like David Letterman . . ." I cringed, but the blame goes at least in part to the corporate forces that weaken the news media's distinct mission.

And yet, good journalism is still practiced every day in the United States and around the world. Despite common complaints among polled nonnews consumers that newspapers are not global enough, not local enough, not relevant enough, and not political enough,[25] a half hour with the *New York Times*, *Washington Post*, or *Wall Street Journal* belies this sentiment, giving a generalist's view of pressing and important news. With intelligent and aggressive reporters stationed at the gates of power around the country and around the world, these newspapers and others like them report, verify, and interpret a wide range of news. Further, they do so in a way that stands apart from political parties. For example, despite critics on the right calling it leftwing, the *New York Times* was consistently critical of Clinton's administration. And the *Times* is eclectic in its editorial page endorsements of Democrats and Republicans. In 2002, for example, it supported the Republican candidate for governor of New York, George Pataki, over his Democratic rival.[26] The same can be true of the *Wall Street Journal*, which leans right on its editorial page but was nonetheless highly critical of the rightwing president George W. Bush. Hearing a perspective apart from the binary partisan options is crucial during times of crisis and change: Watergate, Vietnam, Iran-Contra, the breakup of the Soviet empire, the Gulf War, the widening gap between rich and poor in the 1990s, the impeachment of Clinton, the contested presidential election of 2000, and the aftermath of the September 11 terror attacks. Understanding how the government works and how to hold it accountable are essential ingredients in any democracy. Although citizens should be skeptical consumers of news, to reject all news means to reject the underpinnings of democracy.

The Decline of Social Capital

Robert D. Putnam's 2000 book, *Bowling Alone*, charted the decay of what the author called "social capital," the important resource of public and quasipublic dialogue. For example, Putnam discovered that more people bowl than

ever before, but fewer bowl in leagues; hence, the title of his book. But bowling is just the start. The last half century has seen a decline in membership
in unions, Elks clubs, and PTAs; fewer people give dinner parties, speak in
public, go to church, and attend the theater. The list goes on and on, en-
compassing the whole range of civic activity. Although city dwellers and sub-
urbanites are most affected, even residents of traditionally high civic areas,
like the rural parts of my own state, Vermont, have been hit hard. Putnam
convincingly demonstrated a correlation between the lack of social capital
and news consumption. The same people who join groups and write their
representatives also read newspapers. The same people who have trust in the
system, and their ability to change it, use the news for ammunition. The
same people who distrust each other, drop out of society, and become isolated, find news irrelevant to their lives.

The problem with Putnam's work in this area is that it establishes correlation but not causality. In other words, we do not know whether dropping out
of the once-fertile social fabric of society pushes us to abandon news or if the
reverse is true. For an analysis of this, we would need to move beyond the data
and actually interview young people. This is an aim of this book.

Television, Radio, Air-Conditioning, and Indoor Plumbing

As Putnam and others have shown, the decline of civic involvement runs par-
allel to the rise of television. Television reached a saturation point in the early
1950s. Soon after, news consumption began its steady decline. Putnam shows
a close correlation between those who avoid television with those who have
worked on a community project.[27] As it turns out, TV watching, particularly
entertainment TV, correlates negatively with news consumption. And as the
most time-consuming activity apart from work and sleep, TV watching has an
enormous impact on leisure time; the average household's TV viewing per day
went from four and a half hours in 1950 to six hours in 1975 to more than
seven today.[28]

But as a suspect, television has an alibi. Long before TV, radio, too, had
given people an excuse to stay home. The rise of radio music, for example, co-
incided with the decline of piano lessons and sheet music distribution. Other
technologies affected communities, too. The rise of air-conditioning in the
1940s and 1950s made the living room more comfortable than the stoop or
porch or rooftop. In communities across the United States, indoor plumbing
and electricity have allowed us to stay at home, to avoid the local community,
to feel less connected with the news. Although these trends accelerated during the age of television, they preceded it. The initial wound to news was in-
flicted before television entered the room.

Suburbia

The decline of news also parallels the rise of the suburbs. Why is that so? Perhaps it is the longer commute, typically by car, making reading the paper more difficult. That fact alone could explain the rise of talk radio in the last decades. But that doesn't explain why fewer people read in the New York City subway system. And it doesn't explain another often overlooked fact: While many older commuters listen to news and talk shows in their cars, younger ones increasingly listen to music instead.[29] Perhaps it has less to do with the commute than the unsubstantial community that the suburbs afford. As Lewis Mumford once remarked, "suburbia is a collective effort to lead a private life."[30]

And here we may have come to a common thread in all the suspects. At the end of one Agatha Christie novel (I'll give away the ending, but not the book), detective Poirot discovers that *everyone* did it. Perhaps the common means of assassination by all of the above suspects is that each of the accused attacked not only news, but community, too.

Imagined Communities

Once upon a time, there was an island in the Pacific on which Europeans from three countries lived and worked as friends. It was 1914, and British, French, and German nationals enjoyed their isolation on the island, far from telegraph lines and newsboys. News from Europe would come to the island only intermittently, by ship, in the form of letters, books, and great packages of old newspapers, aged by time and the salty dampness of the journey. One day, a ship brought the news, six weeks old, that Europe was now riven by a Great War. The islanders, who had bonded in their common European heritage, now learned that Germany was the foe of France and Britain. The islanders were now enemies. Moreover, unbeknownst to them, they had been *de jure* enemies for six weeks. This anecdote comes from Walter Lippmann,[31] who used it to discuss the lag between us and events. But the above is also a great illustration of how our allegiances are shaped by both our immediate surroundings and by our media messages. Further, our allegiances shape our sense of community and our place in it.

Study your own allegiances. You may be an American, a Minnesotan, a Mormon, a Yankee fan, or a Democrat. What these categories have in common is that they are all, in some way, a cognitive construction. As Benedict Anderson wrote in his book, *Imagined Communities* (1992), a large community is an imagined one:

> It is *imagined* because the members of even the smallest nation will never know most of their fellow-members, meet them, or even hear of them, yet in

the minds of each lives the image of their communion. . . . In fact, all communities larger than primordial villages of face-to-face contact (and perhaps even these) are imagined.[32]

The lure of an imagined community can be profound. Mitchell Stephens, in *A History of News* (1997), argues that one of the reasons Alexander the Great's kingdom fell quickly after his death was his failure to create a news community to span the empire; instead of creating a cohesive empire, Alexander's heirs set up their own fiefdoms. A few centuries later, Stephens wrote, Rome strengthened its own union by connecting its citizens with news. That all roads led to Rome (and from Rome) meant that news could unite an otherwise disparate people. When Cicero went to Cilicia (Turkey) in 51 B.C. as a proconsul, he grew homesick and repeatedly asked for more news. And while he claimed a preference for senatorial news and a distaste for trifles ("burglaries," "the adjournment of trials," and "gladiatorial pairings"), presumably all types of news helped to keep him from going native because they helped him to imagine himself as a Roman.[33] Stephens speculates that without these connections, Cicero might "have grown more interested in affairs in Cilicia, where his power and prerogatives were so much greater[.]" Unlike Alexander's officers, Stephens wrote, Roman governors "eventually began marching back to—or on—Rome."[34]

If the inhabitants of Lippmann's Pacific island had lived in the satellite age, they could have seen Archduke Ferdinand assassinated, live, on television. Rather than six weeks, it could have taken less than a second for the news of the war to arrive via satellite; within seconds, the German residents of the island could have adjusted their feelings about their French and British neighbors, and vice versa. The presence of modern news systems on Lippmann's island would have quickly altered the imagined community.

Absence of News in Imagined Communities

But the absence of all news would have a profound effect on Lippmann's island, too. Imagine the state of the island if no news at all had leaked in. Slowly but surely the Europeans, or perhaps their children, would have formed alliances or factions based not on pedigree but on proximity and politics. This sloughing of past ties happens all the time. A Republican Party club meeting in Chicago today might involve people of French, British, and German origin, but they would be united by a shared geographic location and a common worldview, based in part on their consumption and interpretation of general news. News can unite people in powerful ways and create powerful imaginary communities. It happened for a short time after September 11, 2001, when a common "American" identity seemed to seduce even the most cynical of citizens.

What would our world look like in the absence of general news? Let's say we are all islands, each man and woman a separate news entity. Let's say we are each interested in news that interests us, consuming not general news, but a type of publication Nicholas Negroponte called "The Daily Me."[35] People have always mixed general news sources (*Time* magazine, for example) with sources that cater to a more specialized interest (think *Golf Digest*, the Food Network, or *Women's Wear Daily*). But let's say the balance between general and specialized news became skewed. How would a media system based on the individual's needs alter what Jürgen Habermas called "the public sphere," that place between the civic society and the State where people come together to constitute themselves as a public?[36] As it turns out, people who choose entertainment over news are less likely to participate in community projects. They are also far more likely to "give the finger" to another driver. And there is evidence that materialism is on the rise as civic involvement declines.[37]

What is the shape of a public sphere driven by private concerns? One doesn't need to use one's imagination to find the consequences. In 1991, the editors and writers of the *Columbus* (Georgia) *Ledger-Enquirer* planned, wrote, and published a series of reports about the city's most important long-term problems. They offered a detailed account of what experts proposed to do about them. The series was cogent, well written, hard-hitting, and intelligent. It was printed. But nothing happened. In other words, the newspaper's good journalism was faced with a growing problem—a journalist's equivalent of throwing a party and having no one show up. The newspaper then tried to create a viable public by holding its own meetings and forums. Some media experts, the most thoughtful of whom is Jay Rosen, have argued that this medicine, now called "public journalism," is less dangerous than the malady of civic illness.[38] But this is strong medicine indeed.

In late 2001, a poll by the Pew Research Center for the People & the Press found that only 19 percent of Americans correctly understood that the United States ran a budget surplus in the last years of Bill Clinton's administration and in the first year of George W. Bush's. Later, in 2003, when Democratic and Republican lawmakers debated the feasibility and desirability of tax cuts (skewed heavily toward the wealthy), government spending, and an expensive military action in Iraq; they did so with an eye to the 2004 general elections. If 81 percent of the American public did not even have a basic outline of their economy, how could the public be a useful guide? If the political parties make mistakes, how will this kind of electorate hold them accountable on election day?

The answer is that, increasingly, they do not. The electorate is uninformed and fragmented, with less opportunity to inform one another. Family dinners in the 1940s became TV dinners in the 1970s. And increasingly, the many TV screens in the home provide a separate rhythm for isolated meals: In 1970, 6 percent of all sixth graders had TVs in their rooms; today 77 percent do.[39] And everyone's watching something different: In 1975, around half of all Americans watched network news every night; today only a quarter of us do.[40] We have become more balkanized and apolitical and our water cooler conversations increasingly revolve around our narrowly defined selves. Our citizens are uninformed about general news and deprived of the means to discuss their opinions of it with friends, family, and coworkers.

Book Outline

Chapter 2: How Tuned Out Are They?

We must guard against nostalgia. There was never a time in American history when every voter paid attention. We must also acknowledge that while most young Americans are tuned out, older Americans are not exactly tuned in: In January 2000, during the presidential primaries, only a fraction of Americans of any age could identify more than one candidate in each party among the crowded race. Nevertheless, the polling data and anecdotal reports are unequivocal: When young people are asked about current events, particularly political affairs, they are *far* less likely to know the facts than their elders are— and further, young people are far less likely to care about their lack of knowledge. This runs alongside a declining interest among young people in the consumption of the various news media, from newspapers to radio to television. While the Internet remains the exception to this general decline, even this medium has failed to close the gap between generations. I have analyzed data from the General Social Survey, a massive database of social habits put out by Roper; polls from the Pew Research Center for the People & the Press; and other data which Robert Putnam and other researchers of this trend have used. Chapter 2, by using polling data and other broad measures, shows the depth of the generational divide.

Chapters 3 and 4: Talking with Young People

In trying to determine how people use the Internet, Dhavan Shah suggested that scholars "check what individuals do with this new medium, not simply what it does to them."[41] This is the aim of chapters 3 and 4—to discover, through interviews with young people, the nature of their news consumption or lack thereof. I have interviewed young people who are politically active, and college students of all political stripes. I have visited Brandeis University to investigate news habits of students in a program that provides them with free newspapers. I have also analyzed the news habits of college students in Boston, Burlington, and Los Angeles; bankers in Kansas City; and actors in Los Angeles. Finally, I have spoken with the youngest of news consumers, 10- to 18-years-old, in areas as diverse as New Orleans and Colchester, Vermont, to get an idea of how they have come of age with the new computer medium. At the start of the nineteenth century, de Tocqueville was the first to travel around America to chronicle its robust journalism and civic life. At the start of the twenty-first century, I have embarked on a similar (but admittedly much more modest) exploration of the dearth of this kind of engagement. In this journey, I have discovered not only what kind of information young people avoid, but also what they embrace. It will be these issues that will shape America for generations to come.

With the possible exception of diarists, nearly all writers write for an audience. The extent to which they pander to their audience's tastes is one of the things that defines their style. Chapter 3 explores this continuum, looking at the desire to inform against the desire to entertain. Through an exploration of

"Didn't this use to be the time slot for his news briefings?"

the past and present forces driving the media markets in the United States, we can see a marked shift away from journalism that fills the public's needs to one that fills its desires. In 1983, Tom Brokaw only had Dan Rather and Peter Jennings to compete with. In his words, he "didn't have to worry about people going 'click.'"[42] Brokaw's successor, Brian Williams, will contend with CNN, Fox News, MTV, ESPN, the Cartoon Network, the Playboy Channel, the Food Network, Rush Limbaugh, and Nakednews.com, among others. Chapter 3 explores what the entertainment does to young people.

Chapter 4 continues the discussion with young people by evaluating their news habits. To what extent are the media choices of young people influenced by workplace demands, conversational norms, childhood education, and new technology? Young people themselves provide some of the best answers.

Chapter 5: Television, the Internet, and the Eclipse of the Local

The world is much smaller now. In 1930, a phone call from the United States to London cost $300 in today's dollars; today, we can "chat" for free over the Internet with Australian Christians and Iranian Shiites. Indeed, we can even find Australian Shiites and Iranian Christians. As Thomas Friedman reminds us, the Berlin Wall fell not just in Berlin, but everywhere. The world's old metaphor, the Wall, has been replaced by a newer one—the Web.[43] Satellites let us view, in a flash, the world's most beautiful women, the world's biggest floods, the world's strangest sights.

But what does the faraway signal do to the nearby? As Mitchell Stephens has said, we are increasingly more likely to know what the president had for dinner last night and increasingly less likely to learn why the ambulance pulled in to the house down the street.[44] The distant can usurp the nearby.

Chapter 5 looks at how the national and international entertainment systems affect community. Here we are informed by Thomas Bender's distinction, borrowed from a German scholar, between community and society. In a community, people "remain essentially united in spite of all separating factors," whereas in society "they are essentially separated in spite of all uniting factors."[45] What are the local political consequences to a community bewitched by TV and the 'Net? If we accept Lewis Friedland's assertion that "place . . . not technology, is the critical element in civic and democratic participation,"[46] what does America look like when the local community is so compromised? Finally, some scholars have argued that Internet communities, with their "low barriers"[47] to entry and exit, discourage accommodation and compromise, necessary in any bricks-and-mortar community. How well do virtual communities serve as a model for the long-term commitment of information and perspiration required of palpable democracies?

Chapter 6: The Decline of General News and the Deliberative Body

Journalism's primary goals may be information, verification, and analysis,[48] but its most important by-product may be democracy itself. One of the ways journalism promotes democracy is by engendering an awareness of shared interests. If a citizen understands his or her thread in society's fabric, that citizen will be more likely to see common goals and understand the need for reciprocity, a notion reflected in Yogi Berra's famous phrase, " If you don't go to somebody's funeral, they won't come to yours."

But journalists can only promote democracy and reciprocity if their rights to know and report are supported in the courts: the state courts, the federal courts, and the court of public opinion. Against the tenuous right to know come competing forces. As cable TV and the Internet provide more opportunities to pursue personalized paths, we see the promotion of another potent right, the right of individual choice. As John Perry Barlow wrote in his *Declaration of Independence of Cyberspace* (1999), "leave us alone."[49] The right to privacy goes back at least to Louis D. Brandeis's famous Supreme Court dissent of 1928 in which he coined the phrase, "the right to be let alone."[50] The tension between the right to know and the right to privacy is a useful one in any democracy; the problem emerges when one side overpowers the other. This happened at the height of "yellow journalism" in the 1890s when Brandeis first began to write about the subject, defining (some would say "inventing") the constitutional right to privacy.[51]

At the start of the twenty-first century, the cornucopia of cable and the Internet tilts the balance the other way, making the right to inform far more difficult: What does democracy look like when its information is self-selected? John Dewey once wrote, "no man and no mind was ever emancipated merely by being left alone."[52] Quoting this line from Dewey, Cass Sunstein worried about the consequences of the "Daily Me" to democracy.[53]

The fragmentation is easy to see in television in general and TV news in particular. The most popular TV show of 1960s, *I Love Lucy*, garnered two-thirds of all viewers. The most popular show of the 1970s, *All in the Family*, was watched by half of all viewers. By the 1990s, *Seinfeld*'s share was only one-third. The fragmentation in news is even more precipitous; rarely do we gather around the television for news, September 11 notwithstanding. After watching Walter Cronkite's carefully worded conclusion in 1968 that the United States was "mired in stalemate" in Vietnam, President Johnson grew despondent. "If I've lost Cronkite," Johnson reasoned, "I've lost middle America."[54] Can any one journalist today command such a following? September 11 notwithstanding, our nation is unified not by a common attention to news, but by our inattention to it.

In one section of *Leaves of Grass*, Walt Whitman sings an embrace of all Americans, of deacons and drovers, prostitutes and presidents.[55] In a nonlinear world, we can click on the presidents and deacons and leave out the rest. Or perhaps we're only interested in prostitutes. Through self-selection, we can build an impressive expertise in one narrow area, but building a well-rounded, generalist's gaze is less likely. What do we miss when we self-select? Sunstein argued that self-selection minimizes one's opportunities to encounter unexpected ideas and unpopular opinions, a necessary ingredient in any democracy.

Here's one example from history: In the 1890s, nearly every white person in the United States believed that blacks were lynched in the South because they raped white women. Ida B. Wells, an anti-lynching crusader, presented clear evidence that (1) despite the *belief* that most lynchings were a response to blacks raping whites, the fact was that rape was not even the stated cause in most cases; (2) black victims were often charged with rape only *after* the lynchings became public; and (3) charges of "rape" were often cases involving a black man and a white woman caught in a consensual relationship. Although these facts took more than a decade to reach progressives and more than two decades to persuade the general public, they eventually changed Americans' perceptions; journalists, despite their prejudices, began to understand the force of the facts and presented them to the public.[56] Imagine how much longer it would have taken to convince dubious whites if they had gotten their lynching news from Web sites only reporting the "lawlessness" of Southern blacks. Chapter 6 takes the arguments of Sunstein and others and puts them in a historical and then contemporary frame. The arguments about the implications of self-selection are not theoretical: Chapter 6, through interviews and research of news habits, analyzes current practices and how news consumers who self-select function as citizens.

Conclusion: How to Tune Back in

"The role of the press," wrote James W. Carey, "is simply to make sure that in the short run we don't get screwed and it does this best not by treating us as consumers of news, but by encouraging the conditions of public discourse and life."[57] How can we push journalists and citizens to report on and read news that matters? How can we set up a news environment that best prevents us from getting screwed?

One of the few outcomes of September 11 we can predict with certainty is that we have entered a long era that will force collisions between security and civil liberties. The good news is that despite their declining interest in news, Americans are more tolerant than their parents and grandparents were. For example, in 1937, only 46 percent of voters surveyed by Gallup said they would be willing to vote for a qualified Jewish candidate for president; in 1999, 92 percent said they would.[58] However, despite the general rise in tolerance in a generation that consumes less news, Putnam has found that within the generations, the more one is engaged in society, the more tolerant one is.[59] That is, people who are civically involved tend to be more tolerant than their age peers. Presumably, news consumption positively correlates, too.

We live in pivotal times and are faced with important decisions. The fall of communism forced the world to remake itself; so too does the long shadow of September 11, 2001. This book is about the tuned-out generations who will lead our children and grandchildren. Its conclusion proposes the tools we will need to give them to tune back in.

CHAPTER 2

How Tuned Out Are They?

In late 2001, I was interviewed on CNN about how young people are following the news in the wake of the September 11 terrorist attacks. Miles O'Brien, the anchor, mentioned that there was an upward "trend" in news consumption among young people and he backed it up with the following statistic from the Pew Research Center for the People & the Press: Two months after the terrorist attacks, 61 percent of people under 30 were following the news of the terrorist attacks "closely." Anyone in America on September 11 and during the days that followed knows that almost everyone was glued to their televisions. But, as I told O'Brien that day, Pew's findings painted a mixed picture about how young people consume news.[1] Consider the following findings from that poll by Pew:

NEWS INTEREST AMONG AMERICANS BY AGE

Age	The terror attacks	Anthrax	The economy	The capture of Kabul	Debate about federalizing airline security
<30	61	32	32	20	21 (307)
30–49	67	38	41	37[a]	27 (573)[a]
50+	69	50	46	43[a]	40 (599)[a]

Percentage following each news story "very closely," November 2001 (Number: 1500)

Pew Research Center for the People & the Press, *Terror Coverage Boosts News: But Military Censorship Backed* [Web posted report and data] November 2001, available from http://www.people-press.org.

$p < 0.05$, [a] = significantly different than age <30

O'Brien cited only the left-hand column, the only one that suggests an active involvement in news among young people. But while most of the under-30 crowd did follow the terror attacks very closely, most yawned through the news about anthrax, the economy, the capture of Kabul, and the debate over whether to federalize airline security workers. The reports of the capture of Kabul and the debate over airport screeners present the starkest difference by age: twice as many older Americans cared as younger Americans. Rather than bucking the long-term trend of declining news interest among young people, these data confirm it.

The evidence for the long-term decline in news interest is overwhelming. In order to prove that young people are following the news less than their elders do and less than young people once did, I have devoted an entire chapter to this argument. I urge you to join me in wading through the many statistics because I am convinced, and believe that you will be too, that our democracy is in big, big trouble.

Long-Term Decline, Current News Interest

In 1990, the Times Mirror Center for The People & The Press conducted a series of surveys to chart news interest. Viewing the issue over half a century, the Times Mirror Center saw an increasingly tuned out generation in what it called the "age of indifference":

> It is clear that the news and information generation gap is a product of our own time. The results of 16 individual measures of public attentiveness from 1944 to 1968 demonstrate only small differences between age groups. Over those years, the interest of younger people was less than 5% below that of interest in the population at large. In the forties, political debates in Washington and election news had as large an audience among the under-30s as among older people. In the fifties, the Army–McCarthy hearings generated as much interest among the young as among older people. In the 60s, as many young people as older people said they were following the war in Vietnam very closely.
>
> In the 70s, Watergate was of equal interest to young and old. But soon thereafter, surveys by the Roper Organization began to show diminished interest in current affairs among younger people.[2]

Despite the widespread use of the Internet among young people, the current generation of 18–34-year-olds appears to be no more informed now than 18–34-year-olds were in 1990.[3] DDB Needham, a marketing firm, annually asks thousands of Americans about a wide range of subjects. I am particularly interested in how people respond to the statement, "I need to get the news (world, national, sports, etc.) every day." Of the six possible responses to this question, the two strongest affirmative ones are "I definitely agree" and "I generally agree." Of the people who were asked to respond to the statement over 13 years ending in 1998, 30 percent definitely agreed and 21 percent generally agreed.

Fifty-one percent of the general population definitely or generally needs to get the news every day, but data reveal that different groups are more or less enthusiastic. Given the range of variables in the DDB Needham database, it is possible to get a demographic and temporal breakdown of news interest. For example, we know that news interest is affected by income, gender, and race:

NEWS INTEREST BY INCOME, GENDER, AND RACE*

Under $50,000	Over $50,000		
49	55.0		(number: 47,099)[a]
Male	Female		
54.7	47.9		(number: 49,331)[b]
White	Black	Asian	
51.8	58.1	56.4	(number: 34,956)[c]

*Percentage respondents who definitely or generally agree: "I need to get the news (world, national, sports, etc.) every day."

[a] Author's statistical analysis of DDB Needham, *Life Style Survey, 1975–1998* [Web-posted data and report] 2000, available from http://www.bowlingalone.com.

[b] Author's statistical analysis of Ibid.

[c] Author's statistical analysis of Ibid.

But all these variables have a relatively weak correlation to news interest (in statistical terms, they are all $p > 0.05$, or statistically insignificant). The variable that correlates most strongly is age:

NEWS INTEREST BY AGE*

Age:	18–24	25–34	35–44	45–54	55–64	65+
	31.5	38.9	46.0	52.3	62.1	68.3

*Percentage respondents who definitely or generally agree: "I need to get the news (world, national, sports, etc.) every day," by age (number: 49,331). Author's statistical analysis of Ibid.

$p < 0.05$, all groups significantly different

The table reveals that the oldest Americans were more than twice as likely as young Americans to "need" the news every day. And in the latest years of the poll, the dichotomy has grown: From 1996 to 1998, only 25.2 percent of young people (ages 18–24) said they need to get the news every day.[4] Nearly every poll I have seen confirms the above data: In the first years of this new century, news interest rises unequivocally with respondents who are older.

Although the table shows a strong correlation between age and news interest, it also masks an even stronger disparity when news is more narrowly defined. Because DDB Needham invited respondents to think of news in broad terms—"world, national, sports, etc."—the results may include those interested in sports, entertainment, and gossip in a range of media. When pollsters homed in on the meat of democracy—political news—the data can only be described as striking:

POLITICAL INTEREST BY AGE*

Age:	18–24	25–34	35–44	45–54	55–64	65+
	12.8	17.8ᵃ	18.0ᵃ	21.5ᵃ	25.3ᵃ◆	32.4ᵃ◆

*Percentage respondents who definitely or generally agree: "I am interested in politics," by age, 1995–1998. (number: 2747). Author's statistical analysis of Ibid.
$p < 0.05$, ᵃ = significantly different than 18–24, ◆ = significantly different than 25–34

As we see, 32.4 percent of the oldest age cohort was "generally or definitely" interested in politics. Only 12.8 percent of the 18–24-year-olds agreed.[5]

DDB Needham's political question began in 1975 and the data reveal a modest decline in news interest among young people over that time. However, another poll, given at college campuses across the country, goes back further. It has been asking a similar question of incoming freshman since the late 1960s. In 1968, the first year of the poll, 60.3 percent of incoming freshmen reported an interest in political affairs. In 2000, only 28.1 percent reported such an interest.[6]

Decline of Politics

Starting with the Times Mirror Center's finding that up until the 1970s young people followed political news as much as their elders did, the decline in the last 30 or 40 years is startling. By a range of measures, from voting to political affiliation to political knowledge, the decline suggests a departure from what once constituted full citizenship. Instead, many young people have what Michael X. Delli Carpini and Scott Keeter call a "thin" citizenship, only following the outlines of democracy, and in many cases, not even bothering to engage at all. Further, we see patterns of "thinness" in people in their thirties and forties. These ages used to be more engaged.[7]

In terms of political participation, we cannot draw a straight line from the nation's birth until now. In 1824, before universal white manhood suffrage, only 27 percent of eligible adults voted. Voting records show a number of peaks and valleys over the course of our history. In the contested election of 1876, the one that would decide the fate of Reconstruction, a full 81.8 percent of all eligible adults voted. In each of the first two elections of the roaring 1920s, fewer than half of all eligible adults did. In each of the presidential elections of the 1950s and 1960s, the voting rate was around 60 percent of eligible voters, the highest rates of our times.[8]

The only consistent trend in all the census data that I have found on voting is the trend of the last 40 years. In 1964, half of 18–24-year-olds voted in the presidential election; in 2000, less than a third did. In 1966, 31 percent voted in the midterm (congressional) election; in 1998, 16.6 percent did.[9] The year 1998 marked the first time in recorded history that voting participation had dipped so low. Do the math: 16.6 percent means that for every young person who voted in 1998, five stayed home. The figures for 2002 are harder to produce, but estimates are that—despite September 11, the war in Afghanistan, the looming war in Iraq, and a slight increase in overall voting in 2002—the rate of 18–24-year-old voting *actually went down*, to 15 percent.[10]

The decline in political participation follows the decline in party affiliation, too. In a recent poll, 68.5 percent of older Americans reported that they were either Democrats or Republicans. In the under-25 crowd, only 52.8 percent reported a major party affiliation:

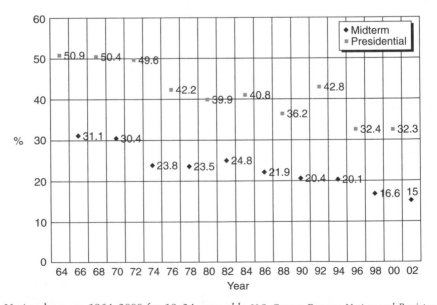

Voting by year, 1964–2000 for 18–24 year-olds. U.S. Census Bureau, *Voting and Registration* [Web posted dated and charts] U.S. Census Bureau, 31 December 2002, available from http://www.census.gov/population/www/socdemo/voting.html. The 2002 figure is an estimate.

PARTY AFFILIATION BY AGE, 2000 (IN PERCENT)

In politics today, do you consider yourself a Republican, a Democrat, or Independent? (number: 8165)[a]

Age:	18–24◆	25–34*	35–44*	45–54*	55–64*	65+*
Republican	24.0	28.8	30.3	26.4	30.1	29.4
Democrat	28.8	17.3	31.9	33.4	36.1	39.1
Total Major Party Affiliation:	52.8	46.1	62.2	59.8	66.2	68.5
Independent	33.9	29.7	27.1	29.2	23.5	17.9
Other Party	0.3	0.4	0.4	0.4	0.6	0.2

[a]Pew Research Center for the People & the Press, *Youth Vote Influenced by Online Information: Internet Election News Audience Seeks Convenience, Familiar Names* [Web-posted report and data] December 2000, available from http://www.people-press.org/. Author's analysis.

$P < 0.05$; * = significantly different than 18–24, ◆ = significantly different than 25–34

This affinity for the "Independent" label is shared by nonvoters as well.[11] This is not surprising given the significant subset of young people who are non-voters. It is difficult to discern which came first: the lack of party affiliation or the general cynicism about politics I discuss in later chapters. What is certain, however, is the extent to which many young people have dropped out of the political system.

How "Thin" Are They?

According to the latest data, most young people have very "thin" political knowledge. In a poll by the Pew Research Center for the People & the Press conducted in January 2000, 76.7 percent of Americans 65 and older could name George W. Bush as a Republican candidate. Given Bush's exposure, it is not surprising that many young people, 44.2 percent, could name him, too. Merely naming Bush is not necessarily a sign of news consumption because that information could have come from a nonnews source. A person may hear a candidate's name from any number of sources, including friends and family, gleaning news tidbits without necessarily getting a deeper understanding.

But Pew not only asked about frontrunners, but other candidates too. In asking a range of questions, Pew's poll allows us to assess the level of political knowledge. In this open-ended question, people who named one candidate were prodded to name others. In January 2000, six Republicans—George W. Bush, John McCain, Steve Forbes, Gary Bauer, Orrin Hatch, and Alan Keyes—were actively seeking their party's nomination. Two others, Dan Quayle and Patrick Buchanan, had recently dropped out. As the chart below reveals, older Americans were more likely to name candidates than younger Americans were. Further, the knowledge gap regarding Bush was relatively modest compared to the names further down the list. Bauer and Hatch, for example, were named by fewer than 1 percent of young people, less than a tenth of the response rate of older Americans. The only exception to this age trend is that young people named Buchanan far more than their elders did. However, Buchanan was no longer a candidate by the time the poll was taken, a fact that presumably most older Americans knew.

KNOWLEDGE OF REPUBLICAN PRIMARY CANDIDATES, FEBRUARY 2000 (IN PERCENT)

Do you happen to know the names of any of the Republicans running for their party's presidential nomination? Who are they? (Number: 1078)[a]

AGE >	18–24◆	25–34*	34–44*	45–54*	55–64*	65+*	Total
1. George W. Bush	44.2	59.1	58.6	68.3	70.9	76.7	62.8
2. Steve Forbes	9.4	11.3	13.3	18.8	22.4	24.7	16.2
3. John McCain	11.6	17.7	24.2	27.5	33.6	40.4	25.5
4. Gary Bauer	0.7	3.2	3.1	4.6	7.5	11.6	4.8
5. Orrin Hatch	0.7	4.8	3.1	5.5	4.5	8.9	4.5
6. Alan Keyes	2.2	5.9	7.0	8.3	12.7	10.3	7.6
7. Other	0.0	0.5	0.0	0.0	0.0	0.7	0.2
8. Dan Quayle	1.4	4.3	3.9	1.8	3.7	1.4	2.9
9. Patrick Buchanan	9.4	6.5	5.5	5.0	5.2	2.1	5.6
10. Could not recall	1.4	3.2	1.6	1.4	3.7	1.4	2.0
11. Don't know/refused	47.1	31.2	28.9	23.4	17.2	17.8	27.6

[a]Pew Research Center for the People & the Press, *Audiences Fragmented and Skeptical: The Tough Job of Communicating with Voters.* Author's analysis.

P < 0.05; * = significantly different than 18–24, ◆ = significantly different than 25–34

Without knowing the names of the frontrunners, a citizen would have a difficult, if not impossible, time of choosing between them. But if knowing the names is essential, it is certainly not sufficient to making an informed decision. For that, one needs to understand at least the basic differences in the candidates' platforms. Another question in the Pew poll can help us plumb the depths of political knowledge: "Do you happen to know which of the presidential candidates sponsored a campaign finance reform bill in Congress?" This question can help us see how "thin" political knowledge is in America, particularly among young Americans. Across age groups, just under 20 percent could identify McCain with his very public position on campaign finance reform. Even older Americans fared poorly, with only 28.1 percent naming McCain.

This suggests that no matter the age, most Americans have an alarmingly "thin" political knowledge. This finding supports the work of Delli Carpini and Keeter who wrote in their book, *What Americans Know About Politics and Why It Matters* (1996), that Americans know very little about the American political system. Delli Carpini and Keeter found, for example, that only 30 per-cent know that Chief Justice William Rehnquist was conservative (and that was in a multiple-choice question!).

KNOWLEDGE OF CAMPAIGN FINANCE REFORM, BY AGE, 2000 (IN PERCENT)

Do you happen to know which of the presidential candidates sponsored a campaign finance reform bill in Congress? (Number 1078)[a]

AGE >	18–24◆	25–34*	35–44*◆	45–54*◆	55–64*◆	65+*◆	Total
McCain (correct)	4.3	12.9	18.0	26.6	27.6	28.1	19.7
Other	8.0	11.8	9.4	12.4	10.4	10.3	10.5
Don't know	87.7	75.3	72.7	61.0	61.9	61.6	69.9

[a]Pew Research Center for the People & the Press, *Audiences Fragmented and Skeptical: The Tough Job of Communicating with Voters.* Author's analysis.
$P < 0.05$; * = significantly different than 18–24, ◆ = significantly different than 25–34

While Pew's question about McCain reveals a general lack of political knowl-edge *across* ages, it also underscores the growing gap, downplayed by Delli Carpini and Keeter, *between* the ages. As the above chart indicates, only 4.3 per-cent of the 18–24-age cohort could name McCain. With a 16.6 percent voting rate in the 1998 midterm elections and a 4.3 percent rate of conversance with McCain's signature legislation, how viable is the 18–24 crowd as a political force?

Pew conducted a similar poll during the 2004 Democratic presidential pri-mary. The poll asked, "Do you happen to know which of the presidential can-didates served as an Army general?" While 42.3 percent of respondents 50 and older were able to answer correctly (Wesley Clark), only 12.6 percent of the under-30 crowd could do so.[12]

The 40-Year Trend

The Pew Research Center for the People & the Press has been evaluating the news interest of Americans since the early 1990s. The Times Mirror Center and the Roper organization did so before it. Together they report that, since the early 1970s, with three notable exceptions, young people have followed the news less than their elders have. The first exception is that young people, for obvious reasons, are a bit more likely than their elders to know what the min-imum wage is. The second exception is abortion. Young women follow news about abortion as much as (but not more than) their elders do.[13] The third ex-ception, mainly involving young men, is sports news. More than a third of young Americans watch ESPN regularly, double the rate of the oldest Amer-icans. Among young men, the rate is even higher, about 46 percent.[14]

It is easy for us to establish a significant downward trend from the early 1960s to now. However—and this represents a potential weakness in the book's thesis—we know the 1960s were an exceptional time; young people were unusually involved in news and politics. It is important, then, to reiterate that we cannot draw any straight lines going back longer than forty years.

Still, there are four reasons why we should pay attention to the 40-year trend. First, as we have seen, the past four decades, a significant part of our nation's history, have witnessed a marked and steady decline in political engagement and news consumption. While there are anecdotal accounts of increased news interest among preteens and young teens, there is no statistical evidence yet to suggest a rebound.

The second reason we need to pay attention to the 40-year trend is that its nadir (today), represents the all-time nadir, too. Since the birth of universal white manhood suffrage in 1824, we have never been so politically disengaged. And for some reason, young people are malnourished with respect to news in a land of information plenty.

The third reason we should pay attention to the trend is that (as I discuss later in this chapter) tuned-out young people in the 1980s and 1990s have still not picked up the news habit today. As the past two generations of young people begin to assume leadership roles in society, their stewardship may be uninformed by news. Andrew Heyward, the president of CBS News, told *Newshour*, "Time is on our side in that as you get older, you tend to get more interested in the world around you. . . . So I think you become more engaged with society as you get older."[15] But Heyward, as I will discuss, is clearly wrong: young people are not picking up the habit and haven't been for a long time. We know this by talking with perceptive witnesses, especially older ones. For this I sought out observers who avoided nostalgia. A high school teacher who has been in the same school since the 1970s does not find students any less intelligent than they were, but he does see a different approach to information, one which now needs to be packaged with entertainment.[16] A geography professor who has been teaching since the 1960s does not see a significant change in students' knowledge of geography; but he does notice that students, when asked to bring in maps, no longer clip them from newspapers or even other news sources.[17] A longtime journalism professor from Indiana said that it is increasingly difficult for her to have conversations about the news with other adults, particularly younger ones.[18] Norman Rosenfeld, a leading architect in New York City, is baffled that his younger associates don't follow the news at all or are

> getting their news from television and from papers like the [*New York*] *Post* or the [*New York Daily*] *News*. A lot are not reading the same stories that I'm

reading. So I'm a voracious *New York Times* person and I clip lots of articles and circulate them and I know that many of these people have not seen any of this firsthand.[19]

Through discussions with young people around the country, I have found many examples of 20-something and 30-something adults who never got the news bug.

Finally, the fourth reason we should pay attention to the 40-year trend is that just because the 1960s represented a high point in political and news engagement, it does not mean that that level could not be realized again, or even exceeded. The 1960s were a decade of war and global threats; so too is ours. Domestically, theirs was a decade that pitted civil rights against the right of states to set their own laws. Ours is a decade pitting civil rights against national security. We, too, live in important times.

Another inherent weakness in the book's thesis is the counterargument about young people: that young people have always had concerns that trump news and politics. "Youth is almost always in deep trouble—of the mind, the heart, the flesh," wrote E. B. White.[20] There is no denying that many young people tend to have a range of obstacles, including their own libidos that prevent them from engaged citizenry. But, as we have seen, news engagement in this group had been much stronger in every decade prior to this one. And self-reported values of young people have changed: one poll of college freshmen showed that in the 1960s and 1970s they listed political engagement and environmental work as far more important objectives than being "very well off." In the late 1990s, making money was three times as important as keeping up with politics and four times as important as working to help the environment.[21] Finally, the disengagement of the youngest adults is not the whole story. As we have seen, many 30-something Americans failed to pick up the news habit as young adults and still have not picked it up. If this trend continues, the very potency of our democracy will be in jeopardy.

Specific Types of Media Consumption

Once we understand that young people are less and less likely to follow the news, it is not surprising that the consumption of individual news media is way down, too. Measuring media consumption is imprecise. With different methodologies, reporting styles, sample sizes and demographics, studies often blur as much as they reveal. Still, by any measure, young people are consuming much less news. As we have seen, only 25.2 percent of the latest crop of 18–24-year-olds say they "definitely" or "generally" agree with the statement, "I need to get the news (world, national, sports, etc.) every day."[22] As can be expected, the decline holds true when we examine individual media use as well.

Newspaper Readership

While researchers offer different reasons for, and measures of the decline in newspaper readership, there is a general uniformity on two points: first, that the readership of each age cohort stays relatively constant over time (that is, as the individuals age alongside their age peers); second, that each successive generation born after 1920 consumes less news than the generation before it.

Both Robert D. Putnam and Wolfram Peiser found that newspaper readership does not drop off significantly as individuals age. Putnam looked at data on four age cohorts from 1986 to 2000 and found little change in intra-cohort readership. Peiser found similar results. Peiser found that the 18–22-year-old age cohort in 1972 read newspapers 46 percent of the time. As the cohort became older, roughly the 48–52-year-olds of 2002, the figure dropped only slightly, to 40 percent. I've shaded that particular age cohort in the next table to show the minimal effects of aging. (Reading the table diagonally shows the effects of aging on individuals.)

READING THE NEWSPAPER EVERY DAY—PEISER'S COHORT STUDY REVISITED (IN PERCENT)

How often do you read the newspaper—every day, a few times a week, once a week, less than once a week, or never?

Year > Age	1972	1977	1982	1987	1991	1996	2002
18–22	46.0	39.8	23.7	32.8	22.4	19.8	21.1
23–27	47.1	38.1	36.1	34.7	29.3	19.7	18.7
28–32	61.7	52.8	49.2*	39.9	31.6	21.3	25.6
33–37	74.4*◆	53.9	44.6*	53.6	41.7	27.7	35.1◆
38–42	73.9*◆	67.1*◆	47.2*	54.2	55.9◆	40.8◆	45.8*◆
43–47	80.9*◆	63.6◆	61.3*◆	55.3	55.2	44.6◆	33.7◆
48–52	76.1*◆	78.0*◆	58.9*◆	56.5	60.0*◆	53.5*◆	40.2*◆
53–57	77.9*◆	76.8*◆	65.7*◆	71.0*◆	58.5	55.6*◆	41.6*◆
58–62	79.0*◆	82.1*◆	62.7*◆	68.9*	65.7◆	63.7*◆	65.9*◆
63–67	75.5◆	80.2*◆	68.8*◆	63.5	76.9*◆	60.5◆	55.0*◆
68–72	66.7	73.0◆	69.8*◆	57.4	66.7◆	72.3*◆	71.1*◆
73–77	75.0	77.3*◆	57.1	62.7	81.1*◆	72.5*	70.6*◆
78–82	78.8	68.2	74.5*	71.4	66.7◆	63.0	50.0*◆

P < 0.05; * = significantly different than 18–22, ◆ = significantly different than 23–27

The big decline in newspaper readership, Peiser says, comes in "cohort re-placement." That is, as older readers die, younger ones replace them. Forty-seven percent of those who were 23–27 years old in 1972 read a newspaper every day. In 2002, only 19 percent of 23–27-year-olds read newspapers every day. Reading the columns from left to right, particularly the top rows, shows the effects of cohort replacement over time. Cohort replacement, while signif-icant in the 18–22 row, is even more pronounced in the 33–37 row. In three decades, the chart reveals, daily newspaper readership went from 74.4 percent to 35.1 percent among the mid-thirty crowd.[23]

The table "Reading the Newspaper Every Day" shows the percentage of respondents in each age group who read newspapers every day. (number: 27995)[24]

Incidentally, Peiser also looked at readership in Germany and found sim-ilar results: In 1970, 68 percent of 20-something Germans read a newspaper every day. Today, only 33 percent of young Germans read newspapers every day, a higher rate than in the United States, but a similarly steep decline.[25] Other European countries have declines, but the United States leads everyone in circulation declines.[26]

While these data point to a substantial decline in daily newspaper reader-ship, they do not fully reveal the decline in the amount of news that young Americans actually get from newspapers. When we couple these data with time studies, a clearer picture comes into view. The Pew Research Center for the People & the Press asked respondents who read a newspaper yesterday to es-timate how much time they spent with it. Not surprisingly, twice as many eld-ers read the newspaper as did youngsters. What is surprising is that even among newspaper readers, older Americans read far longer than younger ones. Of the minority of 18–24-year-olds who say they read the newspaper yesterday, only 41.3 percent did so for 30 minutes or more. The vast majority of the oldest age cohorts read for 30 minutes or more.[27]

Before we examine other media and see similar declines, it is important to comment briefly on newspapers and how they are structurally different than other media. Even if there weren't declines in all other media, the decline in newspaper reading (whether in print or on-line) would be very serious. This is due to the depth that a newspaper can provide. A half hour of television news produces something like 3,600 words; a top newspaper prints about 100,000 words a day.[28] But more than that, a good newspaper can, and does, go deeper than the headlines in outlining processes and background, and pro-viding analysis. Without this depth, politicians know that they can convince people of anything if they have pretty pictures. Three recent presidents, Ronald Reagan, Bill Clinton, and George W. Bush, have proven that flash often outweighs substance in communicating with an increasingly tuned-out public. "Americans are leading busy lives," said Dan Bartlett, the current White House communications director. "Sometimes they don't have the opportunity to read a story or listen to an entire broadcast. But if they can have an instant understanding of what the president is talking about by seeing 60 seconds of television, you accomplish your goals as communicators."[29] This kind of superficial manipulation is best countered by depth, the kind of depth that a good newspaper provides. Before we write off dying newspapers in an ever-expanding media universe, we must remember that it was usually newspapers that took the lead in revealing and explaining budget deficits, tax policy, war plans, official blunders, and everything else that touches our democracy in significant ways. Television is better for big events, like those on September 11, 2001, but for the underlying cause of terrorism, or what to do about it, we would have no better daily source than an on-line or printed newspaper.

News Magazines

Of the top 10 best-selling magazines in the United States, how many are devoted to general news? One: *Time* Magazine. Of the top 25 magazines, three are—if we include the *National Enquirer* (and we shouldn't!).[30] The combined circulation of the top two newsmagazines, *Time* and *Newsweek*, is about 7 million, a fraction of the national special-interest magazines, a genre that has been rising steadily from the 1960s.[31] More young women read *Cosmopolitan*, and more young men read *Maxim* than read *Time* or *Newsweek*.[32] Magazine demographics are not split as dramatically as the other media are; I believe this is because we are dealing with a much smaller subset of news consumers than the tens of millions who follow news in other media, such as television and the combined circulation of the hundreds of daily newspapers. Still, *Time*, *Newsweek*, *U.S. News and World Report* and *The New Yorker* each attract a median age of between 43 and 47—not exactly young. Compare this to the median age for the nation's fastest-growing magazines: *InStyle* (33), *Maxim* (32), *ESPN* (29), *YAHOO! Internet Life* (35), and *Teen People* (30).[33]

Radio News

I asked my Mass Communication and Society students to listen to two hours of radio: one hour of the local top-40 station and one hour of National Public Radio. While some students objected to the music selections of the former, more found the hour of news to be unbearable, or in the wording of one student, "torture." The national trends support this anecdote. Many radio stations are abandoning news in favor of music simply because the majority of every age group, except the oldest, prefer music. The trend toward music is strongest among the very young.[34] An exception to this trend is the recent popularity of mainly conservative talk shows, most notably the Rush Limbaugh show. These shows comment on the news, but because of their polemic nature, do not provide the range of opinions and balance of the more traditional news outlets. Because the popularity of these shows is often pegged to their combativeness rather than their informational qualities, they are poor substitutes for outlets such as network radio news broadcasts or National Public Radio.

National Public Radio has seen a rising audience across age cohorts, but is nonetheless graying: its median age for weekday news is 49 and its weekend news audience is even older.[35] We can see the problem when we look at NPR's relative penetration into each age demographic:

PENETRATION OF NPR FOR EACH AGE COHORT, SPRING 2001

Age:	12–17	18–24	25–34	35–44	45–54	55–64	65+
Penetration:	3	4	10	11	15	16	14

Percentage of total population of each age cohort that listens to NPR. Arbitron Nationwide, Spring 1996–Spring 2001, Monday–Sunday, 6 A.M.–Midnight, NPR Stations. Data supplied by NPR, February 2002.

Only 4 percent of 18–24-year-olds are listening to NPR, compared with 14–16 percent of their parents and grandparents. Jackie Nixon, NPR's director of Audience Research, told me that one of the most surprising things about the age demographics is the 30-something crowd. Many of them, well into their adulthood, have yet to establish the news habits of their elders. Nixon characterized the NPR audience as "graying."[36]

Television News

When I tell older people that I am working on a book about why young people do not follow the news, one of the common responses is that the younger generations are not reading newspapers because they are watching TV news instead. This, however, is not true. As Putnam explains, consumers of individual news media are likely to be news "generalists."[37] That is, older newspaper readers are also the most likely consumers of television news. The reverse is true, too: younger nonreaders are the least likely to consume TV news.

From 1993 to 2000, regular viewership of TV network news of all ages dropped from 60 percent to 30 percent. Younger viewers are less likely to keep a regular appointment with Dan, Tom, or Peter: While 50 percent of the 65+

crowd still watch the networks' evening news regularly, only 17 percent of the under-30 crowd do.[38] Of course, the big broadcast networks are not the only watering holes anymore. But while many viewers have migrated to CNN, FOX, MSNBC, and CNBC, these stations are hardly a haven for the young. The typical viewer at Headline News is 51-years-old.[39] At CNN's main station, the typical viewer is between 59 and 64.[40] One in four older Americans watch CNN "regularly"; among young Americans, it is one in seven (see table). Also, among those young who do watch TV news, they tend to do it for less time than their elders do. The second part of the table, only includes news viewers, hiding the considerable percentage of nonviewers among the young. But it shows that even if we only take into account viewers, age correlates with consumption.

"REGULAR" CNN VIEWERS; AVERAGE TV NEWS–VIEWING TIME, 2000 (IN PERCENT)

"Regular" CNN watchers						
18–24	25–34	35–44	45–54	55–64	65+	All Ages
14.4	20.9	22.5*	22.4*	23.1◆*	24.0◆*	21.5

P < 0.05; * = significantly different than 18–24, ◆ = significantly different than 25–34

Average daily news viewing time of all television news viewers							
	18–24	25–34	35–44	45–54	55–64	65+	All Ages
30 mins+	67.8	76.5	74.3	83.6*◆	83.3*◆	78.7*◆	77.9

(Note that nonviewers are *not* included [number: 863]) Pew Research Center for the People & the Press, *Investors Now Go Online for Quotes, Advice: Internet Sapping Broadcast News Audience.* Author's analysis.

P < 0.05; * = significantly different than 18–24, ◆ = significantly different than 25–34

Taken with the data on newspapers and radio, we see clearly that most young people do not consume news in these media, and many of those who do are consuming it with less vigor.

The Internet

The Internet is, of course, the 800-pound gorilla when we are discussing the news habits of the young. Or maybe it's the 800-pound chimera. What exactly do young people consume on the Internet anyway? Experts are divided. Putnam argued that, "as usage of the Internet expanded in the second half of the 1990s, usage of it to follow public affairs became relatively *less* important."[41] Others, however, disagreed. So what effect has the Internet had on young people's news consumption? The answer is so complicated that I have devoted a good part of chapter 4 to answer it. But there are three points worth noting: First, the Internet, more than any other medium, allows readers to self-select. Whether you are interested in the early works of J. D. Salinger, the clothing of the Masai, or Israeli research on the intelligence of dolphins, there is a place for you on the Web.

Second, when 18–24-year-olds were asked in 2002 about their preferred news media source, they rarely chose the Internet.

MEDIA SOURCES FOR CURRENT EVENTS

Percentage of 18–24-year-olds who use the following media for current events (U.S.)

Media source	
TV news	82
Newspapers	38
Radio	13
Internet	11
Magazines	10

Roper ASW, *National Geographic—Roper ASW 2002 Global Geographic Literacy Survey*. The survey also lists data for other countries. According to the poll, young adults in the United States are less likely to use the Internet for current events than young people from Canada, France, Germany, Great Britain, Italy, Japan, Mexico, and Sweden.

The third thing to remember about the Internet is that despite that young people use the 'Net far more than their elders do, they still lag far behind in their general news knowledge, as we have seen in this chapter. Despite the nearly infinite choices available to readers—or perhaps because of them—the 'Net has not closed the gap between young and old on knowing which presidential candidate sponsored campaign finance reform in the Senate.

Americans of all ages have more and more media choices. Over time, newspapers were joined by radio, then television, then cable television, then the Internet. We still have the *CBS Evening News*, but we also have MTV's *Jackass*. We still have the *New York Times*, but we also have *Hustler* Online. We still have John McCain, but we also have Ozzy Osbourne. What does the entertainment glut do to our consumption of news? That is the subject of chapter 3.

Talking with Young People I: Striptease News and the Shifting Balance Between Need and Want

Tickle the public, make 'em grin,
The more you tickle, the more you'll win;
Teach the public, you'll never get rich,
You'll live like a beggar and die in a ditch.
—Nineteenth-century Fleet Street saying

Well, Normie, this is the information age. We can get up-to-the-minute
stock prices, medical breakthroughs, and political upheavals from all around
the world. Of course, we'd have to turn off the cartoons first.
                                                    —Cliff Clavin, *Cheers*[1]

In 1990, the Times Mirror Center published *The Age of Indifference*, a study
that revealed "a generation that knows less, cares less, and reads newspapers
less. It is also a generation that votes less and is less critical of its leaders and
institutions than young people in the past."[2] This statement, while difficult to
contradict, only provides a bare outline of the issue at hand. Who are these
young people? Part of the answer can be found in the surveys that the Times
Mirror Center and other organizations have conducted, but a deeper picture
can only be found from talking with young people themselves. In 2002 and
2003, I traveled around the country talking with scores of under-40s from
many different walks of life (for a list, see Appendix A.).

My surveys of and discussions with people, ages 11 to 36, were not intended to strengthen or weaken the strong correlation I and others have found

between age and news interest. Because there is no question about correlation, and because mine was not a statistically meaningful sample, I concentrated on what the statistics, formidable as they are, do not show. So, during these interviews, I was not concerned with correlation, which establishes similar patterns, but causality, the underlying reasons behind behavior.

For example, in my trip to Louisiana, I was less interested in what individuals could tell me about how "Southerners" follow the news, than in the exploration of why two students with the same educational and geographical background take an entirely different approach to news. What role do parents, teachers, and peers play in shaping news interest? We know that political involvement correlates with news interest, but which typically comes first? And most important, if young people are indeed tuned out of the news, what are they tuned *in* to? As far as I know, no one else has bothered to ask young people these questions.

Tuned Out, Tuned In

If the measures I used to assess the young people's political awareness could be compared to a heart monitor, most of the respondents (but certainly not all) would be flatliners. Few had ever heard of Tom Daschle, the Senate majority leader at the time of the interviews. Few could name even their own state's U.S. senators.[3] Few could name John Ashcroft, the most high-profile and newsworthy U.S. attorney general since the Nixon administration. Few could name any of the countries listed by Bush as part of the "axis of evil," a formulation that was defining America's foreign policy during the time of the study. In Appendix B, I have listed the questions I asked of most of the people I interviewed for this study. In Appendix C, I have listed the responses to my news interest questionnaires.

Unlike polling data, real people are wonderfully alive, constantly confounding expectations, as the following two examples reveal. In 2002 I interviewed Lizzie Salzfass and Kanon Cozad, both of whom surprised me. Salzfass, 23, a recent graduate of Wesleyan, had written an article in *Ms.* Magazine about her political activism on her campus. In the article, Salzfass recalled her role in a range of campus activities on behalf of the "Queer Alliance," Wesleyan's gay/lesbian/bi/transgendered caucus. Salzfass helped to organize a "kiss-in" to advocate for extra "queer studies" classes; *Ms.* ran a picture of Salzfass smooching with another woman. In the end of the article, Salzfass wrote, "Wesleyan is one of the best places for a young person committed to social justice to spend four years of her life. Call me an idealistic kid or a raging radical lunatic, but here, unlike anywhere else I have ever been, change truly seems possible."[4] Because of this activism and hope, I expected Salzfass to represent the high end of the news consumption scale.

When I spoke to Salzfass, I was impressed with her idealism, thoughtfulness, and faith in her ability to change the system. When I started to gauge the depth of her news knowledge, Salzfass expressed both interest in the news and skepticism of it ("it's just so biased and so packaged"). Considering Salzfass' activism, it is no surprise that she was critical of the Bush administra-

"Special Report: Ms. *Goes to College." The August/September 2001 issue of* Ms. *featured Lizzie Salzfass' report about her protests at Wesleyan University.* Reprinted by permission of Ms. Magazine. Photographs by Julie Farias, Rene Toussaint, Sung Hoon Kim, Jessica Firestone, Daniela Schmid, Sam Ogden, Diana Silbergeld.

tion. What did surprise me, however, was her limited knowledge of basic political facts: She could only name one of her two senators (Hillary Clinton, but not Chuck Schumer), could not name any of the three countries Bush called the "axis of evil" (Iran, Iraq, North Korea), and could not identify McCain-Feingold (the Senate's campaign finance reform bill). "We're all so pathetic. I know. I realize that," she said, referring to herself and her peers.[5]

Salzfass' news knowledge was not entirely incomplete. She did name one of her senators and, after a hint, John Ashcroft. Although she couldn't name any current Supreme Court justices, she knew about *Roe* v. *Wade* and offered that Byron White, a former justice, had just died. But while Salzfass was slightly more informed than most of her age peers, her news knowledge fell far short of her political passion. Why? A facile explanation would be that Salzfass simply reflected the vast majority of her generation: tuned out and apolitical. But Salzfass was anything but apolitical. She watched Bush (whom she called an "asshole idiot") give the State of the Union Address, and she had to leave the room because it was "too sickening." Certainly Salzfass' dearth of news knowledge was exacerbated by her lack of news-consuming age peers, but it would be a stretch to say that she was tuned out of most news because she resembled her age peers. In many ways, she did not.

People are more complicated than the sum of their data and towards the end of the interview Salzfass felt compelled to explain the lapses in her news knowledge. Her tuning out was a temporary condition, she said, due to her frustration with being unemployed after a lively internship with *Ms.*

> Can I say something that you should maybe take into consideration with this?
> . . . Since I've graduated I have to say it was really depressing being unemployed for four months, and I kind of felt pretty useless. . . . While I was working at *Ms.*, it was totally exciting to keep up with stuff because it was so relevant to what I was doing and I felt like I was doing something. . . . But while I was unemployed it was like I've got my own problems and I'm just trying to find a job. . . . And now, hopefully, that I'm doing something again [Salzfass had just landed a two-year teaching fellowship], I'll start. I'll start reading the *New York Times* again.[6]

The above explanation provides a powerful anti-example of two of the most powerful reasons why people follow the news: First, they follow the news because they are part of a community. Second, they learn things that they will use in their lives, particularly in conversation. Salzfass, isolated, was more tuned out than she should have been. And, she said (and I believe) that she was more tuned out than she will be in the future.

At 36, Kanon Cozad was the oldest of all the under-40s I interviewed. Cozad, a vice president at the United Missouri Bank (UMB) in Kansas City, Missouri, offered me the opportunity to talk with him and some members of his staff. I was forewarned by a mutual friend that Cozad was unusually well-read and interested in the news, but I had expected his staff to be relatively less tuned in for three reasons: first, that the bankers I had met over the years struck me as relatively apolitical; second, that Kansas City was far from any center of power; and third, that Missouri was only slightly above average on Robert Putnam's list of states with strong "social capital," his measure of social and political engagement.[7] But just as Salzfass' lack of news engagement confounded expectations, so did Cozad and his staff's close following of current events.

As I listened to Cozad answer my questions, I kept thinking that he was the ultimate anti-example for my book. A subscriber to 10 magazines (including his favorite, *The Economist*), a watcher of public television news, a listener of NPR, a reader of his local paper, and an active browser of the Internet, Cozad even programmed his personal digital assistant (PDA) to give him

The most tuned-in person I interviewed: Kanon Cozad, vice president of the United Missouri Bank. Photo courtesy of Cozad.

the latest headlines. He could answer nearly all of my questions (except that he could not identify Alicia Keys, the R&B singer, and struggled to name the seventh, eighth, and ninth Supreme Court justices). He was one of only a handful of people out of more than one hundred surveyed to name all three countries Bush called the "axis of evil."[8]

Not only was Cozad an exception to my book's general thesis about most young people being tuned out, he was also an exception to the trend explained in Putnam's *Bowling Alone*. Cozad was engaged in his community more than anyone else I had interviewed. To assess this, I used a number of Putnam's measures: In the last year, had he written a letter to a newspaper or media organization? attended a club meeting? contacted someone in government? attended a rally? spoken in front of a large group? Cozad answered most of these affirmatively.[9]

Although not as engaged in news and politics as their boss, Cozad's staff was unusually tuned in—more so, in fact, than any other group I interviewed. Cozad and his staff, were not, as I predicted, apolitical. Nor did Kansas City's distance from centers of power (New York, Los Angeles, Washington, DC, etc.) seem to impact news interest. Whatever disadvantage they were at geographically, they made up for it by their Web savvy. And these workers were generally engaged in their community and in national politics.[10]

In talking with the UMB staff, I was struck by the power of the workplace to shape news interest. Four of the five workers felt that keeping up with the news was important for work; the fifth did not, and was less informed than the rest. If Salzfass, Cozad, and the UMB staff reveal the diverse and unpredictable nature of news interest, they also reveal a commonality: that social and societal factors play important roles in how we value news. These next two chapters reveal a number of important themes in assessing why young people tune in and tune out; among them are how they interface with the entertainment industry (chapter 3), how they interact with their peers, and how they use the various media, especially the Internet (chapter 4).

Talking with Young People: Entertainment

Young people are growing up in a very, very different media world than their parents did. While 24-hours-a-day news is significant, it is not a huge sea change: older Americans also grew up with plenty of news on radio and television. An even bigger change is the entertainment revolution, allowing young people basically unlimited entertainment options 24 hours a day. In discussions with young people around the country, the topic of entertainment came up again and again. If we want to understand why many young people don't follow the news, we need to understand the lure of entertainment.

You may or may not know who said "Give me liberty or give me death," but it's a safe bet that you know who said, "What's up, doc?" You can probably identify Vladimir I. Lenin; you can certainly identify John Lennon.[11] Chief Justice William Rehnquist has been on the Supreme Court since 1972, since Britney Spears was minus eight. But while Rehnquist has done more than almost anyone else to change the course of recent American history (including writing the decision that ended the 2000 presidential election), he is far less known than the nubile princess of pop. Okay, let's not kid ourselves: entertainment has always been more interesting than politics. But what I am concerned about is how serious news has receded as entertainment has grown exponentially.

A former student of mine, Allison Davis, was photographed in the *Burlington Free Press* cheering as she watched one of the most popular entertainment shows, *Survivor*, with a group of friends. I called her the next day and wangled an invitation to join her party at a future airing (the women, who knew each other mainly from a gay and lesbian bar, watched together every week). That is how I came to watch *Survivor* with Allison and five other young women.

"How are you going to refer to us, 'six Vermont lesbians'?" asked one.

" 'Six *Survivor*-watching lesbians'?" asked another. The women discussed the relative merits of terms: "lesbian," "dyke" and "queer" were debated, and the majority chose "queer" as a way of co-opting the term. This was a group that was interested in gay and lesbian rights and seemed interested in politics. But most of all, they were interested in *Survivor*. The group of friends got together every week to watch. "There's no Monday, Tuesday, Wednesday anymore," said one. "It's just 'four days before *Survivor*,' 'three days before *Survivor*,' 'two days before *Survivor*. . . .' "[12]

They watched for various reasons. They watched because they enjoyed the challenges. They watched because most enjoyed seeing one of the contestants, Tammy Leitner, in a bathing suit. And they watched because it allowed the women a chance to have a beer, unwind after work, and crack jokes (don't ever say that all television is always antisocial). Many of their jokes were directed at the heavy-handed product placement (in this case, Visa).

While they showed a healthy skepticism about aspects of the show, they did not accept the premise of my question that there might be more important things on the air. The news media, said one, are "run by corporations." Another explained that the news is purveyed "by Sony, cigarette companies."

On the other hand, *Survivor*, according to one woman, "is real, without filters." Most of the women (although thankfully not my former student) agreed. They accepted the reality, despite the show's choice of contestants and locale, the heavily scripted events, the camera work, the video editing, and the overall commercial nature of the enterprise.[13]

The problem was that these women skipped a healthy skepticism about news and took a do-not-pass-Go ride directly to cynicism. Just like with Salzfass, I was at once heartened by the healthy mistrust of authority and frustrated that it was not empowered by facts. By viewing all political and journalistic information as less important than Tammy's swimsuit, these women had voluntarily ceded power to the very people they denounced: CEOs, politicians, and powerful white men. While knowledge does not always yield power, power rarely comes without knowledge.

Like a fish unaware of its ambient water, young people swim in entertainment and are unaware of its currents. Yet it is impossible to look at changing news consumption without understanding how entertainment has infused media and society. Thus a brief analysis and history are in order.

Frasier's Dilemma: Balancing Need and Want

Journalists need to inform their audience. If their information is boring, they will lose readers and viewers. However, if they pander to audience tastes, they may have an audience but nothing worthwhile to communicate. Journalists without an audience are diarists; journalists without standards are shameless. However, the extremes are not as common as the broad center: Most journalists—indeed most media workers—seek a balance between informing and interesting an audience. Exploring the tension between the two, which is also a tension between an audience's needs and wants, is important if we want to know why young people follow—or don't follow—the news.

My all-time favorite critique of the tension between the desire to inform and the need to pander to an audience's tastes came in a 1991 episode of the sitcom, *Cheers*. The psychiatrist, Frasier Crane, had just walked into the bar and announced that he was the proud owner of a first edition copy of Dickens's *Tale of Two Cities*. As you might imagine, the barflies, Norm and Cliff, were unimpressed as Frasier tried to read the novel to them. " 'It was the best of times. It was the worst of times,' " he read. "Wait . . . which was it?" asked Norm. As Frasier continued to read, his audience quickly lost attention. " 'There was a king with a large jaw and a queen with a plain face on the throne of England,' " he intoned as Norm and Cliff turned away from him on their barstools. Then Frasier took desperate measures. "And there was a blood-thirsty clown who beckoned innocent children into the sewer and swallowed them whole!" To his description of Dickens' novel, Frasier added "four pizza-lovin' turtles who practice martial arts in the sewer" and "an Apache attack chopper . . . [pumping] hot lead into the crowd." By the end of the episode, as Frasier and his wife, Lilith, sat at the bar, we hear Norm and Cliff's exuberant chant of "Dickens! Dickens! Dickens!"

> LILITH: Frasier, I'm impressed. It seems your experiment in cultural enrich-ment has been a success.
>
> NORM: Yep, we're waiting for *Oliver Twist: The Wrath of Fagan*.
>
> LILITH: Excuse me?
>
> FRASIER: Darling, I've done some things the past few weeks I'm not very proud of. Just leave it alone.[14]

What makes this wonderful episode so biting is that it is a dilemma faced by media workers (including the writers at *Cheers*) every day.

It is also the dilemma of journalists. In the late 1990s, my wife, Barbara Richmond, was the producer of an important show on CNN, *Diplomatic License*, about the United Nations. While the show had (and continues to have) a substantial following in Europe and Asia, it had the smallest imaginable au-dience among Americans, who appeared to care little about the international governing body. With the show relegated to the two A.M. slot domestically, my wife and her anchor, Richard Roth, were faced with Frasier's dilemma. They continued to do reports about "peace-keeping forces" and organizational re-structuring, but also included innovative and catchy segments like "Ask the Ambassador." They devoted the body of one show to an airy report on how the United Nations remained a smoker's paradise, despite being in a city in which smokers are asked to step outside. Unlike Frasier, who pandered shame-lessly, *Diplomatic License* maintained its serious and important mission of in-forming its viewers, and it continues to help people around the world under-stand the UN. However, audience retention and even growth remained an important prerequisite to the show's survival. Frasier's dilemma is emblematic of all commercial media: the size of the audience is a consideration in any me-dia outlet driven by capitalist forces.

I am about to argue that young people such as the *Survivor* watchers tune out, in part, because the historical tension between want and need has shifted substantially. To understand this argument we need to explore briefly the his-tory of modern sensationalism and competition.

Historical Tensions Between Want and Need

The oldest surviving document from Gutenberg's winepress-cum-pr\
press is a Bible. But if the 1450s saw relatively traditional uses for the p.
ing press, this did not last for long. Printed sheets, pamphlets and books were
much cheaper than handwritten ones, especially when multiple copies were
made.[15] As more and more printing presses were built for a relatively stable
population size, the law of supply and demand took hold. That is, more and
more printers began to compete for a finite audience. By the 1600s, competition had forced news balladeers to sell their wares on street corners across Europe. To rise about the din and earn a profit, wrote historian Mitchell Stephens,
the balladeers had "to strive not only to be bold, but to be bolder."[16] To this
end, they sang rhyming ballads of shipwrecks and dragons, celestial wonders
and gruesome murders. One ballad, printed in 1624, recounted the "The crying Murther: Contayning the cruell and moft horrible Butcher of Mr. TRAT,"
whose limbs were hacked off and "parboiled" by assailants. Another recalled
a murder "in the strangest manner that ever hitherto hath bin heard of," a
man who poisoned his wife by filling her genitals with ratsbane and ground
glass.[17] One 1584 news ballad wrote of a couple in love. But regular love was
not bold enough: the couple in that ballad that was kissing, fondling, and ca-
ressing was a father and daughter.[18] The *National Enquirer* has got nothing
on the seventeenth century.

In trying to understand the lure of pandering to an audience, it is useful
to understand that sensationalism's primordial soup needed three basic ingredients: (1) a media system that financially rewards people who reach large (or
larger) audiences; (2) a level of competition that puts pressure on media companies and workers; and (3) a willingness on the part of one or more competitors to pander to prurient tastes. The example of early printing meets all
of these criteria.

American Journalism

The early years of America's press represent an interesting counterexample; while
sensationalism has existed in America since 1690,[19] it did not thrive until the
Jacksonian Age (the 1830s). Until that time, the American press was financially
supported by political parties. Most large cities had competing parties that each
funded their own papers to get out the message. Because editors were more beholden to party, and less to audience size, they tended to save their vitriol for
their political columns. Stories of crime, human interest, and international events
were not ignored, but they were not injected with the same breathlessness that

"The Crying Murther," a sensational newsbook from 1624. By permission of the Houghton Library, Harvard University.

stories of Mr. Trat were—and Michael Jackson are. None of the three prerequisites for sensationalism was dominant in America until the mid-1830s and editors, enjoying scant competition and rich patronage, put their newspapers to bed early and went out on the town with their fellow political hacks.

This all changed in 1833 with the birth of the New York *Sun*. Building on the "London plan" of using newsboys to hawk single sales and subscriptions, this newspaper tried to break from the party patronage model. The first criterion, an emphasis on audience, was achieved when the newspaper staked its life on its ability to attract a daily readership. Writing in 1835, de Tocqueville noted that "the spirit of the journalist in America is to attack coarsely . . . the passions of those whom it addresses, to set aside principles in order to grab men."[20]

The *Sun* was successful, but it was the arrival of one of the greatest showmen in American history that sent journalism into a permanent tension between need and want.[21] James Gordon Bennett, like other giants of New York City sensationalism—Joseph Pulitzer, William Randolph Hearst, and Rupert Murdoch—was born far from the city. Like the others, he came to lower Manhattan with a plan—a plan to shake up the establishment by sloughing off the staid and boring practices of existing journalism. Like the others, he would build his success by attracting bigger crowds than any had thought possible. Instead of using a prim Victorian term like "limbs," Bennett would use "legs." Instead of "unmentionables," he would write "trousers."[22] Instead of waiting for news to come to him, he and his reporters would scour the city for juicy tidbits. Upon hearing about the most sensational crime of his day, the ax-murder and burning of a beautiful prostitute, Bennett went to the scene (a brothel) and reported on the news for months.[23]

The salacious press' long tradition of self-promotion rarely matches the excesses of Bennett, who compared himself to Socrates and Moses and billed his own marriage as a "new movement in civilization."[24] While not as politicized as the partisan press, Bennett's upstart paper, *the New York Herald*, ruthlessly attacked individuals, groups, and causes, reminding us of one of the great lessons of journalism: conflict sells. Because these continual attacks included jabs at his rivals, some of his fellow editors actually physically attacked him on the streets of New York. One party-press editor, James Watson Webb, beat Bennett three times: once with a cane, once with a bull whip, and once by shoving him down a flight of stairs. Bennett, ever the showman, splashed all the details—at least his version of them—on the *Herald*'s front page. By his account, the *Herald* had grown within a year to three times that of the hitherto largest circulation paper, Webb's.[25]

Clive James once said that calling someone "the greatest tabloid journalist of all time" is akin to " calling a man . . . the greatest salesman of sticky sweets in the history of dentistry."[26] But while this is a great turn of phrase, it is not entirely fair. Since Bennett showed that journalism could be disassociated from party patronage, American journalism—all American journalism—

has balanced need and want. Starting with Bennett, the U.S. press has grown to be politically independent. We saw this in Bennett's eclectic endorsements in the 1800s. And we saw it in the *New York Times'* critical coverage of Clinton during the impeachment scandal in the 1990s. But in gaining independence from party, the press has grown dependent on audience. Even the *New York Times* needs to be reelected by its readers every day.[27]

The Need–Want Tension Today

In delineating the "need" side of the continuum, we can begin with a comment by Theodore Roosevelt: "I have no idea what the American people think. I only know what they should think."[28] Similarly, William Shawn, the editor of *The New Yorker*, once said that he produced a magazine that he and his staff would find interesting and important. If others found it interesting, then all the better, he said, but he would cater only to his own educated tastes and political convictions.[29] One need not agree with the old aphorism that journalism's job is to "comfort the afflicted and afflict the comfortable," to agree that part of a reporter's job is to tell people things that are more important than they realize.

The conflict between need and want is constant. Do we need to know that Jesse Jackson had an extramarital affair? The *National Enquirer* thought so, putting the news of Jackson's affair on the front page of its January 29, 2001, issue. After the *Enquirer's* story, and after Jackson admitted the affair, the *New York Times* ran the story, too. But the *Times's* story ran on page A21 without pictures or flashy prose. The *Enquirer* used exclamation points; the *Times* did not. The *Times* was saying that the Jackson story was far less important than the ones it put on the first page. Conversely, the *Enquirer* gave the story much more play than it gave to arguably more important stories at the time, such as the political and judicial appointments by the new Bush administration, which the *Enquirer* ignored.[30]

If the *New York Times* and *National Enquirer* really did represent two neat, clearly defined ends of the spectrum, choosing how to consume news would be much simpler. But the lines are blurry. The *Enquirer* has run headlines like, "26 Year-Old Marries 'the Perfect Woman'—She's 73!"[31] But that same paper often did a decent job uncovering many details of political stories in recent times, including the impeachment crisis of 1998.[32] On the other side of the need-want continuum, the *New York Times*, despite producing a lot of good journalism on the impeachment, seemed at times to catch some of the breathlessness of the tabloids. In 1998, oral sex had its big *New York Times* premiere when the paper printed every grisly detail of Bill/Monica.[33] And apart from the impeachment crisis, the late 1990s and early 2000s saw the *Times* switching to color printing, adding cartoons and personals on its Web site, and devoting an entire section of its Sunday paper to the explication of nuptials, sensuality, and young libido, the "Sunday Styles" section. The *Times* is one of the world's best newspapers, but it does not avoid "want" completely.

The Shifting Landscape

With an ever-expanding universe of entertainment choices, news outlets that ignore "want" do so at their peril. One of the top-rated television shows among the 18–24 crowd, *Friends*, was all about libido. In March 2002 when Joey confessed his love for Rachel, 27 million people were watching. They watched because they wanted a piece of the friends' camaraderie. They watched because the characters are funny and beautiful. And they watched to gain entry into the Hollywood dream factory. For on the flickering screens, ordinary Americans consume media, lots of media, that reflect their deepest loves, fears, and passions; there is something terribly primal about American entertainment. We are titillated by Britney Spears and Ricky Martin, tickled by Joan Rivers and Chris Rock, and thrilled by Sigourney Weaver and Arnold Schwarzenegger. Young people, and a great many older ones, too, tune in to entertainment because it speaks to their realities, their fears, and their dreams.[34]

At Brandeis University, in Waltham, Massachusetts, I sat with a group of a dozen or so students and discussed their news habits. I was impressed by their intelligence, thoughtfulness, and ability to examine their relationship with the news and entertainment media. These traits came in handy when they tried to describe why they tuned out from the news to concentrate on entertainment. News is stressful, said one. Another argued that it is not the level of stress but the engagement that mattered. Even though video games can be stressful, he said, "I'd rather play video games than read a newspaper because . . . it engages you more."[35]

The theme was repeated over and over again. With *Friends*, one student said, there is a "sense of emotional investment and . . . instant gratification." Against this is the "detachment" of "campaign finance reform, . . . CNN . . . [and] Peter Jennings." Given the choice between the two paradigms, said another, you are going to choose entertainment because it's "instantly gratifying and . . . resolved immediately. . . . I mean if you have a choice between two of them, you're going to pick the immediate one right away." A few of the students and their professor noted how some of the students presented Peter Jennings as simply a choice within the entertainment universe, just another stock figure. Given that perspective, Jennings, the worldly but aloof uncle is not nearly as engaging as Britney Spears, Chris Rock, or the *Friends* characters.[36]

Let's face it: most news guys are old. The 20-something "reality" show hosts Ryan Seacrest and Monica Lewinsky (yes, *that* Monica Lewinsky) are much younger than the leading names in news: Larry King (69), Peter Jennings (64), Dan Rather (71), and Barbara Walters (72).

This theme of news not being as much fun as entertainment came up not just at Brandeis but repeatedly throughout my interviews and in my informal discussions about the project. And it raises a key issue: For much of the last two centuries, journalism has been marching towards detachment and what it calls objectivity. Blatant political and partisan voices, engaging as they were, gave way to cooler voices. The reader is now asked to sift through balancing quotes or sound bites and make up his or her own mind.[37] The *Wall Street Journal*, CNN, and National Public Radio are all staffed by humans, but they all try to be detached and nonpartisan. They don't always succeed, but if detached reporting is done correctly, we are unable to say with certainty how a reporter voted or what he or she feels about a certain issue. What journalism is facing now is that fewer people understand the importance of being politically informed and more people are judging journalism's entertainment value against that of *Friends*. It's a losing proposition.

Farai Chideya, a longtime journalist who has worked in print, television, and online journalism, told me that the CNN/network television news model often treats young people as passive receivers of news. Unlike the reality shows, which depict people (often young people) being acted upon, the news excludes young adults:

> I did a study where we looked at representative samples from the year's worth of network news and found that even cases where young people should have been the focus of the story, say education . . . older voices were featured so the young people were b-roll; you know, they were shown strolling across the college campus and the older voices, the professors and the administrators, were actually the voice on tape.[38]

According to Chideya, the rituals of objectivity are not as compelling as the "humanity" of the other paradigms. "Whether it takes the form of an argument or whether it takes the form of another type of direct address, people are looking to be . . . part of the process of television instead of just being sort of passive; people want to be actively included," said Chideya.[39] It is worth noting that Chideya herself is a prime example of how one can depart from objectivity and still be deeply engaged in politics and news. A political junkie from childhood who seems to care deeply about her subjects, Chideya's own journalism is infused with the "humanity" she advocates.

Farai Chideya, author and journalist. Photo courtesy of Chideya.

While most news is not as primal and emotional as entertainment, lines have become increasingly blurred. Unfortunately for journalism, this blur does not usually involve getting more passionate about politics; it too often means getting excited about lifestyle and entertainment. Today, *Time* and *Newsweek* are seven times as likely to share the same cover topic as *People* as they were 30 years ago.[40] And lest we forget, it was *Time* and *Newsweek* that became more like *People*, not vice versa.

To understand this shift, we need to see how media have changed in our lifetimes. If you are old enough to remember when Nixon was president, you also remember a time in which there were only six or seven channels on television, a device that typically had a black-and-white screen. Because modern remotes hadn't yet been invented, changing the channel involved calf muscles and hamstrings. Because stations shut down for a few hours each night, there was literally nothing on in the wee hours of the morning. These facts astonish my students, who see television today as an unbounded tube of plenty.

The more media outlets, the more they need to compete with each other for viewers' attention. To illustrate this concept, let me take an example from everyday life. In the 1970s, beggars in large American cities would hold out a hand and ask for change. By the early 1990s, the explosion of homelessness forced beggars to use more potent forms of communication. They would bare wounds and jostle passersby.

Similarly, as the half-dozen TV stations grew to the hundreds currently on some cable packages, it became more difficult to assemble a mass audience for a discussion on the Supreme Court. Entertainment, roughly the modern

equivalent of the balladeers' dragons and shipwrecks, became too much of a distraction. To combat this, AOL Time Warner totally revamped its *Headline News* to look like a Web page, crammed with information; it hired an actress, who struggled to read the news,[41] to be its star anchor; and it started using catchy graphics that appeared to be written by over-caffeinated junior high school students. For example, a report about the war in Afghanistan was coupled with the graphic, "This one's for the boys: Latest air strike." A report about the former CEO of Enron, Kenneth Lay, used puerile ad hominem wordplay: "will testify LAY-ter . . . testimony de-LAY-ed."[42]

Cable TV and now the Internet alter the balance between need and want. Journalists have traditionally held the role of "gate-keeper," the guard who assesses information and lets it through to the public.[43] But, as Tom Rosenstiel has asked, what if journalists perform the role of gatekeeper in the absence of a fence? When Walter Cronkite visited Vietnam in 1968, declaring that the United States is "mired in stalemate," he did so to a captive audience. That evening, February 27, 1968, television viewers had only a few other choices. New Yorkers, for example, had seven channels—2, 4, 5, 7, 9, 11, and 13. At seven P.M., New Yorkers had three news choices, a public affairs show, and repeats of *F Troop* and *I Love Lucy*; when Cronkite appeared again in his report from Vietnam, at 10:30 P.M., he faced competition from only discussion shows and movies.[44] Today, young people are faced with hundreds of stations and fewer than one in ten are devoted to news. And then there are the thousands of choices for text, sound, and video on the Internet.

What does the increased competition do to the media world of young people? As we have seen, competition and its rewards are insufficient to bring about pandering; one also needs willing journalists. Unfortunately, corporate parents of news have been killing their young. Take Disney, for example. On the one hand, in 1995 they inherited some of the most professional news shows in the business. While Peter Jennings has admitted to abandoning some hard news in search of a larger audience, his news show has done it with less enthusiasm than, say, NBC News.[45] And since 1979, Ted Koppel and his staff at

What if journalists perform the role of gatekeeper in the absence of a fence? 404 College Street, Burlington, Vt. Photo by the author.

Nightline have produced thoughtful, intelligent, and informative news programming. Right from the start, however, Disney made it clear that want
trumps need, that entertainment is paramount. When ABC News uncovered
in 1998 that its parent company hired convicted pedophiles at its theme parks,
Michael Eisner, Disney's CEO, tried to squelch the reports. "I would prefer
ABC not to cover Disney. . . . I think it's inappropriate for Disney to be covered by Disney," he said. "We don't have a written policy . . . ABC News knows
that I would prefer them not to cover [Disney]."[46]

In 2002, when Disney thought it could lure David Letterman from CBS,
it was ready to cut *Nightline*, with one Disney executive saying, "The relevancy of Nightline just is not there anymore."[47] With Letterman's show attracting a median age of 46 and Koppel's a median of 50, Disney was willing
to demolish its premier news show for this four-year margin.[48] In 2002, it appeared that Disney saw not only *Nightline* as less relevant, but the entire news
division, too. David Westin, the president of ABC News, learned about Disney's offer to Letterman from a *New York Times* reporter.[49] These Disney executives are to news as silverfish are to books.

In an Op-Ed article in the *New York Times*, Koppel quickly replied to the
unnamed Disney executive who questioned *Nightline*'s "relevancy":

> I would argue that in these times, when homeland security is an ongoing con-
> cern, when another terrorist attack may, at any time, shatter our sense of nor-
> malcy, when American troops are engaged in Afghanistan, the Philippines,
> Yemen and Georgia, when the likelihood of military action against Iraq is
> growing—when, in short, the regular and thoughtful analysis of national and
> foreign policy is more essential than ever—it is, at best, inappropriate and,
> at worst, malicious to describe what my colleagues and I are doing as lacking
> relevance.[50]

From a purely business perspective, the Disney executive did have a point.
If the entire game is about ratings—and not about integrity or democracy—
relevancy and ratings are synonymous. For four decades, the government
had imposed an ethical standard on broadcasters, that they perform a public
service. Thus, it is no surprise that Cronkite and his generation had a lot of
shows about politics and public affairs. It is equally not surprising that in
the 1980s after the Federal Communications Commission (FCC) overturned
its "public trust" requirement, the broadcasters began to conflate ratings and
relevancy.[51] In the end, David Letterman decided, in March 2002, to stay with
CBS, in part to avoid being the man who brought Koppel to the chopping
block. It wasn't a studio head or news executive who suddenly felt the sting
of conscience, but an entertainer. It was a victory for news, but a tenuous
one at best.

Chasing Young People

The combination of all of these factors—competition, the end of the "public trust" requirement, a plethora of choices, and a willingness to pander—means that many in the media crowd are, like their ballad-selling ancestors in the seventeenth-century, trying to out-scream their competitors to reach an audience. Because young people are more malleable in terms of products—less likely, for example, to have decided which carbonated drink to pledge their life-long allegiance to—advertisers follow media outlets that can attract the under-30 crowd.

What does this pursuit of young people look like? We saw it in the 1990s with the explosion of MTV and ESPN. We see it in the marketing of pop star Britney Spears for Pepsi and Tiger Woods for just about everything else. And we see it in the latest TV shows marketed for the 18–34 demographic: *Jackass*, *The Real World*, *Survivor*, and *Temptation Island*. The assumption is that what attracts young people has little to do with news and a lot to do with their own wants. Even Jackie Nixon, NPR's thoughtful director of audience research, had this to say about the 18–24 demographic:

> When you're an 18- to 24-year-old, you're not thinking a whole lot about who's going to be the next president of the United States. You're really trying to think about, Am I going to get married? Am I going to have a successful job? Am I going to be able to afford my apartment? How am I going to pay for my car? And, How cute is the chick or the guy at the end of the bar? And will they go home with me? Their head is in a different place.[52]

Most media players seem to agree with this assessment, but they take it one step further. The strategy for reeling in young people has less to do with car payments than with chicks and guys at the end of the bar. Unfortunately, the strategy seems to be working, with young people consuming more *Jackass* and *Real World*, less Jennings and Rather. But even if we admit that young people rank social life and dating above nearly everything else (20 years ago, I did), we can still expect that young people will be interested in the news if it is presented to them (20 years ago, I was).

The big problem is when "want" drives the show. When I spoke with Chris Rose, a *New Orleans Times–Picayune* entertainment reporter, he likened the "Grammies, Oscars, the romances and the breakups" to sugared cereals. "And I like to have that [sugared cereals] every now and then," he said.[53] Rose is right, but his media diet appears to be well rounded: his playful yet intelligent writing seems to be informed by wide reading. Rose's talk of breakfast cereal reminded me of a study in the 1970s in which children were asked to choose between two bowls of cereal. The researchers discovered that the sweeter the cereal, the more it was preferred. If researchers pandered to a child's taste, the bowl was practically all sugar.[54] The only thing coming between a child and bowl of Cap'n Crunch is often a parent. But the 18–40 crowd does not have a policing parent and television executives seem to have a dearth of integrity and restraint. Older folks, including Rose, have already developed healthier habits, but most young people have been weaned on sweet media since before they could walk. According to Robert Entman, in *Democracy Without Citizens* this creates a "vicious circle," with no pressure on either side to create quality journalism:

> Because most members of the public know and care relatively little about government, they neither seek nor understand high-quality political reporting and analysis. With limited demand for first-rate journalism, most news organizations cannot afford to supply it, and because they do not supply it, most Americans have no practical source of the information necessary to become politically sophisticated. Yet it would take an informed and interested citizenry to create enough demand to support top-flight journalism.[55]

But Entman's worry, real as it was when he was writing in 1989, is far more serious in the 2000s: As the industry chases young people and discovers that the young won't, on their own, clamor for news, who will break this vicious circle?

In recent years, Entman's vicious circle has become increasingly entrenched. Whereas the best newspapers have always tried to shield their editors from business pressures, this separation, often called a "wall," has been increasingly compromised by brazen quests for more money. In 1999, The *Los Angeles Times* embarrassed itself by printing a magazine devoted to praising a new business center; the *Times* would secretly share profits in this endeavor. Increasingly in newsrooms across America, editors' pay is tied to profits. And in 2000, when the on-line magazine, *Salon*, needed to downsize its writers, it did so after assessing their popularity as much as, and perhaps more than, their quality. *Salon* investigated how many "page hits" each writer attracted.[56]

Naked News

In 1982, in a ratings war with his rivals, Dan Rather did something radical to boost his ratings: He tried wearing a sweater with his suit and tie.[57] But a sweater is only important if your competitive universe consists of two other middle-aged white guys in suits.

Even setting aside the varied competition from entertainment, the news business itself has provided both rhetorical and sartorial challenges. The rhetorical includes the many news outlets that allow attitude to trump detachment and objectivity. *Fox News*, which has seen its numbers growing, particularly among the young, injects its news with opinion. Conflict sells, and Fox's shows tend to have a gloss of attitude, even belligerence. It is not a coincidence that both Fox and most of the successful radio talk shows tend to be right-wing. When Rush Limbaugh fulminates against welfare moms and "feminazis," his combativeness is far more engaging than the left's thoughtful and tolerant defense of these groups. I will argue in the conclusion of this book that while these departures from objectivity can be troubling, they provide clues to creating new kinds of journalism for young people.

With or without a sweater, Dan Rather looks conventional next to Victoria Sinclair. On October 14, 2003, Rather opened with a report about the U.S. Supreme Court hearing a challenge to the "under God" line in the Pledge of Allegiance. Sinclair's first story was about Bush's comment that he was "in charge" of Iraq policy. As the two anchors continued to deliver the news, viewers would have noticed that both were concerned with telling the news with a straight face and both had an interest in international affairs (although Sinclair read more international stories than Rather did). Despite their similarities, however, there was one glaring difference: throughout his newscast, Rather remained fully clothed. During her second story, however, on the United Nations Security Council's vote to increase its presence in Afghanistan, Sinclair had nonchalantly unbuttoned her blouse, slipped off her skirt and slipped off her purple bra. Sinclair, fit and youthful looking at 37-years-old, was the anchor of Nakednews.com, a service that broadcasts a daily news show over the Web. As she read her third story, on Iran's nuclear program, she had slipped off her purple panties and was standing naked. It may not surprise readers to know that while Rather's show has seen a decline in young viewers, Sinclair's show has seen an explosion.[58]

At first glance, viewers might actually be impressed with the news content of Nakednews.com. After all, what American news show would lead with five international stories in a row? But Nakednews.com is not a news organization. It reads but does not report. It undresses but does not uncover. It is a show dog, not a watchdog. If journalism's ultimate goal is to make sure that "we don't get screwed,"[59] Rather and his news organization are better protectors than Victoria Sinclair will ever be. September 11, 2001 ushered in a period of tensions between security and civil rights, massive outlays of public money, and the potential for an endless war against terrorism; we will need responsible journalists to help us see how far the pendulum swings in either direction. Despite the entertainment value of Nakednews.com, we need our journalists clothed for battle.

With a range of entertainment and news-as-entertainment options, the political universe of young people has changed substantially. While we can acknowledge that serious topics have always had an element of entertainment

Victoria Sinclair, the lead anchor at NakedNews.Com. Courtesy of Naked Broadcasting Network Inc.

(for example, even the highly literate Lincoln-Douglas debates took place alongside a carnival), we must still admit that today's climate is substantially changed. Bob Dole announced his candidacy on the *Late Show with David Letterman,* Clinton played the saxophone and revealed his preference for briefs over boxers to television audiences,[60] and Colin Powell appeared in 2002 before a huge international audience via MTV to defend the U. S. war aims.

The "Long Island Lolita"/Slobodan Milosevic Inverse Correlative

In January 1993, The Times Mirror Center found that 40 percent of Americans had seen at least one of the three TV movies made about Amy Fisher, the young woman who shot her lover's wife and was dubbed by the press the "Long Island Lolita." The Times Mirror Center found a fascinating correlation: The more Amy Fisher movies watched, the less a person knew about was happening in Bosnia. In the words of the study, "Those who viewed none [of the films] knew more about the Balkan conflict than those who viewed one film, and they, in turn, knew more than those who saw two Fisher movies, etc."[61] As young people continue to replace the news with entertainment, the "Long Island Lolita"/Slobodan Milosevic inverse correlative becomes more pronounced. Nearly half of people under the age of 30, Pew found, use late night comedians as a major source of news. This trend has been somewhat aided by the clever and biting *Daily Show*, hosted by comedian Jon Stewart.[62]

Dhavan Shah, an expert in media usage, wrote that there is a correlation between the kinds of entertainment shows people watch and their views on politics, engagement, and presumably, news. In other words, it is not only the amount of entertainment we watch that is important in predicting civic values, including news viewership, but also the kinds of shows watched. Viewing dramas such as *ER, Law and Order*, and *The West Wing*, Shah wrote, correlates to civil engagement. Sitcoms, on the other hand, do the reverse.[63] Although my sample is too small to support Shah's larger one, I did see a lot of evidence of this in talking to young people. *Friends* was the number one show of the tuned out; an eclectic mix of drama that stresses process and information (*The West Wing, Six Feet Under*) dominated this list for the tuned in.

One of the innovations that the Web has brought to journalism is the tracking of the "most popular" news stories. According to CNN, four of the top 10 most popular news stories on its Web site during the month of August 2001 were about the death of Aaliyah, a young pop star. Other pieces included an article about multitasking, a list of the top party colleges, and a profile of someone who could translate the language of dogs.[64] On the morning of September 11, I was driving to the Saint Michael's College library, just outside Burlington, Vermont, to make sense of this odd and frivolous list, particularly what it said about how young people follow (and don't follow) the news. It was only later that morning, after I learned that terrorists had crashed planes into the World Trade Center and Pentagon, that I began to realize that frivolous news would disappear for a while. In October, *The Onion*, a satirical newspaper, announced, "A SHATTERED NATION LONGS TO CARE ABOUT STUPID BULLSHIT AGAIN."[65]

The United States didn't have to wait long. In January and February 2002, CNN's most popular story was about a woman who became stuck to a toilet in a transatlantic flight. Here is the full list of CNN's "most popular stories" of January–February 2002:

1. Jet passengers [sic] transatlantic toilet trauma—January 22
2. Alert issued for potential teddy bear bombs—February 14
3. Florida town casts out Satan—January 29
4. First cloned cat is born, scientists say—February 15
5. Jeb Bushs [sic] daughter arrested on false prescription charge—January 29
6. Canadian skaters get gold; judge suspended—February 15
7. Personal jetpack gets off the ground—February 6
8. Friends cast back for ninth, final season—February 12
9. Getting a new face after rare infection—February 4
10. Kansas woman expecting 2 sets of identical twins—January 25[66]

This list is remarkable when we consider that all of these stories trumped the military maneuvers in Afghanistan. Remember, these are not the most popular stories in *People*, but among CNN.com consumers. Even among regular news readers, many don't read well. Max Frankel, the executive editor of the *New York Times*, discovered that his readers often avoid reading beyond the front page and often needed an interesting picture to get them to read more. But unlike journalists who tend to pander, Frankel used this information to help him sell serious news to his readers. They will read about Cambodia, reasoned Frankel, but they might need to be helped by a visual to do so.[67]

The Kind of Stories That Lure

People look for stories that shock, titillate, and pull at the heartstrings. This is one of the oldest truths about narratives, a truth that precedes the printing press. Aristotle called a subset of this kind of narrative a "reversal of the situation."[68] The most compelling of these, Aristotle wrote, is the fall of a great and powerful man, in part self-induced (think Oedipus, Lear, Nixon, and Clinton). Looking at human interest stories in general, Roland Barthes, the French semiologist, said that they always involve "disturbed causality," an astonishment that confounds expectations. A man dies in a pool—during a party for lifeguards. A robber breaks into a blowtorch company's safe—using a blowtorch. A man joins the French Foreign Legion—to avoid spending Christmas with his mother-in-law.[69] The problem with this kind of story comes when this astonishment becomes the main objective.

Robert Darnton, a historian who started his professional life as a cub reporter, lamented the overuse of archetypes in journalism. "It was like making cookies from an antique cookie cutter," he wrote.[70] When NBC and the *Wash-*

ington Post began a partnership to investigate stories that would appear in both media, an NBC *Dateline* producer advised *Post* editors that an ideal story should contain "a villain, a victim and a confrontation."[71] The antique cookie cutter is still in use.

If we accept Entman's view that the pull of quality journalism is weak, we must also worry that the forces of entertainment have heated up as competition has become more intense and the traditional broadcasters are no longer as restrained by the FCC's "public trust" requirements. Competition, as David Shenk explains, turns us away from contemplative thoughts:

> As the competition heats up, people do what they have to do to make their voices heard. They TALK LOUDER. They wear more vibrant color. They show more cleavage—if they can. They say shocking things.
>
> In the immediate sense, pumping up the volume is an effective solution. More broadly, though, it becomes part of the problem, feeding a vicious spiral in which the data smog gets thicker and thicker and the efforts to cut through the smog get ever more desperate. As the people of Earth collectively try to rise above the noise, they unwittingly create more of it. The volume and vulgarity increase notch by notch, alongside the glut.[72]

As I traveled around the country interviewing young people, I came to worry that with information as well as with food, we are what we eat. As many young people consume the media equivalent of sugary cereals, they lose their taste for—indeed their ability to digest—serious news.

The "Long Island Lolita"/Slobodan Milosevic inverse correlative that the Times Mirror Center had established was evident time and time again in my discussions with young people. Most people who selected *Cosmopolitan* or *Maxim* as their favorite magazines had a difficult time naming Tom Daschle and other political figures. The clearest examples of this are the junior college basketball players and actors I interviewed in Los Angeles. All were big consumers of entertainment media. None could name more than one or two political facts or figures. For example, all of them could identify Alicia Keys and Allen Iverson, none could identify Tom Daschle or John Ashcroft. Not all shared one actor's view that the news "is all crap"[73]; at least one of the junior college basketball players was deeply disturbed by her lack of political knowledge.[74] But of all the people I interviewed in Los Angeles, the lack of nonentertainment news knowledge was universal.

Actually, that is not entirely true. One person, Aaron Harper, 23, an assistant to the head of casting for Universal Pictures, was as steeped in entertainment as the others I interviewed in Los Angeles. But Harper was tuned in to news. Why? Chapter 4 examines why some people tune in to news while others tune out.

CHAPTER 4

Talking with Young People II: Who Follows the News and Why

Finding a young person tuned in to news is like searching for Waldo and his friends in the *Where's Waldo?* series. They're there, in every crowd, but are half-hidden and very much in the minority. Who follows the news and why? I pondered this question in early May 2002 as I sat at the bar of the Newsroom, an actors' hangout on North Robertson Boulevard in Los Angeles. I was in the middle of interviews with L.A. residents—the basketball players from L A. Pierce Junior College, the actors, and later that day, the assistant to the head of casting at Universal Pictures. The Newsroom had CNN on over the bar and newspapers and magazines for sale by the front door. But although the daily circulation of the *Los Angeles Times* is about a million,[1] there were none in sight, except on the rack. Nobody was watching CNN. The Newsroom appeared to be practically news-free that day. With the exception of a young woman checking e-mail at the restaurant's one terminal, and an older man with slicked-back hair scanning *Variety* at the bar, people were consuming and producing only the most primal of news sources: They were sitting and talking.

Of course, news is often passed orally, especially in a city in which the most important stuff is often the gossip. As I was leaving, Kato Kaelin (whose burgeoning film and television career, spurred by his role in the O. J. Simpson trial, is a great testament to the blur of news and entertainment) walked into the restaurant, creating a buzz.

An hour later I went to interview Aaron Harper, the assistant to the head of casting at Universal Pictures. As I sat in a rented car at the gate of Universal, while smartly dressed security guards passed mirrors under the car's chassis, I pondered whether news could possibly trump entertainment in the glitz capital of the universe. In my quest to find at least one person who follows the news in Los Angeles, was I looking in the most unlikely place of all? Since I had been completely wrong about the Kansas City bankers, I told myself to keep an open mind.

Unlike everyone else I had met in Los Angeles, Aaron Harper was tuned in. Not only could he identify Allen Iverson[*] and Alicia Keys, but Tom Daschle and four Supreme Court justices—not bad for a 23-year-old. The reasons for his news habits reflect some of the most significant divisions between those who are tuned in and those who are tuned out. One of the great dividing lines is the power of the workplace.

Workplace

Harper worked in a place where information mattered. To get a sense of this, I asked him about how much entertainment news he needed to know for his job. For example, I said, you would really need to know who Selma Blair (an actress) is. "Exactly," Harper said. "You have to know. Even more specifically: What was Selma Blair's last movie? *Storytelling*!"[2] Our exchange was revealing because it showed the power of information in the workplace. I mentioned the then-20-something Selma Blair in part to demonstrate that I knew something about the latest currents in Harper's field (mentioning Meryl Streep would only have shown my age). Not only did Harper know Blair's name, but he parried my information with something much more specific, a relatively obscure fact: that Blair's last movie was called *Storytelling*. Just as my question to him aimed to get information and establish competence, so did his reply. As evidenced by his ability to name Supreme Court justices, Harper's information was not confined to entertainment. But, like the Kansas City bankers, he worked in a place where information exchange was paramount. Keeping this in mind, it was no surprise that of five Kansas bankers, four felt that keeping up with the news was important for work. It is also not surprising that they were far more informed than their colleague who did not feel that keeping up with news was essential for work.

Norman Rosenfeld, an architect since 1961, told me that keeping up with the news is crucial in his field. "We're involved with sophisticated clients, so-

---

[*]In July 2002, Iverson was arrested on multiple charges. The interviews I conducted were completed before these legal troubles. At the time of the interviews, Iverson was known principally for his unrivalled abilities as a basketball player.

Aaron Harper, tuned in despite being at ground zero of the dream factory. Photo by
Liz Salem.

phisticated projects, we're involved in a changing world and the more you know
about it, the better armed you are to serve your client needs," Rosenfeld said.
"Reading something in the paper in the morning and going to a meeting in
the afternoon shows how smart you are, that you really know what's going
on in their business." Rosenfeld offered a specific example. A hospital he was
working with was considering installing exercise equipment in its building. He
circulated a *New York Times* article about that trend before he and his associates were to meet with representatives of the hospital. Because Rosenfeld's
younger associates don't read the *Times*, he himself needs to serve as a news
source.[3]

The case of Andrea Alford is a useful illustration of how a workplace can
shape news use. In 1999, Alford, who was a college student at the time, landed
a summer internship at the Washington, DC, offices of Ducks Unlimited, a
nonprofit environmental group. Alford, who was the youngest in the office by
five or six years, quickly learned that she was the only one in the office who
did not read the newspaper:

> When I got there I was the youngest in the office and a lot of times people
> would talk about current events. . . . So that I could keep myself up to date
> and perhaps not stick out as such a young individual, I started reading. I don't
> even remember what paper I picked up every morning. But every morning
> before work I'd go have a cup of coffee and read the paper before I went to
> work. . . . It also helped if you were talking to congressional aides, to know
> what their senator was up to or their congressman, and try to find out if they'd
> want to support the bill that you were working on.[4]

In contrast to Harper and Alford, most people I interviewed for this project put a low premium on the exchange of news. Among the interviewees were the L.A. actors who worked as waiters to support themselves. Banter was important in their field, they said, but news played little or no role in their conversations. This, in turn, was fortunate for them, because they were almost entirely tuned out.[5]

Conversation

The role that news plays in conversation, and vice versa, can be seen in its absence. In the summer of 1945 a newspaper strike almost completely shut down the news in New York City. While their primary news medium was shut for 17 days, New Yorkers felt in the dark as the world events marched on. The United States was still mopping up from the bloody Battle of Okinawa. In Europe, the full horrors of the Nazi atrocities were starting to be revealed. Meanwhile, Churchill was voted out in Britain, replaced by Attlee. In Potsdam, Stalin and Attlee met with Harry S. Truman, who had just replaced Roosevelt as president. The leaders discussed, among other things, the Cold War, and the newly constituted Germany and Poland. Against this news background, the sociologist Bernard Berelson studied how New Yorkers coped with the dearth of news.

They did not cope well. "I am like a fish out of water," said one New Yorker, "I am lost and nervous." Another said, "If I don't know what's going on next door, it hurts me. It's like being in jail not to have a paper." Some respondents spoke about loneliness ("You feel put out and isolated from the rest of the world"), while others reported physiological changes ("I am suffering! Seriously! I could not sleep I missed it so!").[6]

Information has always been fodder for conversation. But what kind of information are we talking about? I asked everyone I interviewed about the types of information they feel they have to know to keep up with the various conversations of the day. As I mentioned, the workplace was a strong factor here. But there were also a few people who seemed to thrive on knowing information as an end in itself. Joel Senesac, a former student of mine who is now a freelance writer, was a case in point. "I've always been interested in finding out the latest news items, being the first to tell somebody about them," he said.[7] For Senesac, whose muscular dystrophy confines him to a wheelchair, information, including news, seems to be a means of recouping some of the loss of physical mobility. Keeping up with the news aids Senesac in many areas of his life, from his considerable advocacy on behalf of physically challenged students, to his growing reputation as a reporter, to his ability to more than hold his own in any news-related discussion.

Joel Senesac, who liked to be first with the news.   Photograph by the author.

People have a primal need for conversation, but they do not appear to have such a need for traditional news. In fact, if my interviewees are to be believed, the lip-loosening, tongue-wagging properties of political and general interest news are limited, especially in comparison to other kinds of information. This was evident throughout my interviews, particularly in my conversation with Chris Rose, the *New Orleans Times–Picayune* entertainment reporter. Rose had been a general news reporter for 18 years, writing about crime, politics, race relations and economic issues. During the period he wrote hard news, he rarely got any response from readers—maybe a call a week. Now, as an entertainment reporter, Rose said "I can write a story about Britney Spears opening a restaurant in New York City, and I mean [I'm] flooded with e-mail, and people stop me and talk to me about it."[8]

It is impossible to figure out which came first, the lack of conversation about news or the lack of news knowledge; I assume that these two are mutually reinforcing. Whatever the teleology, however, we can see the effect on news consumers: when your age peers do not follow the news, there is less incentive for you to do so, too. One Brandeis student told about her difficulty in getting friends to pause their discussions of entertainment so that she could talk about the news: "There are some friends of mine that I just go there and I mention anything about the news and they're like 'alright, next,' like they want to like flip a channel changer." Another woman at Brandeis agreed: "There are definitely people who are content to spout *Simpsons* references till the cows come home. . . . And maybe there's a sense that *Simpsons* quotes can be applied to normal conversation, and then it launches into 'did you see that one . . . it was so funny.' But let's say you saw something on *Nightline,* like 'did you know that blah blah blah blah,' and then it's like, sort of maybe a little bit, but then it's finished. It doesn't have that sort of recurring effect."[9]

This may explain why so many more people tune into entertainment than news. I asked everyone why some people don't follow the news. By far, the number one answer was that young people are far busier than their parents were. Their lifestyles are "faster-paced," said a 29-year-old Kansas City banker.[10] "It really has a lot to do with time and being really busy," said a 25-year-old from New Orleans.[11] While time was cited as the main factor by the tuned in and tuned out alike, the latter seemed especially pressed for time. "I don't have time to watch it and I don't make the time," said a 22-year-old junior college basketball player.[12] It is outside the scope of my study to offer a detailed analysis of generational shifts in leisure time. However, this was a goal of Putnam's and he concluded that people are not as harried as they think they are. In fact, the busiest people are often the ones who follow the most news and engage the most in their communities.[13] It is also reasonable to point out, as Putnam did, that the average American watches four hours of television a day; the average family has the TV on for seven hours a day.[14] If there is something that is making the lives of young people too busy to follow the news, it is most likely television and other entertainment media. The "time displacement" influence of television, wrote Robert Kraut, is significant.[15]

Like Putnam, I find the "time" excuse incomplete. My interviews with young people suggested that priorities, rather than time, may have been the prime factor. In this way, the respondents did correctly understand that a generational change had occurred, but it was not the one they had envisioned. The main change may be that while the entertainment culture has grown, the social need for news has shrunk. Looking at it this way, we can come to the conclusion that it is not that young people have too much responsibility, but not enough. Lizzie Salzfass spoke to me about college being a "bubble," where world events do not touch you personally.[16] Demographers have made a lot of how the latest generations begin careers and marriage later than their elders did. Perhaps this prolonged adolescence can help to permanently deprive people of picking up the news habit by pushing them away from the conversations and responsibilities that would make them inclined to follow the news. By the time many of them have entered the world of adult responsibilities, they are past the age at which news habits are usually formed.

Childhood Habits

Prolonged adolescence can push people away from news, but preadolescence can be important, too. Parental interest in the news appears to be a significant factor. Ann Colbert, 59, remembered how her parents took three newspapers—two dailies and the local weekly—and discussed issues at meals. "I wanted to know what they were talking about," said Colbert. "Later, I added my own thoughts [to her parents' conversations] and was able to contribute to the conversation."[17] Of all the students I spoke with in Colchester High School (Colchester, VT) the most informed was an 18-year-old who avidly discussed the news with his father. The two had emigrated from Bosnia in the late 1990s, and kept a strong interest in international news; for example, this student knew all three countries Bush mentioned as being part of the "axis of evil," the only one of the four I interviewed from his school who could name all three. And despite that he had been in the United States for only five years, this student also did better than his peers in naming his state's senators' and the U.S. attorney general, John Ashcroft. The nightly conversations between father and son helped mutually reinforce their news knowledge, the student said.[18] Mike Long, one of this student's teachers agreed and added, "kids have political views usually because their parents have political views."[19]

Since many of the children and young adults in my study are merely picking up where their parents left off (that is, many of their parents began the trend of tuning out) it is useful to remind ourselves about the trends involving 30-something and 40-something adults. As Putnam has pointed out about civic involvement, the disengagement started decades ago.[20] Many of the youngest people in my study are reaping what their parents started to sow in the 1970s.

The other strong influence on children appears to come from teachers. In the 1920s, a newspaperman visited a high school to preach about the importance of his craft. Young Walter Cronkite was a student there and the rest is history.[21] For David Brinkley, inspiration came from a writing teacher. "A world turned for me in Mrs. Burrows Smith's English class at New Hanover High School," he wrote.[22] Max Frankel, the former executive editor at the *New York Times*, was primed by experience and family to be engaged in journalism: He had escaped from the Nazis and had a father with whom he argued over politics. But his early dream of becoming a journalist competed with aspirations to become a politician, an opera singer, and an artist. What tipped the balance? Perhaps it was the civics class in which the teacher converted America into a "grid of blackboard lines and boxes, illustrating a diffusion of power among competing institutions and peoples—power that [the teacher] thought was properly mistrusted, checked, and balanced." Or perhaps it was the journalism class in which Frankel read *New Yorker* articles, analyzed them, and tried to emulate them. Whatever the precise reason, Frankel's school provided him with ample opportunity to develop a lifelong news interest, and in his case, a career in journalism.[23]

In an on-line discussion in 1999 with his readers about the many choices available over the Internet, Jon Katz asked, "Would you ever read a newspaper again?" Many of the responses dwelled on technology, but some of the respondents who still followed the news gave a more prosaic reason for doing so: a habit formed in school. "I read TONS of news daily," said one respondent. "I've been a news hound ever since the 4th grade (thanks, Mrs. Briggs!). . . . As big as the net is getting, there's nothing like holding that paper in your hands, feeling nice and calm sitting AWAY from the computer, and flipping the pages."[24]

Many of the people I interviewed had similar stories. At Colchester High School, a required civics class appears to be making progress in helping students care about the news.[25] At Bishop Perry, a Catholic middle school that serves African American boys whose families are below the poverty line in

Students in front of the Bishop Perry school in New Orleans.   Photo by Rilda Letourneau. Reprinted by permission of Bishop Perry.

New Orleans, the students were, for the most part, closely engaged in news and politics. This may be because of the many endeavors of the school, including "Focus Afghanistan," in which students presented projects on terrorism, Islam, the Taliban, and other issues relating to the war in Afghanistan. Another such project was "Examples in Excellence," in which successful black men from New Orleans came to Bishop Perry to lecture. Students were expected to be prepared to ask the speaker informed and intelligent questions.[26]

One of the simplest ways to get young people interested in news is to introduce them to the news habit and hope that it sticks. It often does. One of the eighth graders I spoke with in New Orleans mentioned Donald Rumsfeld, the secretary of defense. "You know Rumsfeld?" I asked him. Yes, he said he saw his name on the Nytimes.com Web site. "You read the *New York Times?* When did you start?" I asked, trying to hide my surprise. Remember, this was a poor eighth grader from New Orleans. "Back in sixth grade," he explained. "It was a class project and ever since then we get e-mail from the *New York Times.*" When I asked him why he was still a subscriber two years later, he replied that the *Times* is free on the Internet, and besides, "we could get world news from it."[27] Of the five eighth graders around the table, four had taken that sixth-grade class. All were still subscribed to the *New York Times* two years later.

Other Factors: Defining Oneself Through News Knowledge, September 11, etc.

Aaron Harper struggled with the question about Supreme Court justices. "I know Scalia, there's Thomas, there's Rehnquist, there's . . . Ginsburg," Harper said. "Four out of nine is bad."[28] Actually, four out of nine is not bad; of all the people I interviewed, only three people named more.[29] What is interesting about Harper's reaction is that he felt that this was something he should know. Kanon Cozad, the vice president at United Missouri Bank, could name six and said he would think about it all day until he got the other three.[30] Joel Senesac, the former Saint Michael's College student who expressed his desire to be first with the news, got four and struggled with what he did not know.[31]

The people who were the most informed often felt the most guilty about what they did not know. However, the correlation in my sample was weak; even many of those who did not follow the news felt like they should. "I feel so stupid," said one of the L. A. Pierce basketball players,[32] a sentiment echoed by others. What is important to remember, however, is the difference between the desire to know more and actually following the news. In a survey of Brandeis students, 89 percent said that "reading newspapers is very important or important to their education." However, when students at that institution were given the opportunity to read papers free of charge, only a minority did so.[33]

Some factors that I had thought would loom large in my interviews did not. Robert Putnam wrote about how civic involvement correlates to trust in the government and faith in one's ability to promote change; I looked, unsuccessfully, for a similar correlation in my interviews. The people who followed the news most closely were generally confident in their ability to make a difference politically. However, many others did, too. Lizzie Salzfass, whose news knowledge did not match her political convictions, told me about her protest activity and how she felt that the protests affected the intended target. "I think that people like me do make a difference," she said.[34] Even the two Los Angeles actors who were by and large tuned out agreed that they could make a difference.[35]

Despite the many polls showing that September 11 had little long-term affect on news consumption, I had been hopeful that it would. After all, it was the most significant news day of our lives. While earthquakes and floods have caused more death and destruction, none has been as dramatic and a visually shocking as watching, live, the destruction of two colossal buildings with thousands trapped inside. While the United States was faced with a greater civil rights challenge—the suspension of habeas corpus in the Civil War—in 2001–2002, we were faced with de facto suspensions of habeas corpus and due process at a scale not seen since those days more than 140 years ago.[36] While the United States has seen its share of whodunits, including those involving the Lindbergh baby and O. J. Simpson, none can top the questions surrounding the 19 mysterious men who hijacked four planes on September 11. Taken together, we were left with a day that ought to have changed behavior.

Unfortunately, most of the respondents reported little or no change in their habits. As with other factors mentioned above, the people whose news habits were changed the most by September 11 were those who were already tuned in. Aaron Harper, suspicious of government sources, became more likely to check alternative media outlets; Joel Senesac and Kanon Cozad, convinced of the increased need for international news, started following stories about the Middle East and Central Asia, respectively.[37] But most of the people I spoke with reported only short-term changes in their news habits. One student at Brandeis likened the September 11 attacks to news about reproductive rights, citing the "immediacy" of both: "That's personal, like a . . . 'get your hands off my body' issue," she said.[38] For most respondents, September 11 was nothing less than the worst day of their lives. That said, for many it was *nothing more* than the worst day of their lives. In other words, it was seen as a horrible, but discrete, event. Because of its horror, September 11 competed successfully with entertainment television for readers' and viewers' attention. Because the shock faded and the drier political ramifications came to the fore, many young people went back to their old habits.

The Internet

Everything you have read in this book up until now is complicated by the introduction of the most powerful new media force since televisions hit the shelves in the late 1940s. The Internet changes everything because, to borrow Whitman's phrase, it "contains multitudes"[39]: it has substitutes for all the traditional news media and it has the full spectrum of information, from hard news to sports to music to child porn. In 1995, 14 percent of all Americans went on-line to access the Internet (including the World Wide Web and e-mail). By 2002, 66 percent had done so.[40] In the 1990s and early 2000s, newspapers, while maintaining profitability, have seen declines in circulation. At the same time, Web sites, while making far less profit, have seen an explosion in readership. At Nola.com, the Web site sponsored in part by the *New Orleans Times–Picayune*, the monthly page views have seen a hundredfold rise in four years:

NOLA.COM'S MONTHLY PAGE VIEWS FOR JANUARY, 1998–2002

1998	222,458
1999	4,380,790
2000	15,141,681
2001	17,690,818
2002	24,761,705

John Donley, personal interview, 8 May 2002. Data supplied by Donley.

Nola.com's median user age is 38; half of the users are college graduates and about half are female.[41] These statistics reveal the changing demographics of the Web: that it is no longer dominated by young, educated, white males. By 2000, the Internet's demographics began to resemble that of the overall U.S. population. About 50 percent of all users were female, 40 percent were college educated, and 69 percent were over 30 years old.[42] Even in the school I visited in the poor, black neighborhood of New Orleans, everyone was wired. Within a short time, with initiatives in libraries and schools across the country, and with computer prices continuing to drop, Internet connections may very well become nearly as available as television.

But What Is on Their Computer Screens?

But with the United States zipping towards Internet access for all, it is important for us to remember that far more young people log on than follow the news. At the height of the 2000 presidential election, 26.5 percent of 18–24-year-olds who logged on accessed election news at least once a week. We must remember, however, that if 26.5 percent of 18–24-year-old on-line users logged on weekly to get election news, 73.5 percent did not.[43]

What is the wired under-40 crowd doing over the Internet? E-mail is the primary use, with more than 90 percent of all Internet users sending and receiving mail on a typical day. This is also true among the youngest Internet users, 12–17.[44] Most of my interviewees agreed, citing e-mail and AOL Instant Messenger as their primary activities over the Internet. These activities appear to have increased in the last few years.[45] This makes sense because until the mid-1990s, few people had e-mail; by 2002, the vast majority of Americans were connected via e-mail and the World Wide Web, creating a critical mass necessary in any mass medium. Coupled with the fact that greater and greater segments of the population are logging on is a shift away from using the Internet primarily from and for work. By the mid-1990s, the majority of 'Net users were logging on from home and this trend continued in the early 2000s. According to Jonathon Cummings and Robert Kraut, this trend "domesticated" the contents of the Web: "buddy lists," e-mail messages (including forwards), and music exchanges became increasingly important in the early 2000s.[46]

Much like what happened with television in the 1990s, entertainment and personal interests seem to be making news a smaller and smaller part of the Internet's universe. Even at Brandeis University, where everyone is wired, 41 percent of students say they seldom or never access newspapers on the Internet.[47] When I asked students there about their primary uses of the Internet, e-mail and chatting were, by far, the most common answers.[48]

Why Do Some Follow News over the Internet?

In looking for factors that affect news habits among young people, researchers and other observers increasingly look to the Internet as a strong determinant. But what does the Internet do to young people's news knowledge? Because the Internet is so vast, and so complex and so new and so much a part of our everyday lives, making sense of it is extremely difficult. Even those who try to examine the new media seascape are only now realizing how complex it really is.

Until about five years ago, leading researchers tended to see the Internet as a neutral or negative force in civic involvement and news consumption. In their landmark article, "Internet Paradox: A Social Technology That Reduces Social Involvement and Psychological Well-Being?" (1998), Robert Kraut et al. wrote about how the Internet promotes isolation and disengagement. Like television, wrote Kraut, "the Internet generally implies physical inactivity and limited face-to-face social interaction." With this comes "isolation" and "loneliness," wrote Kraut.[49] In 2000, Putnam concluded that young people's news consumption and civic involvement are either unaffected or adversely affected by the Internet. Moreover, Putnam argued, "unlike those who rely on news-papers, radio, and television for news, those few technologically proficient Americans who rely *primarily* on the Internet for news are actually *less* likely than their fellow citizens to be civically involved."[50]

Beginning in 1998, researchers began to take a different tack, under-standing the subtler currents within the various new media. Pippa Norris and David Jones (1998) divided Internet users into four categories: "researchers," "consumers," "political expressives," and "party animals." Although Norris and Jones were not very optimistic about the overall picture, they did see one area of hope, finding that "researchers" had more political knowledge and were more likely to vote than the other groups.[51]

Another team of researchers, Dhavan Shah, Nojin Kwak, and R. Lance Halbert, see "information exchange"—similar to the "researcher" category of Norris and Jones—to have a "universally positive impact" for all ages.[52] Another important development in this area came in 2002 when Kraut et al. revisited their theory that the Internet promotes isolation, loneliness, and disengagement. In this newer study, the authors found that the negative effects of the first study had dissipated and that people "generally experienced positive effects of using the Internet on communication, social involvement, and well-being." However, Kraut et al. reported a "rich get richer" model wherein extraverts and those who were connected to a community became more engaged, while others became less so.[53]

Shah found something that is crucial to understanding the influence of the Internet on young people: that the great predictor of civic involvement is embedded in how people consume the media of their youth. For example, the level of civic involvement of the so called "greatest generation," those who came of age just before or during World War II, is connected closely to that generation's newspaper readership. The civic involvement of "baby boomers" correlates most closely to their TV habits. And information exchange over the Internet is the primary predictor of civic involvement among today's teens and young adults.[54] With this in mind, Shah believes that more researchers need to develop a deeper understanding of young people's relationship to the Internet. "Studies on the psychological and sociological consequences of Internet use have tended to view the Internet as an amorphous whole," wrote Shah, "focusing on *hours of use* as opposed to *patterns of use*."[55]

Unlike the naysayers of the late 1990s or the optimists of the early 2000s, I have found, above all else, that the medium does not independently pull or push the consumer. Instead, what happens is closer to Kraut's "rich get richer" theory: Because the Internet is basically infinite, people appear to have a great deal of independence to express their preexisting needs and values. While this concept is not complex, it is unsettling to some. Robert Putnam (2000), in trying to understand the Internet's role in the future of civic life seemed like he needed to give form to the basically formless medium: "Will the Internet in practice turn out to be a niftier telephone or a niftier television? In other words, will the Internet become predominantly a means of active, social communication or a means of passive, private entertainment?"[56]

The only way to answer Putnam properly is to do so like a Buddhist: Yes, the Internet will be (and already is) a telephone. And yes, it will be (and is) a television. And no: The Internet, like a magic wand, changes the telephone and television (and all other media) by digitizing everything and making it into something new and unprecedented. And yes and no: The new digital telephone allows us to send and receive television images. And the new digital television allows us to talk to and entertain one another.

In the 1960s media theorist Marshall McLuhan divided various media into two categories, "hot" and "cold." Hot media included movies, stereos, and all those that are intense enough to overwhelm the audience, paradoxically creating a passivity or "low participation." Cold or cool media include telephones and 1960s televisions and media that are less complete in terms of the vibrancy of the media message. McLuhan wrote that those media are low intensity but "high participation."[57] While we can quarrel with these categories (and I imagine McLuhan might have made his classification of television hotter if he had lived to see Zenith's new 60-inch Plasma High-Definition TV), we can agree with McLuhan that certain media are hotter and colder than others. Not so, however, for the Internet. While the Internet's interactivity has been disparaged by some (compared by one critic to a big candy machine[58]), it is in some ways the coldest and most interactive of media. Despite how self-indulgent and superficial a chat room can be, it is nothing if not interactive. On the other hand, we can get any number of high intensity/hot media experiences, too.

My point here is that the elasticity of the Internet allows it to be a sort of Rorschach test for one's preexisting wants and needs. I do not deny that the medium itself plays a part in shaping news habits, but after discussing this issue with young people around the country, I found that the Internet does not in itself drive news use. We know this because most people do not use the Internet for news. Instead, their news consumption seems to be driven by work requirements, conversation, political connectedness, and the other factors outlined in these last two chapters.

Making the Choice on the Web

Before exploring the role of "choice" on the Internet, it is important to acknowledge that we have always had some independence in media choices. As we have discussed, the rise of cable television and the plethora of special interest magazines afford us ample choices, from the Cartoon Network to *Windsurfing*

magazine.[59] Even within a single newspaper, readers pick and choose. Jon Donley, the editor of Nola.com, who had been a newspaper editor for years, remembered well choices some of his readers made: "One of the humbling things I used
to do was . . . [go] to the newsstand and watch people take the paper off the rack.
Some would throw out everything but the sports section, or the coupons."[60] And,
of course, even within the sports stories and coupons there are choices.

But the Internet is unparalleled in offering a near-infinite number of choices
about a wide range of topics. The Internet satisfies the most specific of needs. People only interested in nature could be sated by the newspapers' many articles on
the subject, but for narrower interests, we need more specific media. When I finished reading *The Trumpet of the Swan* to my son, we went to the Internet for
more information on trumpeter swans. There we found detailed descriptions, action newsletters, videos for sale, academic papers, and even recordings that dis-
tinguish the trumpeter from its cousin, the tundra swan.[61] The hallmark of the
Internet is its ability to fulfill the most personal interests imaginable.

In this way, the Internet can be seen as the logical conclusion of the mass
media explosions that were started with movable type in the 1450s. Although
Gutenberg's printing press is popularly seen as the birth of the mass *public*,
it can also be seen as the birth of the mass *private*, allowing readers to follow

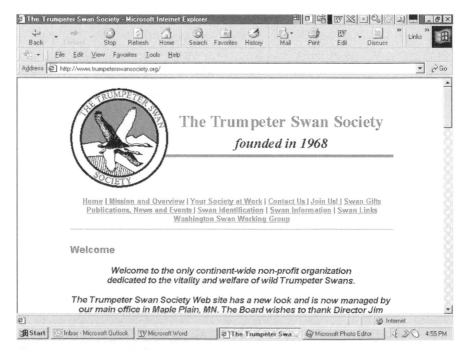

The Trumpeter Swan Society home page downloaded. May 2004. Reprinted with permission.

one's own interests, by taking home books and other media. As we have seen, the rise of specialty media, particularly in the last 40 years, has paralleled the rise in stories that aim not at the head but at the heart. One of my interviewees, Ann Colbert, the journalism professor who witnessed a generational shift in news interest, also noticed that conversations are veering away from news, toward "personal stuff."[62]

In trying to figure out what television does to the country's social fabric, Kraut et al. (1998) concluded that "time displacement" was the most significant factor.[63] The same appears to be true on the Internet, with entertainment displacing news and politics. Down the hall from Jon Donley at Nola.com is Cory Melancon, an Internet journalist whose specialty is the streets (and thus the parties) of New Orleans. In some ways Melancon is a traditional journalist and follows traditional practices. "I'm going to give you these facts," she said of her relationship to her viewers, "and I'm not going to change them, and I'm going to be as objective as possible."[64]

I agreed with her assessment of her seriousness as journalist. But while she brings integrity to her craft, the focus of her show was on the fey and fantastic street life of New Orleans. Day after day, night after night, Nola.com points its Webcams at Bourbon Street, chronicling the parade of colorful pedes-

Cory Melancon, New Orleans street journalist.   Photograph by Sarah Griffin Thibodeaux. Courtesy of Melancon.

trians. This is not something she created; it was enabled by the Internet. Because the Internet is a great medium for voyeurs, and because Bourbon Street is a great locale for voyeurs, it follows that a growing number of the Internet throng would gravitate towards Cory Melancon, standing on Bourbon Street, interviewing the clothed and the unclothed, the drunk and the near drunk.

Tuned in on the 'Net

Despite that the prevailing current on the Internet is away from news and toward frivolity, some people swim upstream. Actually that metaphor is not exactly right; there really is no "upstream" on the Internet, which provides ample crosscurrents to satisfy anyone's news appetites, no matter how expansive they might be. Kanon Cozad, VP at the United Missouri Bank, probably the biggest news junkie I interviewed, used the Internet as one of his main news sources and set up alerts from various news organizations. When he leaves the computer, the alerts are automatically sent to his PDA. And the Internet allowed Cozad to dig deep into news, getting extra information about Afghanistan and Pakistan.[65]

At Universal Pictures, Aaron Harper gained his expertise via the Internet and a proprietary database used collectively by the major studios. Like the free and popular Internet Movie Database, the studios' version includes data on films, actors, directors, and writers. But it goes much further, allowing Harper and his colleagues to get information on agents, who is represented by whom, studio executives associated with each project, and anything else executives might need. "It's unbelievably extensive," said Harper.[66] For Cozad, Harper, and others who value information flow, the Internet and computers in general have helped them become even more informed, and more engaged in news and politics than they would be without new technology. And while the median age of news readers and viewers continues to climb, there appears to be a core group of informed citizens from every age of adulthood.

The *New York Times*, the preferred national newspaper of the educated and well-heeled, has a median age of around 48, roughly the same as the national news magazines[67] This relatively low median age reflects what we have always known: that a core group of close readers exist at every age.[68] But even if we discount the overlap in those who subscribe to these publications, their total circulation is a tiny percentage of the total U.S. population. For the less elite news operations, the ones that reach far greater numbers, such as the TV network news, the average viewer has one foot in the grave.

What does it mean when only a small minority is engaged and informed? Specifically, what does it mean to our governing process, both on the local and national political stage? This is the focus of chapters five and six.

CHAPTER 5

Television, the Internet, and the Eclipse of the Local

Begin with a clear conception that the subject of deepest interest to an average human being is himself; next to that, he is most concerned about his neighbors. Asia and the Tongo Islands stand a long way after these in his regard. It does seem to me that most country journals are oblivious as to these vital truths. . . . Secure a wide-awake, judicious correspondent in each village and township of your county. . . . Do not let a new church be organized, or new members be added to one already existing, a farm be sold, a new house be raised, a mill be set in motion, a store be opened, nor anything of interest to a dozen families occur, without having the fact duly though briefly chronicled in your columns. If a farmer cuts a big tree or grows a mammoth beet, or harvests a bounteous yield of wheat or corn, set forth the fact as concisely and unexceptionably as possible.[1]

—Horace Greeley, 1860

In some important ways, the early twenty-first century seems the fulfillment of Greeley's statement. More and more specialized media, including the Internet, allow us to follow our own particular preferences. If Horace Greeley were to look over the shoulder of the typical Web user and see the typical exchange of e-mails, he would find that some of what he wrote was corroborated. He would notice how personal the news has become—the twenty-first-century equivalent of the "mammoth beet" he mentioned—and he might smile in recognition of his principle at work. Internet users have become even more personal than the reporters of Greeley's time. E-mail, Instant Messenger, and countless Web sites give us a "daily me," tailored to our particular tastes; we are all beat—or excuse the pun, "beet"—reporters now. After noting the triumph of the personal, Greeley might also remind us of the other half of his point, that distant lands—"Asia and the Tongo Islands"—are still beyond the interests of most Americans.

But then Greeley might admit to two major surprises. First, Americans *do* involve themselves in the lives of the faraway. Hollywood and London churn out stars about whom we care deeply, sometimes too deeply, sometimes more deeply than we care about our neighbors. And the same can be said of our concern for the personal lives of some politicians, too. Those who liked Clinton spent considerable time thinking about him, wrestling with his politics, trying to discern his motivations, and pondering the dynamics of his marriage. And for many of those who despised him, he may have loomed even larger in their imaginations.

While Greeley correctly described (and predicted) our enduring interest in ourselves, he might be surprised about how much of the interest in local politics has evaporated. After learning about themselves and their friends, most Americans, particularly young Americans, have only a facile understanding of their local community. This void includes the oil of local democracy: news that makes communities work. This chapter examines the failure of citizens, and journalists, to keep up with local news and the consequences of this neglect.

In previous chapters we discussed the connection between the media's need for ratings and the audience's desire for entertainment, and we've mentioned that Entman (1989) called this connection a "vicious circle." The problem with local news today can be better described as a "vicious triangulation." Civic decline, tuned out young people, and facile, ratings-driven local news outlets each contribute to the decline of local news.

Local News

In my discussions with young people around the country, very few said they valued local news. Some, of course, did not value any news at all, as reflected in the comment of one of the Los Angeles actors: "I don't like the news 'cause I think it pretty much gets me down; it's all crap, to tell you the truth."[2] But even among young people who were tuned in to national news, there was a lot of frustration about the local stuff.

It is not surprising that the most tuned in of all my interviewees, Kanon Cozad, the vice president of the United Missouri Bank, followed local news closely. He was even able to discuss the particulars of the Kansas City school system, though he was not a parent himself. But when asked about the local newspaper he reads daily, the *Kansas City Star*, Cozad told me that it was a poor product: it "is essentially a cut-and-paste from the wire system," he said.[3] Aaron Harper, the tuned-in studio assistant at Universal, also was frustrated with local news, in this case the local television news: "I cannot watch local news here simply because you turn it on and it's Kevin Spacey on the morning news, or Julia Roberts, or for two hours, they're following a beat-up truck with ten police cars chasing it. I think one of the biggest things that turns people off is how frivolous it can be. This is not news, you know."[4]

In chasing viewers, local news outlets have long ago learned three things: First, newspapers and local television news stations can (and do) make lots of money. Second, cutting corners and dumbing down the product does not seem to drive away consumers. Third, and most important for local television news: sex, celebrities, and especially violence sell. The old adage is generally true, "If it bleeds, it leads." From 1990 to 1998, as the national murder rate declined by about 20 percent, stories about murders (not including the O. J. Simpson murder trial) increased 600 percent on the network news; on local news, the percentage increase may have been less, but the sheer amount of violence was certainly more.[5] Not only that, wrote Phyllis Kaniss, a media critic, "it is the corollary that should concern us: If it doesn't bleed—or choke with emotion—it doesn't air."[6] Because local news avoids a lot of important items, including city council meetings, policy decisions, and local initiatives—in short, the blueprints of local democracy—we are civically poorer. Young people are not given stories that would allow them to understand the process of government; instead they are merely frightened by gore or pandered to with celebrities. No wonder many young people turn away from local news.

Bad News

Study after study have charted the decline of respect for journalists.[7] As we have seen in chapter 3, some of this is because journalists pander to their audience's desire for entertainment. Some of this, however, has more to do with the local media's business decisions. In 1999, when the *Los Angeles Times* printed a magazine devoted to praising the new Staples Center and secretly shared profits with Staples, journalists all over were aghast. But as much as journalists were *shocked, shocked* that this kind of behavior was going on in their newsrooms, a significant minority of local news organizations were engaging in this kind of practice regularly. The magazine *Editor & Publisher* found that one-fifth of all editors it surveyed felt that the Staples fiasco was an "acceptable" business practice for newspapers. Worse still: half of the polled publishers felt the practice was "acceptable." It is no surprise, then, that many of those polled found a decline in traditional separations between the business and editorial aspects of newspapers; many also admitted to using good copy to cuddle up to advertisers and coddle them.[8]

In their recent book, *The News About the News* (2002), Len Downie Jr. and Robert G. Kaiser looked carefully at the business practices of local newspapers and television stories and concluded, "News is the most important profit center for local stations, and profit is more important than news." They provided ample evidence of ethical lapses. WCBS in New York City, for example, promoted the services of TLC Laser Eye Centers after that firm gave the station $300,000 in advertising. One station, WBAL in Baltimore, received hundreds of thousands of dollars a year in advertising from Mercy Hospital. During this time, WBAL set up a thrice-weekly feature, "The Woman's Doctor," featuring doctors and patients from Mercy.[9] Mercy's homepage linked to WBAL and vice versa.[10]

Why should we be concerned with the WBAL/Mercy arrangement? After all, the hospital got its advertising message out (Downie and Kaiser say its ranking for women's health went from seventh to first among the public). The station got money. And the public got informed. But what kind of information was disseminated? In a city in which other, arguably better hospitals exist (Johns Hopkins, for example), should the medical advice come from only one hospital or should specialists from other institutions be interviewed as well? Just as we need our news organizations to be an independent voice as a check against politics, so too do they need to provide a check against business.

As Dan Rather told Downie and Kaiser, "Once we begin to see ourselves as more of a business and less a public service, the decline in quality is accelerated."[11] What Rather was referring to was a decline in how much corporate executives valued news. But we must also remember that this internal change is coupled with an external change as well. A common theme running through my discussions with young people was that the news is bought and paid for by big corporations. In the hands of some young people, this argument is often overblown—after all, good journalism is practiced every day—but it is no wonder why many young people are discouraged. Too many news outlets, particularly at the local level, are infusing their news with advertising and other business considerations.

One of the most disturbing trends is the dilution, and in some cases elimination, of local programming. In the 1990s, when the FCC deregulated the radio industry, consolidation transformed the field. Clear Channel Communications went from 36 stations to more than 1150. Clear Channel saves a lot of money by substituting local content and talent with national content and talent. A Clear Channel DJ may be in a studio in San Diego, for example, remotely broadcasting as if he were next door. Television news has recently embraced this model, too. Many weather forecasts are now piped in from remote locations, and the trend is toward buying syndicated news or in the case of large media companies, using in-house national talent. One company, Sinclair Broadcast Group, owns 62 stations and uses reporters, anchors, and weather forecasters from its studio in Baltimore. The company calls this practice "Central Casting."[12] The FCC ruling of June 2003 allowing further consolidation will almost certainly further erode the amount and quality of local programming.

Violent News

Even more noticeable than the advertising-editorial blur is the pervasiveness of violence in the local media. Watch any big-city local station and you are struck with the parade of slashings, slayings, rapes, murders, assassinations, and various other misdeeds. Living in a big city, one is often hard-pressed to separate a city's reality from its funhouse mirror image in the local news in which crimes, violence, and celebrity are magnified and the other everyday workings are reduced to nothing. Journalists need to be reelected every day and as we watch blow-dried and breathless television news reporters rush from corpse to celebrity to corpse, we get a good picture of what they think getting elected entails.

On some level, they must know what they are doing: many of us, young and old, keep coming back. But what kind of news do we get? Taken together, violence and business totally dominate most local news stations. A recent analysis found that more than 90 percent of all local television news stories came from police scanners or public relations events. Less than 10 percent of all stories came from initiative reporting.[13] If young people take a dim view of local news, calling it frivolous, violent, and depressing, can we argue with them?

Decline in Governmental Coverage

One of the easiest ways to see the decline in local reporting is to examine how the news media spend their money. The *American Journalism Review* did just that, counting the number of full-time reporters assigned to each newspaper's statehouse. In 1998, the magazine found a steep ten-year decline and this decline had not reversed at the time of the magazine's last survey, in 2002.

In 2002 James Pindell, a reporter for West Virginia's *Dominion Post, did* cover the statehouse and when House Bill 4322 okayed a complex land transfer from the state university to a private consortium, he had the contacts (and the job!) to untangle what was actually being proposed. By the time Pindell was through, everyone in government had the opportunity to understand the environmental, legal, zoning, and business ramifications that had not previously come to light. While a version of the bill did pass, the provisions were no longer a secret and the suspicions about the deal being a ploy to bring a Wal-Mart to town, were aired and debated.[14]

When the third largest newspaper in West Virginia, a fairly typical state in this trend, ceased to cover its statehouse, it created a reportorial void. As the *American Journalism Review* report stated, "The [West Virginia] governor, like politicians elsewhere, has been quick to fill the areas of reportorial vacuum with information churned out by his own publicity machine."[15] Our communities suffer when we do not know what is going on. "There's less desire for nuts-and-bolts government news," Jonathan Salant told the *American Journalism Review* in 1992. At the time, Salant was a DC–based federal policy reporter for two Syracuse, New York, newspapers. "There is no request to write, 'The Defense Appropriations subcommittee today voted on a bill that would mean X dollars to Syracuse.' This year I decided not to cover a single appropriations story until the final bill passed, and nobody noticed,"[16] said Salant.

In the year 2000, one study examined how much time the local television news stations devoted to the close race for New Jersey's U.S. Senate seat. The answer? The top-rated stations devoted an average of 13 seconds a day. A similar study of California local stations found that in 1998 they devoted an average of .5 percent of their news time to their governor's race.[17] Not all gubernatorial races are ignored by local television news. California's 2003 race involving Arnold Schwarzenegger and others received considerably more than .5 percent of news time. However, unless movie stars, former child actors, strippers, and other sensational figures become fixtures on the campaign trail, such civic enthusiasm among local news outlets may be short lived.

Young People and Local News

African Americans, young and old alike, tend to watch local TV more than whites and Hispanics do.[18] This may have something to do with the main subject matter of local news—crime and violence. This makes sense when we consider that blacks are the most likely victims of such mayhem. The junior college basketball players in Los Angeles whom I talked with, all African American and/or Hispanic, had no knowledge of local or national politics that I could measure. However, about half of them expressed an interest in following crime news, to see " . . . if they are any killings."[19] In New Orleans, the young African Americans I spoke with were very interested in local news—not only the blood and guts but the politics, too. However, I will treat New Orleans as an exception, and discuss it later in this chapter.

Overall, the picture for local news is very bleak. True, a few more blacks than whites watch their local TV news, but local TV news, with its 90 percent crime and PR content, is useful only if we value the staccato reports of crimes and press conferences; it is a poor way to learn about the workings of a community. Further, while the local newspaper does provide some political information, that kind of news is shrinking fast. And remember, the vast majority of young people are not reading the newspaper anyway.

The practices of local news outlets listed in this chapter—the increase in advertorials and violence and the decrease in political reporting—may be some of the reasons why young people are less interested in the local news. According to a recent poll by the Pew Research Center for the People & the Press, regular viewership of local news was at its lowest level in decades, at 56 percent. Among 18–34-year-olds, the figure is even lower: 45 percent.[20] All in all, the picture for young people is that many do not follow local news; those who do don't get much either. It all brings to mind the old Woody Allen joke about the two women at a Catskills resort. One complains about the terrible food and the other remarks, "yes, and such small portions!"[21]

Decline of Civic Involvement

Running alongside the dearth of quality local news is the decline of civic life in America. One of the most widely reported reasons for this decline is the flight of the middle class out of the cities and into the suburbs. This is not only because, as Lewis Mumford said, that "suburbia is a collective effort to lead a private life,"[22] but also because it tends to come with a long, roots-weakening commute. Every minute added to a commute, wrote Putnam, correlates to a weakening of the civic structure of a community.[23] The same can be said of journalism: With the flight out of the cities, especially in the 1960s and 1970s, came the loss of local businesses and local advertising.[24] As people spread out into the suburbs, community, civic engagement, and journalism were weakened together. Local media are still profitable, but remaining so was not a bloodless process. Once upon a time, most communities, no matter how small, had multiple newspapers, often connected to or supported by political parties. Today 98 percent of all American cities have no more than one local daily newspaper.[25]

The general decline in civic life has been widely documented by Putnam and others. That our local communities are at the front lines of this decline is reflected in the greater attention given to national rather than local or state political elections. In the 2000 presidential election, about half of registered voters actually voted; in the 1998 midterm elections, only about a third voted. And as we have seen, among young people, only 16.6 percent voted in 1998.[26] But voting is just the most quantifiable of the many problems that weaken our communities.

Membership in the various Parent-Teacher Association chapters (PTA) reached a peak in 1959, wrote Putnam (2000). Now, membership is a third of what it was, even though the U.S. population has increased. Putnam also looked at the "mean membership rate" in 32 national chapter-based associations. With the exception of a dip during the Great Depression, Putnam's chart of association membership resembles a neat bell curve, rising to its peak in 1960. By 1997, membership rates had retreated to World War I levels.[27] Finally, if you attend a club meeting, lecture, book signing, political rally, or other public event, you may be heartened to see 50 or so people in attendance. But the more you go to the various events, the more you start to see many of the same faces in the crowd over and over again. Just like news consumers, public events attendees tend to be generalists.

During our 40-year period, more people are bowling than ever before, but fewer are bowling in leagues. Putnam sees similar trends everywhere. Watching sports is up, doing sports is down. Church membership is down modestly, 10 percent, but attendance is down significantly, 25–50 percent. Political parties are wealthier, but fewer people participate in them as volunteers. Associations such as NOW and the NRA are flush with cash, too, but they are rapidly becoming checkbook associations; as Putnam wrote, if your neighbor belonged to one of these organizations, you'd probably never know. Drinking alcohol is up, drinking in bars is down. Education is up, the civic engagement and knowledge (which had once been connected to education) is down. Betting in casinos is up, card games with friends is down. Stay-at-home dinners are up, dinners with friends and neighbors are way down. From the mid-1970s to the mid-1990s, fewer people had written a congressman or senator (-23%), signed a petition (-22%), served as an officer of some club or organization (-42%), or worked for a political party (-42%).[28]

The impoverished civic life of local communities can be palpable and its evident effect on young people is everywhere. On a recent snowy day, I went to my parents' apartment in New York City and saw the nearby sledding hill, one of the best on the Upper West Side; unlike during my childhood, the hill was practically vacant. Even high schools, where social mingling is a matter of necessity, not choice, have seen declines in group activities. According to a news account in the *New York Times* (1996), high school students still sweat, but they rarely shower in groups, leading some schools to consider dismantling their showers altogether.[29] It is as if the students are unused to being amidst others in public. Perhaps they are.

The New Model for Young People and Local News

In the face of these marked declines in civic society, we are left with an important question: How do the media of young people affect their involvement in local affairs? Certainly the national television news system has had a role. Fifty years ago, Edward R. Murrow's radio news show, *Hear It Now,* became *See It Now.* To demonstrate the reach of the new television medium, Murrow's show broadcast live split-screen images of the Brooklyn Bridge and the Golden Gate Bridge.[30] It is seen as a moment in which TV helped to unify America, and it was. But it was also a moment at which the two coasts of America were spectacularly highlighted, muting thousands of small communities in between. This may remind us of the way Walter Lippmann described a trip in a hot-air balloon: As you go up and see farther, you see fewer details.[31]

Television allows us access to the seats of American politics. However, there is a cost: it erodes the human connections we had to the seat of American political power. The rise of television, wrote Downie and Kaiser,

> was accompanied by the decline of the institutions and individuals that, in a pretelevision age, served as intermediaries between statesmen or big events and the public at large. . . . But when television gave everyone the same exposure to national and international leaders . . . those intermediaries lost their role, and their status. Your precinct captain (if you still had one) wasn't your connection to the governor or the president; Walter Cronkite was.[32] (2002)

Edward R. Murrow and his simultaneous live images of the harbors of San Francisco and New York. During this first broadcast of See It Now, *Murrow also displayed simultaneous images of the Golden Gate Bridge and the Brooklyn Bridge.* Courtesy of CBS-TV.

What Downie and Kaiser were suggesting was that television can take even an ardent political junkie and loosen his or her grip on the local scene. This is the media world in which young people have entered—a world in which politics are increasingly personal or national, with local concerns receding. Further, Downie and Kaiser were also suggesting that the relationship between politics, civic involvement, and media is complex. But despite this complexity—or because of it—this relationship is worth exploring, especially how it relates to young people.

One of the great paradoxes of my study and others is that while young people are less and less engaged politically, they are more and more likely to engage in volunteerism. In 1998, 74 percent of college freshmen, for example, said they volunteered during their senior year of high school, up from a low of 62 percent in 1989. This is something that Putnam (2000) took as a hopeful sign but conceded, "Why this welcome and encouraging increase in volunteerism has occurred is not yet clear."[33]

I posed this paradox to Brandeis students and found what is probably the most plausible explanation. It is not because young people are suddenly more politically involved. They are not. It is not because young people are following the news. Certainly not! Rather the reason is more prosaic, as one Brandeis student explains: "In National Honor Society, there is a requirement to volunteer and it seems like if the time was set to do volunteering, you'd keep doing it."[34] At first glance, this reason seems a disappointment. They are volunteering simply because they *have* to? But perhaps there is hope in this, too. Imagine how informed young people would be if civic and news knowledge were a requirement for the National Honor Society!

> **Service** This quality is defined through the voluntary contributions made by a student to the school or community, done without compensation and with a positive, courteous, and enthusiastic spirit.
> —From the National Honor Society Web site, http://www.nhs.us/membership/, downloaded 20 October 2003.

Civic Society and Media

As it turns out, civic knowledge is one of the best predictors of being a good local citizen. Why does civic knowledge matter? Delli Carpini and Keeter offer five reasons: political tolerance, active participation, consistency, the ability to identify interests, and the ability to act on interests. Delli Carpini and Keeter set up a test to measure respondents' political tolerance. They asked, which group—communists, atheists, or the Ku Klux Klan—do you like the least? Then they asked whether a member of this least-favorite group should be allowed to teach in a public school or give a public speech in the respondent's city or town. Finally, Delli Carpini and Keeter tested the correlation between this tolerance and a respondent's understanding of courts and civil liberties. They found that this correlation was stronger than any other they tested (age, race, income, and education).[35] Because Delli Carpini and Keeter's research is now more than 15 years old, I was eager to reexamine this question. After all, young people have continued to become more tolerant than their elders were (or are).[36] My similar question (see Appendix B, question 10) found only five young people out of more than a hundred surveyed who would not let their least favorite group's representative make a speech. Although my sample was small, it is interesting to note that four of the five "intolerant" respondents were among the most tuned out of more than a hundred respondents.

What is the correlation between local news consumption and civic participation? Given the near-total absence of meaningful local news on television, it is no surprise that researchers found little correlation between that medium and civic participation. In fact, one group of researchers found that daily local TV news viewers were *less* informed and *less* politically active than those who do not watch daily.[37] But they did find a very strong connection between newspaper readership and all kinds of civic participation.[38] Shah, McLeod, and So Hyang Yoon (2001) examined a range of variables correlating to civic engagement, including income, employment, home ownership, residential stability, and other factors. They found that among both the oldest and the youngest in the sample, news consumption rated second only to home ownership and residential stability in terms of its connection to civic involvement.[39]

As I have mentioned, Robert Putnam found a strong inverse correlation between the number of times a person volunteered last year and the number of times he or she "gave the finger" to another driver.[40] I went back to Putnam's source, the DDB Needham "Life Style Survey" (2000) and evaluated the data for other correlations as well. It turns out, not surprisingly, that bird flippers are less likely to have family dinners together or keep up with the news.[41] Obviously, we should not try to exaggerate the importance of these facts, but they do point to one of the central theses of those who study the connection between civic engagement and media: That those who are most engaged in the news and in their communities are often also those who trust in the good of others and in the ability of the political system to be responsive. While too much trust can be a liability, we do need some trust, some level of cooperation, to function as a society.

Delli Carpini and Keeter's fourth and fifth benefits of civic knowledge—
the ability to identify interests and the ability to act on interests—are prob-
lematic. De Tocqueville (2000) once said that one of the goals of civic participation is to discern one's "self-interest, well understood."[42] Certainly, we need
to understand our interests, and a debate over competing self-interests can help
clarify issues and serve democracy. However, while self-interests may be well
understood, they do not always serve the community interest, well understood.
For example, each of the following statements may be good for the individual
but bad for society: "I'm a convicted felon but I want a gun," "I want the government to pay for my child's private school tuition," "I want to be able to
pollute," "I don't want to support the military with my taxes." A generous
view of local TV news would be that it keeps us safe, giving us reports of violence so that we in turn will not go down those dark alleys. But for any level
of community interest, including what might be done about the violence, we
need to read a newspaper or go to a Web site that actually spends money on
reporters who cover the seats of power and hold them accountable.

In understanding how individuals balance self- vs. community interests,
it is important to consider two trends in society, "massification" and "progressive differentiation." These two trends, as outlined by James W. Carey
(1969), are different, indeed nearly opposite. The first, "massification," suggests the "eclipse of the local . . . by the growth of national centers of power
and communication."[43] We avoid local news, in part, because we are seduced
by national events and media. We can watch *Friends*.

The second trend, "progressive differentiation,"

> emphasizes the crucial role of the division of labor in creating distinct worlds
> of work and community. It stresses not the sameness of social life but its over-
> whelming variety; not the centralization of power but its dispersal; not the
> threat of totalitarianism but the exceptional opportunities for individuality
> and freedom. . . . [44]

Massification beckons us to Hollywood and Washington. Progressive differentiation beckons us to the mirror of our own tastes and desires. But we must
remember that neither necessarily beckons us to our community. Despite the
many differences of massification and progressive differentiation, they share
one essential quality—both can weaken one's membership in a local community. Taken to their logical conclusions, these trends could force us to share little with our neighbors. One critic of these trends asked, "What are you going
to talk about in the carpool?"[45] Although the question is slightly dated by recent declines in carpooling, it does provoke important questions: What do we
share? What binds us together? What do we work together to achieve?

While researchers have established a strong correlation between tuning
out of local news (especially newspapers) and dropping out of society, I also

wanted to find out from my young respondents which came first, tuning out or dropping out. I asked this question of everyone but got nowhere. Based on dozens of answers, I concluded that since most of these young people had always lived in a world in which most of their peers (and many of their parents) were disconnected from both news and politics, they could not give illuminating answers about cause and effect. So I am left with an unanswered question and a less-than-satisfying conclusion: Tuning out and dropping out are inextricably connected and probably mutually reinforcing.

Internet Communities and Real Ones

Within the lifetime of today's teenagers, the Internet has gone from an academic enterprise of a few professors and tech heads to a series of fully formed and interconnected communities with their own rules and opportunities for civic engagement. It may be hard for us to imagine a time when the Internet did not figure prominently in our lives, but as recently as 1995 only 14 percent of all Americans had gone on-line. By 1999, more than half of all Americans had logged on. By October 2002, nearly two thirds had.[46] My own daughter, by the time she was 12, had started to spend time communicating with friends over AOL's Instant Messenger. Among college students and 20-somethings around the country, the vast majority are building on-line communities. As they spend more and more time on-line, many are consuming less news but making more relational contacts. How does membership and communication in these virtual communities impact real ones?

Charles Kuralt, the peripatetic correspondent for CBS News, once said: "Thanks to the interstate highway system, it's possible to travel across the country without seeing anything. I wonder if the information superhighway will offer a corollary."[47] Indoor plumbing may be wonderful, but as Marshall McLuhan has pointed out, it takes us away from the communal well.[48]

However, in 2002 Kraut et al. found that the negative effects of their first cautionary study had dissipated and that people "generally experienced positive effects of using the Internet on communication, social involvement, and well-being." In part this was because, as we have seen above, Internet users had reached a critical mass. No longer, wrote Kraut et al., were Internet users an isolated minority.[49] Indeed, one could argue that the isolated ones are now those who are not on the 'Net.

What kinds of communities are being built? Even though e-mail communities are generally seen by their inhabitants as less effective than real ones in terms of social life, they are seen as extremely effective for information exchange.[50] And we have all seen examples of what Thomas Friedman (2000) has called, "super empowered individuals," people who use the Web and other new technology to compete with huge corporate or governmental forces. As an example, Friedman offered Jody Williams, who won the 1997 Nobel Peace Prize for organizing a global ban on landmines. How did she do it? In part, by organizing over e-mail. Another example was the lobbying effort by a small group of Vietnam veterans against Cable News Network. In 2000, CNN reported that American troops had used poison gas in Vietnam. Through the e-mail lobbying effort of five retired generals, veteran groups forced an apology from CNN, a subsidiary of AOL Time Warner, one of the world's largest corporations.[51] Some of the people I interviewed for this book were "super empowered individuals," most notably Kanon Cozad, Aaron Harper, Joel Senesac, and Farai Chideya. The Internet allows them to leverage information from virtual communities into real ones.

According to John Dewey, the philosopher and educator who wrote so eloquently about the public, the chief grist of democracy is not what the various media tell us; instead, it is the conversation that ensues.[52] We are more likely to hold government accountable if its workings are part of our daily dialogue. Thus the Internet, with its opportunities for information exchange, would be an ideal medium for citizen involvement. As Jay Rosen has written, the ethics of journalistic fairness and accountability achieve an even greater significance when the public becomes an active part of the equation.[53] Journalists are most accountable to their audience when that audience has access to them.

But for all the advantages of the Internet as a tool for promoting *communication* and its linguistic cousin, *community*, its ease of use poses a significant drawback as well.

Some Drawbacks of Internet Communities

The kind of in-your-face politics that Lizzie Salzfass was involved in at Wesleyan—the protests, the kiss-ins, etc.—requires courage, hard work, compromise, and all the other efforts involved in bringing a public campaign to an eclectic and skeptical community. Real communities require a level of work, sacrifice, and accommodation that virtual ones do not always share. This is, quite simply, because in the real world you often encounter a lot more opposition than you do in the virtual. As the following passage from de Tocqueville suggests, there was a time in early American history when people waded into their communities, ready for a discussion with the allies and opponents in their neighborhood:

> To meddle in the government of society and to speak about it is the greatest business and, so to speak, the only pleasure that an American knows. This is perceived even in the least habits of life: women themselves often go to political assemblies and, by listening to political discourses, take a rest from

household tedium. For them, clubs replace theatergoing to a certain point. An American does not know how to converse, but he discusses; he does not discourse, but he holds forth. He always speaks to you as to an assembly; and if he happens by chance to become heated, he will say "sirs" in addressing his interlocutor.[54]

In a virtual community, life is very different. The barriers against engagement are dropped. In the real world we struggle against or compromise with neighbors because they will be our neighbors tomorrow, too. On the Internet, we are more likely to drop our virtual neighbors completely to get someone else who will agree with us. As Cass Sunstein has pointed out, when individuals are polled on issues, their conclusions are often very different than when they are asked to discuss issues in a group setting. That is, when people hold their views up to one another's scrutiny, they may become strengthened or softened, but certainly altered. Against this model of deliberation and civic engagement, Sunstein contrasted the self-selected views put forth over the Internet.[55] A perfect example of this paradigm came in the 2004 Democratic primary. For much of the early primary season, Vermont Governor Howard Dean enjoyed a lot of support, fuelled by enthusiasm from self-selecting virtual communities. However, during the Iowa Caucus in January 2004, Democrats all over Iowa deliberated in meeting halls, civic centers, gymnasiums, and living rooms. After face-to-face discussions, a consensus emerged that John F. Kerry, the Massachusetts senator, would be the strongest candidate to face George W. Bush.

That may be why Lewis Friedland noted that place, not technology, is the most important sphere of civic and democratic participation.[56] And while some observers have felt that the Internet offers "commonality of interests rather than the accidents of proximity" others have felt that "a community is people who have greater things in common than a fascination with a narrowly defined topic."[57]

Summing up these and other perspectives, William A. Galston questioned whether the 'Net strengthened or weakened communities. Galston found the answer complicated. First, he rejected the idea that the medium, because it is not face-to-face, cannot promote community. But Galston nevertheless was worried about the Internet's landscape. For Galston, the ultimate problem with the Internet in terms of its civic and political ramifications is that its communities are so easy to exit. "One of the great problems of contemporary American society and politics," wrote Galston, "is the proliferation of narrow groups and the weakening of structures that create incentives for accommodation."[58] One of my students once told me that the beauty of the Internet is that it allowed him to avoid walks to the library in inclement weather. We might draw an analogy to the Internet's effect on communities.

The picture I have painted in this chapter is bleak: Few young people are reading the newspaper, the best link to their local communities. Local television news attracts more young people, but its contents are a morass of crime and advertorial. The Internet allows for narrow interests to be explored, but few people use it for local news. And the easy entry and exit of the Internet is a poor model for civic commitment and accommodation. All this is against the backdrop of real communities that are in civic decline. Well, not all communities. Next stop, New Orleans.

New Orleans and the Promise of Local Engagement

While it is impossible to overstate my surprise that the poor, black boys from Bishop Perry Middle School in New Orleans were reading the *New York Times* (see chapter 4), I was probably even more surprised and impressed with their command of local news, which greatly exceeded their understanding of national issues. True, they said they watched between four and eight hours of mostly entertainment TV every day on their very own sets in their rooms. And it is true that the little local news they watch is dominated by violence. One boy said he watched local TV "for the killing."[59] But all of these kids also belonged to households in which adults subscribed to the local daily, the *Times–Picayune*. All their parents voted. And these kids all plan to vote, too. As one said, "It took us a long time to get to vote. . . . African Americans . . . suffered to get black people to vote. So I think we should take advantage of the opportunity we have."[60]

There is evidence that these boys will be informed voters. When C. Ray Nagin was campaigning to be mayor of New Orleans, he visited Bishop Perry Middle School. John Fitzmorris, then the principal of Bishop Perry, was surprised by the kids' specific questions about Nagin's rival, Chief of Police Richard Pennington. "One of the kids asked, 'What do you think about Chief Pennington saying this about you in the campaign?' And I thought: wow!"[61] They also asked Nagin whether he would appoint his opponent to another term as chief of police. During my interviews with the boys, they discussed an impressive range of specific issues, including local minimum wage laws, the backgrounds of Nagin and Pennington, the term limit law that forced the previous mayor out, and his political maneuvers to avoid this limit.[62]

How did these kids get so invested in the news and politics of their community? Their comments about getting involved after the civil rights strides of their elders seem like an answer, but not if we consider that nationally and regionally, blacks are less likely to vote than whites.[63] The media habits of these boys do not fit, either. They are tremendous users (abusers even) of entertainment TV and local TV news. And yet, they buck the trends regarding these media: they are tuned into local politics.

And this brings us to one of the great truths of the media-community relationship: A community as tightly woven and compelling as New Orleans can drive news consumption. As I mentioned earlier, I met with Chris Rose, the *Times–Picayune* reporter, while I was in New Orleans. The interview was outside as he and his wife chased their small child around Lafayette Square. A great local band was on stage and the park was ringed with food and drink booths from locally owned restaurants and bars. The crowd was an admixture of whites and blacks, young and old, rich and poor, locals and tourists, suits and jeans. As Rose spoke to me, a parade of people came up to him to say hi. It was as close to a small town setting as I have ever seen in a big city. Here I was, meeting with a general interest reporter who had moved to entertainment, discussing the blurring of the two areas, and I was standing amidst one of the last true communities in America. And Rose helped me to see the big countertrend to my book's thesis. He said,

> I think people here are actually more engaged. We have a rarity. I don't know if you've been here before or been here long enough to pick it up, but this is the least American city in America. And we do actually have remnants and dregs of old culture. People sit on their stoops at night and talk to their neighbors. . . . It's a small town, and people cross paths a lot. There's a lot of rich and poor crossing, a lot of black and white crossing. I'd almost think that maybe here for all the rap we take for our lack of education here, which is well deserved, because our schools are shit, just depraved and embarrassing . . . adults do meet in a . . . there is some remnants of the town square, not your town hall meeting, but the town square, people seem to cross paths, you know, and talk. I get in cabs, I chat up the meter maids, the cop, the guy who gets my crawfish in the sack. It's certainly opinionated, so I don't know if informed is the word, but people tend to know what the issues are there. . . . One of the famous lines and stereotypes about New Orleans and Louisiana . . . is [that we've] never had a good professional sports team, because politics is our sport. . . . We talk. . . . Tomorrow night I'll have 10, 12 friends over. I'll boil 30 pounds, 40 pounds of crawfish, we'll sit around, have some beers, and we'll talk. I'm sure that with the exception of my maniacal Yankees-loving-fan friend, the rest of us will be talking about our new mayor.[64]

But maybe Rose's description is not a countertrend or weakness in my book's thesis at all. Maybe a lot of the answer is that if you create a community in which people "cross paths," and talk, you set the stage for junior high school kids who know the issues, interrogate mayoral candidates, and care about politics.

And maybe these "crossings" and conversations create an environment in which people vote. New Orleans has long been known for its high voter turnout, especially in local elections.[65] And maybe this creates a need for good local journalism. What is the only CBS affiliate to broadcast its own local morning show to compete with the networks' national ones? That would be WWL-TV in New Orleans. Until recently, with the introduction of another local morning show (an NBC affiliate), WWL was getting about 70 percent of the market audience.[66]

I wrote earlier that virtual communities often serve as a poor model for real ones. Real communities benefit from the need for accommodation, compromise, and one's tendency to confront views that are not one's own. But in one significant way, New Orleans resembles and benefits from one characteristic of the Internet, the tendency for people to seek out like-minded people.

New Orleans, like other cities around America, is a destination. If you are in a mixed marriage in Biloxi or Mobile, New Orleans beckons. If you are gay, or an atheist, or a Jew, or a saxophonist, or a communist, New Orleans beckons. Like the Internet's ten thousand small communities of Hyundai mechanics, Anoushka Shankar fans, or journalism historians, New Orleans gives people a home no matter how obscure their tastes. Like the Internet, New Orleans sates even the most obscure desires and interests. But unlike the Internet, New Orleans demands something in return: that the Jews, saxophonists, communists, Hyundai mechanics, Anoushka Shankar fans, and journalism historians live with each other, shop at the same stores, struggle over the same taxes, deal with the same crime rates and listen to the same street musicians. Rather than the insularity that the Internet sometimes breeds, New Orleans takes its disparate ingredients and creates a great, giant gumbo.

And isn't this the essence and the beauty of America? To be able to flee from a thousand small towns around America and ten thousand small towns around the world and find a common ground? We walk down Decatur Street, make a left onto Toulouse and then we are on Bourbon, walking amongst the throngs. Like in Whitman's "Song of Myself," we walk among all Americans; like Whitman, we walk among "deacons and drovers," "prostitutes and presidents."[67] On the Internet, we choose our company. In New Orleans we choose, too, but we cannot completely avoid.

And that, too, is the beauty of the mainstream press. We need our separate identities, but we are also so much richer because of our connections. For me, while the front pages of the *New York Times* and hundreds of local newspapers around the country can be frightening, maddening, or terribly depressing, they are also things of beauty. They are a daily reminder of our mutual membership in the American gumbo. In this book's final chapter, we will look at how the American gumbo is diluted by our inattention to the nation's news.

CHAPTER 6

The Decline of General News and the Deliberative Body

In 1965, CBS ran a story from Vietnam showing U.S. Marines burning the village of Cam Ne. The report, by correspondent Morley Safer, brought CBS's huge audience face-to-face with marines as they were setting the thatched roofs afire with Zippo lighters. Villagers, mainly women and children, watched in horror. The next morning, Frank Stanton, CBS's president, was awakened by a telephone call. "Frank, are you trying to fuck me?" said the voice, which Stanton, in his sleepiness, did not recognize. "Frank, this is your president, and yesterday your boys shat on the American flag." Lyndon Johnson was on the line.[1]

Despite that it frequently displeases heads of state, we need good journalism. We need it because it gives us information about whether we should support our country's war plans. We need it because, as in the case of Watergate, it's important to know when our leaders are corrupt. And most of all, we need it because without it, there is no reliable information of any kind. And without reliable information, we have no democracy.

But what does all this have to do with young people? Journalism (and hence democracy) needs three things from our young people: First, that they consume the news, something I and others have established that most are not doing. Second, that they pay for it, because good journalism is expensive. And third, that they care deeply, and elect people who care deeply, about our First Amendment right to gather information and hold the government accountable for its actions.

The Fourth Estate

When the majority of multiple generations ignore the news, we lose more than just journalism. The baby that is being thrown out with the journalistic bathwater is the strongest formal check against power that citizens have: the information that empowers our votes. This check on authority came relatively recently in history. Walter Lippmann viewed the history of the press in three stages: Publication as a monopoly of government; publication as the privilege of political parties; and independent publications, supported by a vast readership and advertising.[2] In 1734, when a newspaper editor, John Peter Zenger attacked the New York colonial governor William Cosby, he was arrested for "seditious libel." When Zenger was arrested, the colonial government was still operating under the assumption that the press was a government monopoly and that in terms of criticism, "the greater the truth, the greater the libel."[3] But a few months later, when an American jury rejected the established law of "seditious libel" and acquitted Zenger, they were moving the press out of Lippmann's first stage and into his second. The second stage lasted a hundred years, until about 1835. During this time, political parties dominated journalism in America. Just like there is an inherent bias in a government-controlled press, the partisan press was beholden to its paymasters. Literally on the payroll of party bosses, partisan editors received government contracts, patronage jobs, and other sinecures.

We can trace America's independent journalism back to the 1830s and the New York "penny press."[4] That the commercial press gave birth to both sensationalism (see chapter 3) and independence is neither coincidental nor surprising. The same commercial forces that pushed editors to pander to a wide audience pushed them to recognize the greater economic power of nonpartisanship. Why talk to half the town with party slogans, reasoned the editors, when you can reach them all with sensationalism and/or balanced reports?

This paradigm explained why James Gordon Bennett, the founder of the *New York Herald* in 1835, used his newspaper to poke fun at his party-press rivals for being so boring and hidebound. It explained why Bennett championed sensational crime reporting and juicy tidbits about society balls. And it explained why Bennett endorsed a Democrat in 1836, a Whig in 1840, a Democrat in 1844, a Whig in 1848, a Democrat in 1852, and a Republican in 1856. Finally, it explained why rival James Watson Webb, the party press editor, beat up Bennett three times on the streets of New York City.

Having No Friends

My favorite motto from our stage of journalism, the commercial one, comes from Joseph Pulitzer's newspaper, the *New York World*. A large sign posted in

Pulitzer's newsroom announced, "The *World* has no friends."[5] Being friendless has its advantages: Without friends, a newspaper uncovers corruption, vice, and incompetence wherever it finds them. For obvious reasons, neither the government controlled press nor the partisan press could say that they were friendless; they were in the pocket of others. The commercial press, of course, is not totally independent, relying on government officials for access and advertisers for funds. But still, the better elements of the commercial press regularly resist pressures and have provided our democracy with what we need to make decisions.

When the *New York Times* and the *Washington Post* obtained the 47-volume study that came to be known as the "Pentagon Papers," the Nixon administration attempted to thwart its publication. But the *Times* and the *Post* resisted. After a judge blocked the *Times'* publication of the documents, Katherine Graham, the publisher of the *Post*, decided to print them, despite her own lawyers' objections.[6] Later, when the *Post* went full throttle in its investigation of Watergate, the Nixon administration tried to pressure it by a number of regular and irregular means, including manipulating the *Post'* stock price by getting citizens to challenge the newspaper's TV holdings.[7] Despite this pressure, the *Post* persisted, helping to produce one of the greatest accounts of governmental excess and wrongdoing in modern American history.[8]

Incidentally, Lippman believed that the third stage, the commercial one, would not be its last. He predicted that the next level would be an "objective" stage, in which experts (sort of like Lippmann himself) would offer readers an analysis free of commercial pressures.[9] His dream has not been realized. In fact, rather than the pressures abating, they are intensifying. Journalists still resist governmental and commercial pressures, but as fewer and fewer young people support the enterprise, business executives are beginning to think the unthinkable, like when in 2002 when Disney was willing to ditch Ted Koppel to make way for David Letterman and his slightly younger demographics.

We need good journalism because it seeks the truth. Some, like Todd Gitlin, a social critic, see this brand of truth as "partial, superficial, occasional- and celebrity-centered truth,"[10] but this is not entirely true. Good journalism offers us nonpartisan political information, too. From the early years of commercial press, it has offered a distinct view from that of the political parties. Abraham Lincoln had to satisfy himself that fellow Republican Horace Greeley, whose paper would be a natural ally, gave him at least lukewarm support. "Uncle Horace," said Lincoln, "is with us at least four days out of seven."[11] While the *New York Times* and *Wall Street Journal* are regularly accused of being Democratic- and Republican-leaning, respectively, their support for politicians of their own party is often less than the four-sevenths enjoyed by

Lincoln. In their editorial pages, Bill Clinton and George W. Bush have been frequently criticized by both papers. And in their news stories, it is often impossible to guess the allegiances and sympathies of individual reporters who are taught to balance the views of their news subjects fairly.

Despite claims by the left and the right, journalists do not generally hold extreme political positions, unless we count the extreme center.[12] While we certainly need some outlets that are partisan and opinionated, the benefit of a nonpartisan source is immeasurable. When Robert Torricelli, a Democratic senator from New Jersey, engaged in a pattern of questionable campaign practices in 2001 and 2002, we needed the *New York Times* and *Wall Street Journal* and other news sources to inform us and hold Torricelli accountable for his actions. This is especially true when we consider that both the Republicans and Democrats were so concerned with the mechanics of holding and losing power that they mainly spouted empty rhetoric at each other; neither side spoke with clarity about Torricelli. We needed a third view to help us and the senator's colleagues decide how to react to the charges.

Good journalists go to great lengths to guard against governmental and business pressures. In his autobiography, Max Frankel reported that in the 1950s the *Times* mandated its employees return any gift worth more than $10. By the 1970s, *Times* reporters were told that they could not accept freebie tickets to events. And Frankel himself was required to submit a list of his personal investments to the chief financial officer of the *Times*. When Linda Greenhouse, the *Times*' Supreme Court reporter, wanted permission to march in relative obscurity in a rally for abortion rights, her editors said no.[13] It is all about maintaining a critical detachment. As Abe Rosenthal said about his firing of a reporter who was dating a politician on her beat, "I don't care if you fuck elephants as long as you're not covering the circus."[14]

The great payoff for political detachment in news stories is, as Daniel Hallin explained in the *"Uncensored War"* (1986), greater access to voices in both parties. Starting in the 1830s, reporters gave up their party affiliation and their right to speak with a partisan voice. In return, wrote Hallin, journalists got greater political access than they ever received as partisans.[15] We, as news consumers, are in turn granted access to clear information to help us make political decisions and hold our leaders accountable.

Economic Consequences of Ignoring Good Journalism

It would be an exaggeration to say that when good journalism happens it is always ignored. Hard-hitting stories often provoke real change. However, as Robert Bellah and his colleagues wrote, "democracy means paying attention."[16] Sometimes, as in the example in my first chapter of the 1991 reports in the

Columbus (Georgia) *Ledger-Enquirer,* good journalism is greeted with a yawn. When the *Ledger-Enquirer* published its investigative pieces, there was not only no public outcry, there wasn't even a public discussion. This all compelled the journalists themselves to rally the public to take notice. Increasingly, good journalism is lost on many in the under-40 crowd, and as we have seen, this problem is showing no sign of letting up. But the problem affects not only the young, but everyone: If young people turn away from the news, they drain the journalistic enterprise of its economic lifeblood.

Good journalism is expensive. In 1835, James Gordon Bennett could start up a newspaper cheaply, with $500 and a desk made out of packing crates.[17] But today, good journalism requires huge expenditures of cash. For every news story on CNN, for example, there are more than a dozen staffers working behind the scenes. When I worked for that network as an assignment editor, I was part of a large team putting together the news. Our team included anchors, reporters, PromTer operators, camera and sound operators, field producers, futures editors, assignment editors, writers, editors, font operators, directors, producers, production assistants, tape deck operators, service technicians, and countless others. The big three broadcast networks are even more labor intensive. While newspapers can do without many of these players, their daily output of words is much more prodigious, somewhere in the vicinity of one hundred thousand.[18] And the cost of newsgathering is only the beginning. A newspaper needs to be printed, trucked, and delivered before seven A.M. the next day.

To maintain profits while costs remain high and news consumption is down, corporate executives have had to make decisions that sacrifice content. For example, the average 30-minute nightly newscast, minus commercials, was 23 minutes and 20 seconds in 1981. In 2000, it was down to 18 minutes and 20 seconds.[19] To further cut costs, the networks cut expensive international stories. And as fewer and fewer people showed interest in political process stories, these stories were cut, too.[20] It is no wonder that when Tom Brokaw was asked about his mission, he answered, "To survive."[21]

A newspaper's central business challenge today is how to maintain its integrity and high standards while maintaining profits. In the midst of a reader exodus, something has got to give. What gives, wrote Max Frankel, is often the news:

> Unless they are specially educated and restrained, stockholders care most about a company's customers—and readers are not a newspaper's main customers; advertisers are.
> . . . When profit margins slip and stock prices stagnate, emergency measures are invoked. News bureaus are closed. The space allotted to news is reduced.

Reporters and editors are "bought out," and hiring is "frozen." Since most American newspapers no longer face any other paper's direct competition, this dilution risks no immediate reader revolt, only a slow erosion to which bonus-seeking managements and transient stockholders are usually indifferent.[22]

The managements and stockholders have done well for themselves and their bottom line. The average operating profit margin of America's biggest newspaper companies is about 22 percent.[23] In its 1997 annual report, Gannett boasted that its operating profit margin was "the highest in the industry." This figure was nearly 30 percent, with more than a dozen of Gannett's papers making in the range of around 40 percent or higher.[24] How does this happen in the midst of a dying and shrinking readership? Part of it relates to what Frankel alluded to, above, and what I discussed in the previous chapter—staff cutbacks. The corollary is the shrinking news hole, the term describing the percentage of a newspaper actually devoted to news. As I am writing this, a copy of the *Burlington Free Press* (a Gannett paper) is sitting on my desk. A banner advertisement pollutes its front page in the place where news used to be. This might be okay if the hundreds of thousands of dollars in new revenue were to be used to hire new reporters for the local newspaper. But as of this writing, Gannett had not hired additional *Free Press* reporters. The money had gone to Gannett's bottom line, to further the *Burlington Free Press'* obscenely high estimated 45 percent operating margin.[25]

It is easier to avoid corporate and governmental pressures if you are flush with cash. When Frankel was the editor of the *New York Times Magazine*, he refused to warn the *Times'* ad sellers before stories that were critical of sponsors would appear. That kind of integrity is easier when you are not risking the bank. "The only free and independent press," Max Frankel wrote, "is a profitable press." And yet, wrote Frankel, greater profits do not equal greater freedom and independence.[26] Keeping up profits in the face of a declining readership pushes companies to hire people like Mark Willes, who, as the General Mills executive turned Times Mirror CEO, infamously called for "closer cooperation" between the editorial and business sides of his company's paper, the *Los Angeles Times*.[27] The logical conclusion of Willes' remark came in the form of the Staples Center deal in which the Los Angeles *Times* printed a magazine devoted to praising the new complex. In this secret deal, Staples and the *Times* would share profits in this endeavor. The *Los Angeles Times* could not claim, as Pulitzer did, that it had no friends. That's because the *Los Angeles Times* not only had a friend, but a secret best friend.

Despite that the United States leads every European country in the percentage of college-educated citizens, it is near the bottom of daily per capita newspaper readership and at the bottom of daily per capita TV news viewership.[28] And our rates of news consumption are dropping. What does this mean for the future of American journalism (and, yes, the future of democracy)? Pippa Norris, in her book, *A Virtuous Circle* (2000), asked, "have sagging sales in the print sector fuelled down-market pressures towards tabloid sensationalism in the pursuit of readers and a decline of traditional journalistic standards?"[29] This is a useful question, especially when many corporate parents are seeking to maintain and even increase their profit margins. And as the FCC allows further deregulation, corporate parents are increasingly likely to care more and more about the bottom line.

Norris's book title, *A Virtuous Circle*, reflects her ultimate optimism that new media interactivity and more news options will create more civic engagement and better democracy in the future. But I am far less optimistic. Good journalism requires money and fewer people are paying. Somebody needs to pay for the reporters who dig for corruption and incompetence at the statehouses and courthouses around the country. Somebody needs to pay for the 186 full-time correspondents that American newspapers currently station overseas.[30] Because you and I cannot go around the country and around the world looking for malfeasance, somebody needs to pay someone to dig. And somebody needs to pay well because reliable, intelligent, and interpretive journalists do not come cheaply.

They Will Pay if They Perceive a Need for It. But Few Do

In one of the most climatic scenes in *Citizen Kane*, a film based on the life of newspaper mogul William Randolph Hearst, the drama critic and boss's buddy Jedediah Leland sits down, drunk, to write a negative theatrical review. The review is of Kane's gal, an actress. Audiences saw the tension between integrity and loyalty, a tension lubricated by alcohol. Nowadays, as journalism becomes increasingly lost in a vast sea of media, a drunken reporter is only unsettling insofar as journalism is perceived to matter. For increasing numbers of young people, it does not. Even within the news business, the focus on the hard news stories seems to be eroding. Tom Brokaw, the NBC News anchor, observed: "Curiously, the people who are coming to us [to work at NBC] are smarter than they've ever been, well educated. . . . They're children of television and they really want to come to work here. And a lot of them, unfortunately, don't give a shit about the news. They want to do magazines or they want to do talk shows."[31]

As I mentioned in the last chapter, there is great support among young people I spoke with for freedom of speech. Few would deny an opportunity for their least favorite group to speak at a town meeting. When I asked Lizzie Salzfass, the recent Wesleyan graduate, this question, for example, she both supported a hate group's right to speak and her own right to drown them out.[32]

This laissez-faire attitude can be seen in John Perry Barlow's widely quoted *A Declaration of Independence of Cyberspace* in which he wrote, "On behalf of the future, I ask you of the past to leave us alone. You are not welcome among us. You have no sovereignty where we gather."[33]

Three years ago, I taught a media law and ethics class in which the vast majority of students were big proponents of the First Amendment's free speech rights. But when presented with the press's right to print names of people who are arrested, a student in the class told the story of how the *Burlington Free Press* printed the names of college students arrested for drinking, underage, at a downtown bar. In part because she was one of the arrested drinkers, she could not imagine any good reason for the newspaper's printing of the names. Nor could most of class. Even though these were intelligent and thoughtful students of journalism, they did not understand some of the central roles of the press: to inform, to verify, and to clarify. With some success, but probably not as much as I would have liked, I argued throughout the semester that without names, all college students would be suspects. By printing the names, the paper was not taking sides about underage drinking, but merely telling what the police did, when they did it, where they did it, and to whom. Without this kind of information, police (and thirsty students) would be far less accountable to the public.

The right to be left alone, important as it is, should never eclipse the responsibility to stay informed and engaged. The women with whom I watched *Survivor* did not feel invested in the news. For them, and many others like them, the daily political information in the newspaper was suspect (because of the news organizations' corporate sponsors) and worthless (because all politics is corrupt). This abdication of political responsibility means that these women and many others like them would not get to learn about the differences between political parties. No wonder Ralph Nader, who made claims about how the two parties were indistinguishable, was so popular among young people in the 2000 Presidential election. If you never read articles about how far apart Democrats and Republicans are on gun control, tax breaks for the wealthy, abortion rights, and Medicare, to name just a few issues, you might buy Nader's outrageous argument that Washington is run by a one-party system.

"I don't think about politics," says Rabbit in John Updike's *Rabbit Redux*. "That's one of my Goddam precious American rights, not to think about politics."[34] That right, however, makes for a poor democracy. This is because the ability to speak freely should not be confined to what someone else does in some ill-attended public meeting. A citizen cannot attend every single public meeting. An exchange of ideas needs to extend into public places which more than an engaged minority attends. Nor does the workplace provide a free speech forum (two thirds of all employers regularly monitor their workers' e-mail and voicemail.[35]). For general news and the ability to engage in a free and public debate, the best source is still the daily newspaper or a good on-line equivalent.

In broadcast, the declining share of quality news programming and the public's declining perception of its need may very well be mutually reinforcing. Back in the 1920s and 1930s, the FCC established that broadcasters needed to operate in "the public interest, convenience and necessity" in exchange for permission to lease the public airwaves (many people do not realize that the government owns the airwaves).[36] While early radio and television broadcasts were replete with examples of mindless fluff, these media did contain a lot of "public interest" programming, too. Because the government took an active role in the content going over its airwaves, the public was given more news than the market would naturally sustain. By the 1980s, under the Reagan era spirit of deregulation, broadcasters were no longer held accountable in the way they once were. News was becoming increasingly lost in a sea of media.

Since the late 1980s, I have attended academic conferences in which journalism professors talk about the difficulty of getting students (even journalism majors) to care about media history. Increasingly, however, I hear professors concluding that it is not the history that young people are resisting, but the whole reason for studying journalism. One professor, Jay Rosen, told me that as commercialism became more pervasive in the media, many students have become less likely to see the unique mission of journalism, less likely to see "what difference it makes, why it's not the same thing as entertainment or media, why it's important for it to be protected—all those things are perhaps less obvious. . . . [Students] don't grow up with the religion [of journalism], they don't imbibe it in the same way that students used to. Some do, but a lot don't."[37]

Journalism, Arbitrage, and "Imagined Communities"

Much of what we have seen so far relates to what Benedict Anderson called "imagined communities."[38] When younger generations no longer imagine themselves as part of a community, they see themselves as alone, unaffected by others. In two interesting ways, this vision of the world reminds me of the way the world was before the invention of the telegraph in 1844. Just as many young people see themselves as disconnected from politics and news, pre-telegraph cities were insular and distinct in some interesting ways. Before the telegraph made time zones a possibility, each city even had its own "local time"; Boston time and New York time, for example, differed by about 12 minutes. On the morning of November 18, 1883, called the "day of two noons" the nation adjusted to Standard Time, aided by time messages sent across telegraph lines. The rest of the world followed suit with the creation of time zones in the years ahead.[39]

One effect of the telegraph was to nationalize (and later internationalize) time. It took insular localities and made them part of a larger world. As James W. Carey has explained, the telegraph also promoted national and international arbitrage and futures trading.[40] In other words, if pork bellies were selling for a two dollars a pound in Boston and a dollar in Chicago, the telegraph, combined with the railroads, allowed traders to sell Chicago pork to Massachusetts. Further, the telegraph helped to provide an intellectual and cultural arbitrage as well. Ideas and politics and habits flowed quickly from one end of America to the other and back again. The downside, of course, was the decline of regional accents and manners, a homogenization if you will. But the upside far outweighed the cultural blurring.

In the aftermath of the telegraph's arrival, the debate over slavery began to heat up, in part because of the tensions leading up to and following the Compromise of 1850, but also due to the rapid cross-pollination of ideas, both intra- and intersectional. Despite that its paid circulation was minuscule,[41] the famous abolitionist newspaper, the *Liberator*, did as much as any other in spreading antislavery ideas and provoking debates. Before the telegraph's arrival, the *Liberator* spread its message via newspaper exchanges (cross-subscriptions). But after 1844, the *Liberator*'s messages were increasingly carried on electric wings.

In 1850, a famous abolitionist rally, led by William Lloyd Garrison and Frederick Douglass, turned into a debate when a "Capt." Isaiah Rynders, the thuggish leader of a local proslavery group, stormed the stage. The proslavery side suggested that blacks were descendents of apes. To this, Garrison suggested that no white man reply. Douglass then stood up and gave a long speech that essentially argued that Douglass himself was a man. In desperation, Rynders yelled, "*You* are not a black man; you are only half a nigger." Douglass, whose father was white, said, "He is correct; I am, indeed, only half a negro, a half-brother to Mr. Rynders."[42] In the intellectual arbitrage surrounding slavery and freedom, Douglass had successfully argued that he was not a beast, but a man (in fact, Rynders later admitted that Douglass "[gave] me a shot, and it was as good a shot as I ever had in my life."[43]). The struggle to convince the vast majority of Americans of that fact would extend forward in time to the 1950s and 1960s, but the battle surely began as ideas began to be exchanged between North and South, among people who vehemently disagreed with one another.

This may be one of the most important functions of the press: to bring people in contact with ideas that they do not agree with. This is at the heart of John Milton's famous seventeenth-century defense of press freedom. "Let

[Truth] and Falsehood grapple; who ever knew Truth put to the worse in a free and open encounter?"[44] In other words, society always benefits when conflicting ideas are permitted to compete in the open marketplace of ideas, a place in which debate is free and unfettered.[45] Historically, these chance encounters were less frequent when the party-owned press preached to the choir. They rose with the advent of the independent, commercial press and were distributed widely over the telegraph. But while the success of the commercial press promoted diverse views, the recent commercial success of exceptional media choice has not always been good for diversity and intellectual arbitrage. A prime example of this is when modern technology provides Israelis and Palestinians with their own broadcasting news outlets.[46] Israelis and Palestinians might want to consider the efficacy of the early U.S. commercial press model in planning their own exchange of information.

In his book, *The Lexus and the Olive Tree* (2000), Thomas Friedman echoed James W. Carey's view of commercial and intellectual arbitrage. Unlike Carey, who concentrated on the telegraph, Friedman saw the World Wide Web and other new media as fueling what he called "information arbitrage."[47] Friedman's own career may be seen as a shining example of arbitrage; an American Jew by birth, he studied in the United States and Britain (Oxford), and then traveled throughout the Middle East, learning Hebrew and Arabic and trying to make sense of—and find middle ground within—two opposing views. And Friedman takes comfort in everyone's ability to learn from one another.

The problem is, of course, that unlike the slavery debaters and Friedman's examples of what he called "Super-empowered individuals,"[48] most people do not get various opposing views because they do not get much news at all. In late 2002 and early 2003, an interesting debate raged over whether to begin mass vaccinations against smallpox in the United States. Of course, the events of September 11 proved that some people would commit terrible crimes against the United States if they could. And, by reading the newspaper we would know that smallpox is a deadly disease with no known effective treatment. But widespread smallpox vaccinations are not without risk and would almost certainly cause hundreds of deaths across the country, as newspapers reported throughout 2002. And while the threat of smallpox must be taken seriously, the disease itself was eradicated in the United States in 1949 and worldwide in 1977. Surely these important—and conflicting—considerations must inform the public debate about the efficacy of mass vaccinations. But in January 2003, at the height of the national exposure to these issues (President Bush himself was vaccinated in December 2002), came a report that a majority of Americans were woefully uninformed about these issues. A majority (78%) believed that there is an "effective medical treatment" for smallpox. A majority believed that "there has been a case of smallpox in the past 5 years . . . some-where in the world (63%)" and a significant minority believed that the dis-ease had hit the United States in the past five years (30%).[49]

To vaccinate or not to vaccinate? That is an important question. Unfortu-nately, as the above reveals, most Americans are completely incapable of mak-ing such decisions or holding political leaders accountable for theirs. In Sep-tember 2003, after the first wave of hostilities in the Iraq war had ended, the Bush administration disavowed its public relations campaign to link Iraq to the September 11, 2001, attacks. Still, most Americans, 69 percent, believed that it was "likely" Saddam was responsible for the September 11 attacks.[50] What-ever you think about the wisdom of the 2003 Iraq war, you must acknowledge the costs: hundreds of U.S. lives, thousands of Iraqi lives, and more than a hun-dred billion dollars in expenses. These costs were carried by a public that was woefully uninformed.

This all reminds me of how my then-three-year-old daughter used to dis-cuss the "Power Rangers" television cartoon with her friends. None had actu-ally seen the show, but that did not stop them from having long conversations about it. The conversations were wonderful and imaginative, but they had ab-solutely nothing to do with the show. In the same way, the Canadian Broad-casting Corporation (CBC) has a show devoted to making Americans look silly. Rick Mercer, the host of the show, travels around the United States, asking questions like, Should Canada go to a 24-hour clock? What do you think of Canada's new black prime minister? Or its new king, Lucienne Bonhomme? In 2000, Mercer even asked then-candidate George W. Bush for a reaction to the fact that Canadian "Prime Minister Poutine" endorsed Bush's candidacy. "I appreciate his strong statement," Bush said. "He understands that I want to make sure that our relations with our most important neighbors to the north of US, the Canadians, are strong and we'll work closely together."[51] Never mind that Jean Chretien was the actual prime minister and *poutine* is a Cana-dian dish involving fries, cheese, and gravy. Many Americans, Rick Mercer shows us, will talk with confidence about many topics, ranging from Canadian "kings" and "presidents" to whether Canada should be permitted to continue strip-mining Mount Rushmore.

This book has given a lot of evidence about the extent to which Ameri-cans, particularly younger ones, are tuned out. What Mercer and his colleagues at the CBC show us is how many Americans are not shy about topics about which they know little or nothing. The next time you read about a poll pur-porting to divine the public's sentiments on war, politics, or smallpox vaccina-tions, you might want to consider how much information the public has about the issues of the day. Public opinion, in the absence of fact, becomes a farce,

The Far Side® by Gary Larson © 1983 FarWorks, Inc. All Rights Reserved. Used with permission.

and when politicians talk to their constituents, they increasingly resemble the man in the old Far Side cartoon who berates his dog with language that is incomprehensible to it.

In 2004, Jay Leno discussed his show with Marc Gunther, a writer at *Fortune*. Political jokes, Leno told Gunther, are much harder to tell than when he first started hosting the *Tonight Show* in 1992. "Americans don't really know politics," Leno said. "Once you get past secretary of state, they don't know anyone. To do a John Ashcroft joke, you literally have to explain who he is, the position he's in." Leno, who has the benefit of a studio audience to gauge news knowledge, needs to educate as he entertains. A lot has been made of the fact that nearly half of Americans under 30 treat late night comedians as a major news source (see chapter 3). Leno's remarks here illustrate that audiences familiar with late night comedy need to be reminded, again and again, of basic political facts. Leno's sense that things have gotten much worse in the last twelve years may very well be a reflection of what this book has addressed, a broad generational shift away from news and politics.[52]

Imagined Communities

Over and over again we have come back to Benedict Anderson's idea of "imagined communities." It may be the most important idea that informs this book.

When I asked my interviewees whether they could make a difference in American society today, two answers emerged as dominant. The first was, No, my voice (my vote) cannot make a difference. The second was, Yes, our voices (our votes) can make a difference. I do not want to oversimplify the distinction—there were many variants of these themes—but we should not miss the larger lesson either. Those who see themselves as individuals (my voice/my vote) are prone to feel powerless. Those who are part of a wider community (our voice/our vote) tend to see the need for politics and news. And this makes perfect sense: the weight of an individual's vote is minuscule. Even the 2000 presidential election, decided by 537 votes,[53] was not a strong case for an individual to vote. No one person's vote would have tipped the balance to Gore. But if we change our focus from the single voter to an individual's ability to help mobilize communities, get out the vote, and work with organizations to lobby—if we imagine ourselves as part of communities, then our power rises exponentially.

In a recent study, Thomas Patterson found a disintegration of the national imagined community reflected in the news media itself. In a fascinating project, Patterson examined the extent to which news stories used "collectives" words (crowd, humanity, army, congress, country) and "self-reference" words (I, I'm, me, mine, myself). Over the past two decades, Patterson found, the use of "collectives" words has plummeted while the use of "self-reference" words has shot way up.[54] News that stresses the individual and solitary may have some value to *me*, but we should examine its value to *us*, too.

Connected to the Press, Connected to Each Other

In one of his most haunting and lovely poems, "So Long," Walt Whitman wrote

> *Camerado, this is no book*
> *Who touches this touches a man*
> *(Is it night? are we here together alone?)*
> *It is I you hold and who holds you,*
> *I spring from the pages into your arms. . . .*
> *Dear friend whoever you are take this kiss.*[55]

Whitman was trying to make a temporal connection with his readers, saying in effect that he will remain palpable and sexual despite his corporeal demise. Journalism does something similar to Whitman's leap across time. It leaps across space, giving us a connection with one another, allowing us all to become members of a common expanse, to meet at a common crossroads.

When people tune in together, they can—as they did in the 1960s—react together to marines burning a Vietnamese village. They can recoil in horror, together, at the fire hoses and police dogs in Birmingham. There were counterarguments to what journalism presented to the country (*the Marines were provoked, the South has a right to segregation*) and independent journalism, at its best, tried not to take sides. No, in these kinds of stories, journalists don't take sides, they give sides. In the Miltonian marketplace of ideas, journalism provides readers and viewers with different perspectives. In the 1960s, many of these readers and viewers acted like citizens and leaders and the nation decided to end Vietnam and end segregation.

Occasionally ideas are kept out of the mainstream for too long. Many black leaders had strong arguments against segregation and racism well before the civil rights era, but their voices were rarely heard by those in power. In the 1940s, when a waitress told James Baldwin, the writer, "We don't serve Negroes here," he did something he had never done before: He threw a pitcher against the restaurant's mirror and ran.[56] It was only later that Baldwin gained a journalistic avenue for his critique of American race relations. In the 1980s, journalists saw AIDS as a gay disease, and most all but ignored it until they found out that Rock Hudson got it. And even today, members of many groups, representing narrow interests spanning the political spectrum, rightly complain that their voices are sometimes misstated or ignored.[57] But while the mainstream media occasionally fall short of full inclusion of ideas, other media come in to supplement them. "We wish to plead our own cause. Too long have others spoken for us," wrote America's first black newspaper as it started a long tradition of minority journalism.[58] Whether it is the mainstream press or the minority press, if you want to reach a wide audience, the best route is going through the media.

American Crossroads

Although we should acknowledge that not all voices are heard, it still does not obviate the need for a crossroads-like central forum. In fact, the United States itself is predicated on this ideal. In the late 1760s, when a small group of British subjects in North America started to talk about rejecting their king's rule, they needed to convince their skeptical fellow colonists. The charge was led by men and women of all walks of life, but the words were propagated by a small cohort of journalists and writers, including newspaper editors Samuel Adams and Isaiah Thomas, and writers Thomas Paine and John Livingston. The Boston Tea Party was planned in the office of a newspaper editor.[59] British subjects from 13 colonies were slowly turned to revolution by the nationalistic fervor of their newspapers which included expressions like, "JOIN OR DIE!" "THIRTEEN CLOCKS STRIKE AS ONE!" and "UNITED WE STAND—DIVIDED WE FALL!"[60]

There were certainly many competing factions during and after the American Revolution, but journalism provided, above all else, a unifying force. To a great extent, the British colonials became Americans as they read their newspapers. This kind of crossroads is central in any democracy, especially one whose motto is *e pluribus unum* (from many, one). This model may have been what George Washington was thinking about when he set aside money in his will to establish a university that "would have a tendency to spread Systematic ideas through all parts of this rising Empire." Students would learn, among other lessons,

> knowledge in the principles of Politics and good Government; and (as a matter of infinite Importance in my judgment) by associating with each other, and forming friendships in Juvenile years, be enabled to free themselves in a proper degree from . . . local prejudices and habitual jealousies.[61]

America remembers Washington's will because it manumitted his slaves, but we should also remember it for the above passage and its model for a society of shared values, experiences, and news.

It is precisely this model that will allow us to make the case that general news is crucial in any democracy, that we need responsible journalists to give us useful windows onto the nation and the world. We need, in the words of Kovach and Rosenstiel, an "intellectual diversity" in our newsrooms and on our front pages, and for that reason we must shun the undiluted sensational outlets.[62] Good journalism involves us—the many publics—on a common ground, with common points of interest. When you read a good newspaper or listen to or watch a quality news program, the world may seem scary, but at least the news provides a series of common experiences for us to view, interpret, and act upon.

Washington's model promises us that "local prejudices and habitual jealousies" will be eased. In other words, the model promises us that we can shake off our narrow views and come to a common understanding. This is, of course, exactly the opposite paradigm of those who flew planes into the World Trade Center and Pentagon. Whatever you may think about the merits of U. S. foreign policy, American citizens were attacked on September 11, 2001 because what connects every human—culturally, genetically, religiously and politically—was not as strong in the eyes of the terrorists as what divides us. Our response, whether it is war, peace, foreign aid, domestic security measures, or whatever, must be built by people who embrace an opposite paradigm: that we can reach a common understanding. This understanding is informed by good information and analysis—in short, quality journalism.

Above all else, there is one thing that makes America great: our working democracy, built on sound information and common dialogue. We have had dark times in our history, fought ill-conceived wars, enslaved one group and expelled another, but we have always preserved the workings of a democracy that allows its citizens to speak and protest based on information that has become, for the most part, free and unfettered. In return, the only thing we must do is stay informed.

CHAPTER 7

Conclusion: How to Tune Back In

Leonard Downie, Jr. and Robert Kaiser ended their recent book, *The News About the News* (2002), on a hopeful note. They wrote that despite all the pressures—from the government, the corporate boards, and the tabloids next door—journalism will continue to thrive because of tomorrow's news consumers: "In the end, the most important people shaping tomorrow's news won't be the owners or the journalists, but the readers and viewers. As long as they create a market for good journalism, there will be good journalism. That's the good news."[1] Downie and Kaiser were, of course, correct that consumers can make a difference by choosing quality news. However, the authors' last sentence, "That's the good news," caused me to yell back at the still-open book, "No, that's the bad news!" If researching and writing this book has taught me one thing it is that our democracy is on the brink of a crisis and that the problem will not right itself. Nearing the time when 20- and 30-somethings will be given the tiller of the ship of state, we and they might ask, are they informed enough for the journey? We must do something to address the crisis and we must not let false optimism prevent us from acting swiftly and forcefully.

Existing Solutions

The existing solutions range from unimaginative to useless. For all their business concerns, media organizations have done little beyond identifying the demographic shift away from news. One report by the International Newspaper Marketing Association offers an excellent overview of the consequences to the newspaper industry. But the words "democracy," "voting," and "citizen" never appear; the report looks to the industry itself when it outlines the three possible solutions: "continue the current strategy . . . ," "enhance current efforts . . . ," or "treat 'youth' as a current market with unique products and market pitches."[2]

Another report, by the Readership Institute, offers "eight imperatives" to building readership. Many of these are quite impressive, one of which (making the paper easier to read and navigate) I will discuss in my section on improving journalism. But all are too insular, not looking at the society outside the newsroom. For example, the title of Imperative 8 is "Building an Adaptive, Constructive Culture That Is Attuned to Readers and Customers . . . "[3] If the "culture" in the title would refer to the general culture at large, the "imperative" would certainly have a broad impact. Instead, the report suggested a change only in newsroom culture. Newsroom culture is important in itself, but as I have argued, it is insufficient to produce the kind of changes that are needed.

Another typical approach, with all its methodological limitations, is to ask young people who don't read newspapers what they would like to see. One publication, "Recapture Your Youth: How to Create a Newspaper for Future Generations," reported a range of responses. Young nonreaders claimed that newspapers don't provide political coverage, aren't global enough, disrespect youth, "lack information," and are "irrelevant."[4] To make newspapers more hip, the young nonreaders argued, we must consider running ads about the relevancy of newspapers; these ads should run during soap operas and ESPN shows. Some young people suggested that newspapers on CD-ROM would attract a younger market. The only thing worse than these contradictory theories, purveyed by nonreaders, is that they are taken seriously by desperate news executives. These suggestions fail to understand that fine news organizations already exist; the real challenge is to create a society in which young people feel that reading quality journalism is worthwhile.[5] Newspapers across America are adding Britney Spears and subtracting Tom Daschle; in trying to make newspapers matter to young people, they make them matter to no one.

Take the new Chicago newspapers aimed at young readers. Please! In 2002, the *Chicago Tribune* and the *Chicago Sun-Times* started competing tabloids, *RedEye* and *Red Streak*, respectively, aimed at young adults. On January 3, 2003, the *Chicago Tribune* began the new year with a typically diverse front page (see Figure 7–1). The top story (on the upper right of the page) was about the economy. This was balanced by a picture of Senator John Edwards, who had just announced his candidacy for president. Other stories were about lower fares offered by airlines, Britain's sending troops to Iraq, a charge by the State

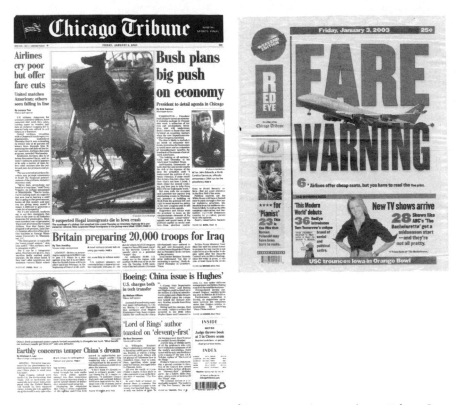

The Chicago Tribune *and its evil spawn*, RedEye.   Copyright 2003, Chicago Tribune Company. All rights reserved. Used with permission.

Department that Boeing had sold sensitive information to the Chinese, J. R. R. Tolkien's 111th birthday, and the Chinese space program.

It would be unfair to compare the diversity of the *Tribune*'s front page with that of *RedEye*. After all, the latter is a tabloid, which naturally stresses fewer stories on its front page. Nor is it unexpected to see that *RedEye*'s lead story (on the airlines) was 11 paragraphs to the *Tribune*'s twenty. Or that *RedEye* had only 40 pages, mostly ads, to the *Tribune*'s 108 pages. No, it's the flavor of the paper that is so very different. "Fare Warning" the transformed *Tribune* article, was less about the financial crisis of the airlines and more about what the airlines are doing for *you* in terms of cheap tickets. The second story on *RedEye*'s front page was "New TV Shows Arrive." The third story was about a comic strip. Inside, *RedEye* has much less about politics (although there is a rare primer on the Democrats) and much more about sports, music, movies, food, television, and celebrities. It is not hard to imagine what *RedEye* thinks about its young readers: that they are not citizens but spoiled, selfish, insatiable consumers wanting TV, fun entertainment, food, and titillation.

The problem with *RedEye* is that it retained little of the *Tribune*'s most important news. We don't learn about Bush's economic plan. Or Britain's plan to send troops to Iraq. Instead, we get "F.Y.I. Nation" and "F.Y.I. World," two pages offering tidbits about orangutans, a Venezuelan firecracker named after bin Laden, and an Italian murderer who escaped his hospital prison. Completely missing is any depth, process, or analysis of politics. The paper has become Headline News and the headlines are mainly about fluff and consumerism. The paper doesn't serve the primary function of journalism, to make sure we can be good citizens, to make sure we don't get screwed.[6] Rather than offer an antidote to the crisis, *RedEye* perpetuates it.

So what are the solutions? I offer four.

Solution #1
Take Back the Airwaves, Desktops, and Newspaper Offices

Robert Putnam, whose otherwise brilliant research and ideas have inspired this and other books, had a strikingly implausible idea about how to limit the media's influence on society: Ask the media moguls to help us get Americans to "spend less leisure time sitting passively alone in front of glowing screens."[7] It is difficult to imagine corralling the CEO of Disney, Michael Eisner, into this cause. After all, limiting screen time is precisely antithetical to everything he is working towards with his television network. But if cajoling Eisner would certainly not work, do we have any leverage? It turns out that we have plenty and it comes down to the fact that the airwaves are owned by us and leased to the TV networks. As I mentioned in chapter 3, the late 1960s saw a much higher percentage of programming that was devoted to news and public affairs.[8] Why? It is because networks were very concerned that the FCC would reject their license renewals, which actually used to happen from time to time. Since the 1980s, deregulation meant a weakening of the imposed ethical standard on broadcasters. As the Federal Communications Commission was overturning its "public trust" requirement in the 1980s, broadcasters were paring their news divisions and public interest programs.[9]

News for Kids

Because of the growing news options, including 24-hour cable news, most people still could get plenty of news and did not suffer. However a subset of them did suffer—kids. As children's programming used to be held to the same "public trust" standard as adult programming, there was a greater percentage of news and public affairs shows among the programs for kids. My own appetite for news was whetted on Saturday mornings in the early 1970s with CBS's *In the News* program for kids, a show that has been discontinued.[10] The show was brief, sandwiched in between Saturday morning cartoons, but that was its strength. While millions of kids were being entertained, they were being informed about national politics and world events. One of the easiest ways to introduce news into a child's diet is to throw it in with the sugary stuff. We should insist that every network (including the Cartoon Network) carry news as a fixed percentage (let's say 5%) of its children's programming. The news would not be like Nickelodeon's *Nick News*—which tends to be lifestyle driven, and apolitical—but geared to the great political issues of the day.[11] Domestically, the children's news would cover decisions by the three branches of government. Internationally, it would provide the latest in geopolitical changes. We may not and should not dictate the exact content of the programming, but we can and should mandate that our own airwaves have some political coverage for kids.

Diversify Broadcast and Newspaper Ownership

During the 1980s and 1990s, the FCC loosened its requirements barring broadcasters from owning multiple stations within a single market. During this time corporations began to gobble up ever-larger shares of markets while arguing that the First Amendment protected them from any regulation whatsoever.[12] In June 2003, the FCC rolled back a series of regulations to make it easier to own media across platforms, greatly accelerating the potential for consolidation.[13] This parallels the ever-increasing corporate influence in the newspaper field. Many media critics, most notably Benjamin Bagdikian, have called for government regulation in these areas to prevent or even roll back consolidation. Bagdikian's view is that corporate centralization of media limits messages, particularly those not friendly to businesses. His solution was to pass laws that make local and national media ownership more diverse. While this book reveals that many young people overstate corporate influence on the media ("they are all bought and paid for"), young people are responding to something real—the corporate and entertainment influences that weaken the purity of the news. We should support legislation that makes it more difficult for major national corporations to edge out smaller local ones, and we must protect against monopolies.[14]

Desktop News, E-mail News

A number of advocates of using the Internet to promote democracy, including Andrew Shapiro, James Fishkin, and Cass Sunstein, have proposed a discussion portal on each home computer, perhaps called PublicNet or Deliberativedemocracy.com.[15] The same could be done for news. We can insist that com-

Google News, 29 August 2003.   Downloaded May 2004.

puter manufacturers and Web navigators include a separate portal for news organizations. In keeping with our tradition of freedom of the press, we would not dictate to the computer manufacturers what news organizations they should choose, but we could and should insist that the news portal be prominent on the desktop and have links to national and local news outlets. Despite the myth that the Internet is driven by private enterprise, its infrastructure was started by and is still supported by the U.S. government, which also is the largest purchaser of hardware and software. Surely the government can insist, like it used to do with television, that computers support the public good. A news portal would make following the news even easier than it is currently. By this same logic, Internet Service Providers (ISPs) might be forced to offer a news option default with its e-mail service. Let's say you sign up for e-mail for Yahoo. Unless you choose to avoid it, you would receive a daily news e-mail with top stories and links to the major news outlets. Incidentally, Yahoo and Google each has a great system for disseminating news, devoting a central location to the news of other sources. However, you'll only find Yahoo's or Google's pages if you seek them out. My proposal would put a portal to pages like these on every desktop. This kind of maneuver, creating a default system of news consumption, greatly influenced the New Orleans kids I spoke with.

Solution #2

Change Our Expectations: College Admissions and Civic Knowledge

Joel Senesac told me, "People learn what they need to know."[16] In some circles, what we need to know is who plays on the Chicago Cubs. In other circles, it is who plays on the Supreme Court. One of the greatest problems is that there is little perceived need to know about news. In other words, news has less and less currency in conversations. As I recounted in chapter 4, a Brandeis student found that when she tried to talk about news, her friends did the verbal equivalent of grabbing for the remote, changing the topic as fast as they could back to lighter fare.[17] Without a critical mass of young people to talk about news, it will continue to feel like a waste of time for most of them.

How do we change this model? If the examples of this book are a guide, we can change news habits if we change our expectations. When Andrea Alford walked into her summer internship at Ducks Unlimited, the nonprofit firm, she quickly learned that the coin of the realm among her older office mates was political news in the *Washington Post*. In order for her to feel connected at work, she needed to buy and read the paper.[18] This is in keeping with the work of Bernard Berelson, who wrote that news is often used as fodder for conversation.[19] One of the quickest ways to change news habits is for parents, teachers, and older colleagues to make sure news matters—to us and to young people. And we need to make sure young people know they will be judged on how conversant they are, too.

Throughout this book I have discussed how the entertainment choices of cable television and the Web can weaken one's resolve to keep up with the news. The Web, in particular, is driven by one's own interests, no matter how distinct or arcane they may be. It is difficult to imagine a change in the media environment that would return us to the limits of the past. In the face of the cornucopia of entertainment, the only way to change young people's habits is to alter our expectations in ways that will make a difference. The Web is a poor medium in which to find news by chance, but an excellent one to find it by choice.

Honor Society Requirements

In chapter 4, we learned that part of the rise of volunteerism among high school students may be due to the simple fact that it is a requirement for the National Honor Society. On the one hand, that college entry, and not altruism, may be responsible for some volunteerism is rather depressing. On the other hand, it can give us hope that the decline of news readership may be malleable too. Maybe it tells us that if we change our expectations about news consumption and political involvement—make *that* a requirement for the honor society—then young people's habits in this area will change, too.

C-SAT

In April 2002, I visited a civics class in Colchester High School in Vermont. Many of the students were able to discuss the issues of the day. Some, too, knew about the First Amendment and other matters as a direct result of the class. It left me wondering why civics is not more universally taught. The answer is that civics and current events are valued by neither national standards nor colleges.[20] In this climate, civics and current events are seen as expendable frills.

It is reasonable to encourage colleges to pay more attention to the civic involvement and knowledge of their high school seniors. After all, our country's first president founded a college based on the idea that it would promote democracy. It is also reasonable for our colleges and universities to demand that their students know the issues of the day. Along with the SAT, colleges could ask for a C-SAT, a civics portion of the college aptitude test. In addition to being able to answer static questions about the makeup of our government and reveal some general world knowledge (where is Iraq, for example), incoming freshmen might be asked to identify the Speaker of the House, which of the two Koreas is communist, the nature of the Human Genome Project, which political party controls the U.S. senate, and whether the United States ran a deficit in the last fiscal year. It wouldn't take much effort: ten civics/news questions appended to the standard SAT, coupled with the colleges' commitment to notice them, would completely transform the news habits of young people. The intellectual diversity and political currency that is the staple of any democracy cannot be fully measured by a C-SAT, but it can be promoted by one. We demand a civics test of everyone who wants to become a U.S. citizen; it seems fitting to have high school students take a news/civics test, too.

Solution #3

Make Politics Meaningful Again

When looking at the problem of young people not following the news, nearly everyone is wrong. The optimists are wrong that young people will eventually pick up the habit. The pessimists are wrong that there is nothing to do about it. And industry believes, wrongly, that the problems and solutions can come from industry alone. They cannot. For example, perhaps the simplest way to making political news matter is to make politics matter.

There was a time when it did. In 1968, for example, the Democratic national convention mattered. As Southern blacks fought to be seated as delegates, many Southern whites resisted this and some even bolted from the party. Outside the convention hall, antiwar protesters clashed with police. Inside, politicians clashed over the platform, embarking on a series of floor fights.

CBS's Mike Wallace was on the convention floor, asking an African American delegate from Minnesota about her support of black challenges to the all-white Southern delegations. The two quarreled over labels, with the former saying "Negro" and the latter saying "black." At one point, the white delegation from Georgia tried to steal its banner and leave the hall. In the midst of all this, Dan Rather tried to get an interview with a delegate who was being forcibly removed from the hall. Rather, in turn, was roughed up and punched in the stomach.[21] This all made for great, riveting journalism, making sense of stuff that mattered.

Today, politics still matters, but so much of it is so scripted that its vibrancy is hidden and its meaning is often shrouded by the nonsense of polling. For example, television ads and lawn signs used to say things like "Jones: Democrat for Senator." Today, there is a near-universal view that touting party affiliation is not an effective way to get elected. Rather than party affiliation, you get "Jones: For a Change," or similar pablum (Dave Barry quipped that his own slogan would be, "A Leader Who Will Lead, by Leading."[22]). This practice may have some strategic worth: swing voters, like nonvoters, often shun party labels.[23] In other words, politicians, once they are reasonably sure of holding their base, strive for the tiny undecided minority. But although this math might work to win elections, it is a terrible calculus for our democracy. One of the reasons why young people do not see much difference between parties is that they are not told the differences by the candidates. And the decision to use focus groups' views to justify shielding party affiliation is hardly comforting. As E. J. Dionne, Jr., has written about focus groups, "the approach to politics is not even Machiavellian; it is Pavlovian."[24] We need to create a system that will look well beyond election day and build long-term generational affiliations with parties.

FEC Intervention on Ads
To break this Pavlovian approach to getting elected, the Federal Election Commission (FEC) should be instructed by Congress to take specific steps to force the announcement of party affiliation. The FEC should withhold any matching funds from politicians who do not include party affiliation on ads. Individual candidates may not wish to unilaterally announce their affiliation, but if everyone is mandated to do so, it will not hurt either side. Similarly, limiting the soft money PACS that don't use party affiliation, one of the cornerstones of campaign finance reform, would help to make political ads more recognizably partisan.

U.S. Intervention on Debates
The most important element of our presidential elections may be our televised debates. No matter how much politicians offer their canned speeches on the

road and their 30-second pabulum over the airwaves, the debates do offer a chance for politicians to have their views held up to scrutiny, live, even if the format is not always conducive to great depth. For 90 minutes, three times each election cycle, the public and the journalists can take a break from horse race reporting, scandals, innuendo, and other superficialities and just listen to ideas. It isn't nearly as useful a window into policy as is the weekly "question time" of the British system, but it is the best window we've got. The problem is that many politicians who are ahead in the polls duck the debates. Congress should pass a law making at least three prime-time debates between major candidates a requirement for federal matching funds. This, along with the intervention on political ads, will go a long way to ensuring that party affiliation and values are on full display each election cycle.*

Open Our Airwaves

The vast majority of industrialized democracies provide free airtime for political advertisements—the United States is a rare exception.[25] Subsidized TV appearances could go a long way in reintroducing political messages into the American dialogue. Unfortunately, the main resistance to this idea comes from the same people who cut checks for broadcast journalists—the television corporate executives. True campaign finance reform would be a good step to breaking the broadcasters' effective veto over free political ads. Another good step would be mobilizing our political will to make it happen. If we join this battle, however, we must remember that broadcast journalists will not be allies, at least not vocal ones.

"Multiply Picnics"

After Robert Putnam laid out, for more than 400 pages, the decline of civic society in his seminal book, *Bowling Alone*, he offered numerous solutions. One, echoing Henry Ward Beecher, was "multiply picnics."[26] Part of the solution, I have come to believe, is following Putnam's advice for re-engaging civic life in America. Many journalists and media critics reject the "public journalism" model in which journalists themselves try to reinvigorate public life. However, we are still left with the fact that a vibrant civic life is to journalism as gasoline is to the internal combustion engine. And vice versa.

Nearly a century ago, Walter Lippmann's and John Dewey's views on the press framed what is still an argument in journalism criticism: Lippmann said

---

*The coupling of the debates with federal matching funds would not, of course, end the discussion of exactly who gets invited to debates (a common threshold is any candidate who holds 15% support in national polling), but it would not necessarily alter the discussion either.

that correct information is paramount in order to engage an elite minority of decision makers; Dewey said that broader discussion among citizens was more important.[27] They were, of course, both correct—and incorrect. Only a marriage of the two would bring a true dialogue to support democracy and provide a check against governmental authority.

Today, Lippmann's side is holding its own. We have reporters digging for the kind of information Lippmann said we need. When Nixon's men planned and then covered up the Watergate burglary, the press was there. The press was there for Reagan-Bush's Iran-Contra, Clinton's Whitewater, and George W. Bush's extrajudicial arrests of American citizens as suspected terrorists. It is Dewey's side of the equation that needs bolstering. True, an engaged minority is as active as ever, passionately discussing issues and e-mailing journalists, politicians, and activists. But the elite minority is actually closer to Lippman's model; we need to greatly broaden the discussion. Putnam's book is a good place to start in our attempt to reinvigorate journalism's lifeblood, the public.

Solution #4
Create, Consume, and Teach Quality Journalism

People say that too much time is devoted to the scandals of the day. When O. J. Simpson fled from the police in his white Bronco, when John F. Kennedy, Jr.'s plane crashed, when Princess Diana died, when Michael Jackson was indicted, we cry "sensationalism." But we eat it up, too. The truth of the matter is that this sort of thing sells; each of these stories generated huge readerships and ratings for the journalists who covered them.[28] This book is not going to make people avoid sensational news. However, there are a few things we can do to counteract its influence.

Do Quality Journalism That is Also Accessible

As we have seen, the rise of narrowcasting (media tailored to specific tastes) provides a series of challenges to journalists. However, it also offers a significant advantage: there will always be at least a niche market for quality journalism. Journalists can (and should) continue to cover O. J. Simpson, Princess Diana, J.F.K., Jr., and Michael Jackson, but they should also remember that, in the words of Kovach and Rosenstiel, "Citizens are not customers." As Kovach and Rosenstiel wrote, "all O. J. all the time—actually leaves most of the audience behind."[29] Some citizens may *like* "all O. J. all the time," but they *need* more than this. They need a great diversity of items, including a substantial amount of political news. There is even evidence that, despite conventional wisdom, quality sells. The Project for Excellence in Journalism, in a study of 146 local TV news programs, graded each show in terms of quality (A, B, C, D, and F) and then evaluated the shows' success, in terms of ratings over a three-year period. Of the newscasts earning a "grade A," 64 percent saw their ratings increase, too. None of the other categories—B, C, D, and F—had a clear majority of stations with a ratings increase.[30]

Too often people in the media seem to think that accessibility means dumbing things down or adding the latest macabre murder or Hollywood hottie. But sometimes responsible journalists don't do enough to make quality journalism accessible to light readers. A thoughtful student once told me that following the news was like trying to keep up with a difficult math class after missing the first half of the semester. It wouldn't kill journalists to provide a few more crib notes. An interesting proposal came from the Readership Institute: put more road signs in the newspaper. Offer more "branded" content, content that readers can quickly recognize to help them navigate around the paper. Offer a "contents" strip running down the left-hand column of the front page. Offer "Follow Up" or "Talking Points" bullets that get tuned out readers up-to-date on stories that they might happen upon for the first time.[31] When reading a story about Kenya, even the best of readers might benefit from a brief sidebar of its history or geography. A profile of a presidential candidate could have a sidebar listing other candidates, or a Web link that lists that information.

Recognize Quality Journalism and Demand It

The only way to get quality journalism is to demand it and pay for it. Max Frankel wrote, "Facts don't inform. Reporters and editors do."[32] Journalists are more than just a window onto the world. They dig, they gather, they uncover, they verify. But they also do far more: they provide an interpretive frame by making sense of the information they get. And the better journalists resist the age-old pressures from government, parties, and marketplace. People who do what I do, media criticism, have gotten very good at explaining to high school and college students how the media can be biased. But too often we do not articulate the benefits and even beauty of a well working and ethical press. We need to help students recognize the value of nonpartisan, ethical, and high quality news. That way, they will be more likely to pay for it. Reporters and editors, particularly good ones, are expensive. We need to teach young people about the importance of fine journalism and how and where to find it.

The Greatest Democracy for the Greatest Numbers

When Barnes & Noble sells a chai latte, it helps introduce more people to books. But if Barnes & Noble were to throw out all its books to make way for a bigger café, it would lose its raison d'être and serious readers would suffer, too. A business executive might ask the question, "does it increase profits?" But there is also another question to ask: "does chai latte help to produce a net gain in reading?" Barnes & Noble is still a great place for books, but we, as citizens, should insist that it stays that way.

Similarly, journalists need to ask whether adding Britney, and perhaps a few young readers, justifies making democracy poorer by the subtraction of serious news. It may be that ventures such as *RedEye* are merely stepping-stones to greater news involvement. Or maybe not. Either way, the litmus test should be a utilitarian one: What brings the greatest democracy for the greatest numbers? In other words, if the *New York Times* or the *Wall Street Journal* added 1 percent more entertainment news and doubled its readership, we can applaud that decision as a great success: many more people would be armed with information needed in our democracy. On the other hand, if they added 25 percent more entertainment news (with the same net loss in serious news), for only a marginal gain in readership, democracy would be the poorer for it. If more journalists (especially editors) would ask themselves if changes pass the "greatest democracy" test, many of the new initiatives to attract younger readers would die a quick death.

An example of this is the successful attempt by Fox News to attract viewers with its flash and attitude. But are the viewers becoming better citizens? A recent study suggests that Fox viewers are considerably less informed than consumers of CNN, network television, NPR, PBS, and newspapers. People were asked about three widely held misperceptions of the 2003 Iraq war—that Iraq was directly involved in September 11, that world opinion favored the war, and that weapons of mass destruction had been found. A full 80 percent of Fox viewers believed one or more of these misperceptions, compared to 47 percent and 23 percent of newspaper readers and NPR/PBS listeners and viewers, respectively.[33] These findings need to be clarified: did Fox News viewers start out much less informed than, say, NPR listeners, or did Fox News actually make its viewers less informed? Either way, these findings would suggest that Fox News must immediately rethink the way it conveys news so as to make its viewers smarter citizens, not dumber ones.

Without Compromising Journalism's Prime Objectives, Follow the Ideas, Attitudes, and Topics of Young People

The young people interviewed for this book, especially the students at Brandeis, described how news doesn't offer the "emotional investment" of the entertainment media. On the other hand, we need journalism that is politically independent. Isn't this a contradiction? The model of political detachment is coupled in networks like CNN with a practiced emotional detachment. But objectivity and political detachment needn't be emotionally detached.

The remarkable success of Fox News, which overtook CNN in 2002 as the nation's most watched all-news network, has been widely misinterpreted by many on the right and the left as an affirmation of that network's conservative values or of its sensationalism. But a more plausible explanation may be that Fox does a great job of showing both the humanness of its reporters and anchors and talk show hosts and that they actually care about the news they're delivering. One could imagine a nonpartisan network with the attitude of Fox. A story about welfare reform, or Americans killed in Iraq, or the "partial birth abortion" debate need not be told in a robotic way; one can be passionate and still remain nonpartisan.

This might be the attraction of something like *The Daily Show*, Jon Stewart's nightly spoof on the news. Like Fox, Stewart has been accused of having a political agenda (in Stewart's case, a left agenda), but the possible leftwing bias is not the secret of Stewart's success—it is that the show is very, very funny and drips with the kind of irony that many young people tell me they appreciate. Another such show is *Real Time with Bill Maher*. In that show, Maher attacks both parties, airs a lot of unconventional pundits, and has an iconoclastic approach that has a much younger vibe than CNN and the networks. Maher's show is not, as far as I can tell, consistently partisan. But it is opinionated, passionate, and entertaining. And its skepticism about power makes it an effective watchdog.

Two other broadcast models are worth mentioning: *Now* with Bill Moyers and *Countdown* with Keith Olbermann. In his show, Moyers takes a decidedly progressive position, which generally jibes with the mainstream and left of the Democratic Party. But while the Moyers model might not work on a major network that seeks political balance, Moyers' empathy for the poor and passion for social justice are not, after all, partisan attributes.

Keith Olbermann opens his show, *Countdown* (MSNBC) with the question, "Which of these stories will you be talking about tomorrow?"[34] This, of course, addresses what young people have told me again and again: that the extent to which news affects conversation is a crucial indicator of news consumption. Olbermann's show is well written and punchy, qualities that seem to have migrated from ESPN's *Sportscenter*, where Olbermann was an anchor in the late 1990s. Any journalism that can increase conversation among young people is worth noting.

Part of this connection may simply be including young people's stories in the news. As Farai Chideya found, a typical television story about education will include shots of young people walking around campus; when the reporter needs to talk to someone, however, he or she will go to the teachers and administrators. "If the news is totally manufactured as a product for older Americans, which is increasingly true, then there's less and less reason for young people to buy into it," Chideya told me.[35] When politicians and the media take the voices of young people seriously, interesting things happen. In 1996, when Clinton answered questions from an MTV audience, he was widely criticized for answering a question about his choice of "boxers or briefs." But along with this politically unimportant question (and response) came a new idea: young people should be included in the discussion. In 2003, when the Democratic presidential candidates debated on MTV, many of the questions were uninspiring. However, many were not. And if young people are included, and not just b-roll, they will begin to make their way back into the process.

One of the interesting aspects of the 2003 MTV debate was that each of the candidates made short videos. Most used fast-cut MTV-style video; most used driving music. Wesley Clark's used humor. Sitting around a table with young people, Clark was depicted on his video as conversant with the issues of the day, including a funny reference to a band: "I am pro-choice, and I am a strong believer in affirmative action . . . it's the right thing to do, it works, it's about the American idea of equal opportunity . . . and I don't care what the other candidates say, I don't think OutKast is really breaking up. Andre 3000 and Big Boi just cut solo records, that's all." Chideya sees this type of engagement as a good step towards getting young people back into public forums.

I agree, but while even facile engagement can be a useful model for journalists who try to connect with young people on a visceral level, it is certainly no substitute for depth and process-related stories. If young people see only superficial references to them and find the majority of the weightier newspaper stories about Social Security, Medicare and other topics that appeal to older readers, they will be left with the impression that the true political process is outside their realm. And because there are many, many entertainment sources that are far, far more viscerally engaging than news, young people will remain tuned out until they are given a compelling reason that they, *as citizens*, should tune back in.

This book's solutions might end with a lot of ideas about journalism, but the problems certainly have more to do with what happens outside the newsroom's walls than inside them. Many reporters reject the advocates of "public journalism" who call for journalists to promote a healthy public life and civic dialogue. But while reporters may conclude that their role should not extend beyond reporting, their bosses—the owners of the print, on-line, and broadcast news media—have no such luxury. Second only to the goal of quality journalism, making sure young people see themselves as citizens should be the priority of every news executive in the country.

It has been said that nothing focuses one's attention like a hangman's noose.[36] Because they have ceded their own political power, the majority of young Americans who are tuned out pose a huge danger to their own generation; when they are ready to become leaders, they will pose a huge danger to democracy itself. This chilling image focuses me and should focus you, too. The problem is that many do not see the scope of the problem. To use another metaphor, we are like a frog that has been unaware of a slowly heating pot. This book has been an attempt to make the problem, and its consequences, clear and immediate. The last solution I offer is to view this book as an opening salvo in the battle to better inform ourselves. If you share the concerns of this book, I hope you will continue to explore this problem. I also hope you will do something about it.

Amartya Sen found that there has rarely been a famine in a country with a democratic press and free elections. Famines are partly the fault of the environment, but also the product of corruption, poor planning, and often, greedy dictators.[37] These inequities could only be foisted on a people with little power and little knowledge. It is not hyperbole to say that if a citizenry unilaterally abandons political knowledge, it relinquishes power as well. It has been said that America is a system "designed by geniuses so that it could be run by idiots."[38] But this is not entirely true. The Constitution does provide checks against our greatest mistakes of the moment. And elections do provide a quick check against the government's neglect of the people. But nothing in our Constitution protects us against the long-term ravages of neglect *by* the people themselves.

Government supported by an uninformed citizenry is not a democracy; it is a sham. This is our crisis. Let us work deliberately and forcefully to hand the mantle of responsible and informed leadership to the next generations of Americans.

People Surveyed or Interviewed for This Project, 2001–03

June 2001	Kathy Pinckert, NakedNews
August 2001	Joel Senesac, Saint Michael's College, '01, Colchester, VT
February 2002	Jackie Nixon, National Public Radio
February 2002	Doug Mitchell, National Public Radio
March 2002	Kanon Cozad and colleagues, United Missouri Bank, Kansas City
March 2002	Professors Jim Rowland and George McCleary, University of Kansas (Lawrence)
March 2002	College students, Saint Michael's College, Colchester, VT
April 2002	Students, Colchester High School, Colchester, VT
April 2002	Lizzie Salzfass, Wesleyan University, '01
April 2002	Andrea Alford, law student, Waco, TX
April 2002	Ann Colbert, journalism professor
April 2002	Mike Socolow's journalism students, Brandeis University
April 2002	Kristine C. Asselin, director of Student Activities, Brandeis University
May 2002	*Survivor* watchers, Burlington, VT
May 2002	Junior high school student, Shelburne, VT
May 2002	Basketball players, L.A. Pierce Jr. College, Los Angeles
May 2002	Actors, Los Angeles
May 2002	Aaron Harper, Los Angeles
May 2002	Chris Rose, columnist, *New Orleans Times–Picayune*
May 2002	Students, Bishop Perry Junior High School, New Orleans

May 2002	Jon Donley, Nola.com
May 2002	Cory Melancon, Nola.com
June 2003	Jay Rosen, New York University
June 2003	Norman Rosenfeld, architect
November 2003	Farai Chideya, author and journalist

Format of the Standard Interview

1. Why do you think many people don't keep up with the news?
2. Think about the political system in your state and in Washington, DC. Is the government responsive to the people? Can someone like you make any difference?
3. Has September 11, 2001, changed the way you follow the news? If so, how so? If not, why not?
4. A lot of people have said that Americans don't follow politics much, but few have tried to figure out what they *are* following. What kind of news do you follow? Do new media allow you to go into depth on a specific topic?
5. What is your favorite form of entertainment? (please be specific)
6. Please name your favorite
   Magazine (if any):
   Radio show (if any):
   TV show (if any):
   Do you read a daily newspaper (which one?)
   Web site (if any):
   What is your default homepage on your browser?
   What is your principal entertainment medium? News medium?
7. If you use the Internet, how often do you use it?
8. If you use the Internet, could you rank your three most important uses? E-mail? Chatting? Education? Meeting people? Politics? Other (please specify):

9. Picture eating dinner at your family's home. How frequently did you discuss the news at dinner (circle one): *Daily, Frequently, Occasionally, Rarely, Never.* Which kinds of news?
10. Circle the group you like the *least*: *The Ku Klux Klan, The Aryan Nation, The Communist Party, Planned Parenthood, Operation Rescue, The NRA, Handgun Control.* Should a representative from that group be allowed a turn to speak in a public hearing in your city or town?

11. Who is Alicia Keys?

12. Who is Tom Daschle and what is his importance in Washington?

13. What is your home state? Can you name your own state's U.S. senators?

14. Who is Allen Iverson?

15. Who is the attorney general of the United States and what does he do?

16. Do you follow local news? Local school news? Why? Why not?

17. In his last State of the Union Address, which countries did President Bush say represented "an axis of evil"?

18. What is *Roe* versus *Wade*?

19. Please name as many current U.S. Supreme Court justices as you can.

20. What is McCain-Feingold?

21. Where did the planes crash on September 11, 2001?

22. Are these questions a fair indicator of your familiarity with what's going on in America? If not, what other questions would be better?

23. In the last year, have you. . . . Check all that apply:

    Written a letter to a newspaper?_____

    Done regular volunteer work?_____

    Attended club meetings? _____

    Spoken in front of a large group_____

    Contacted someone in state government? _____

    Contacted someone in national government? _____

    Attended a rally away from home_____

24. I am going to read a list of some possible goals. Please rank the level of importance in your own life for each of the following goals: *very low, low, medium, high, very high*

    Living in an elegant house ___

    Owning a fancy car ____

    Staying politically engaged ____

    Giving something back to your community ___

    Joining a club ____

    Having friends ____

    Raising a family____

    Keeping up with the news ____

25. *If you keep up with political news,* when did you get into the news habit and why?

26. A lot of people say that people who follow political news are more connected to their local and national political communities. That is, those who are more likely to follow political news are engaged politically, too. Conversely, those who don't follow political news often don't have faith in politics. The problem is that no one has figured out which came first. In your case, do your politics drive your news interest, or vice versa?

27. What types of news (for example, sports) do you feel you have to know to keep up with the various conversations you have over the course of the day?

Responses to Questions 11–21

11. Who is Alicia Keys? [rhythm and blues singer]
    CORRECT: 54
    INCORRECT: 4
12. Who is Tom Daschle and what is his importance in Washington? [Senate majority leader at the time of the interviews]
    CORRECT::   18
    INCORRECT: 40
13. What is your home state _____? Can you name your own state's U.S. senators?
    CORRECT: 21
    INCORRECT: 37 (could not name both)
14. Who is Allen Iverson? [NBA player; my interviews preceded his well-publicized arrest in July 2002 on multiple charges.]
    CORRECT: 39
    INCORRECT: 19
15. Who is the attorney general of the United States and what does he do? [John Ashcroft]
    CORRECT: 18
    INCORRECT: 40
16. Do you follow local news? Local school news? Why? Why not?
    N/A
17. In his last State of the Union Address, which countries did President Bush say represented "an axis of evil"? [Iran, Iraq, North Korea]
    3 CORRECT   7
    2 CORRECT: 7
    1 CORRECT: 8
    NONE CORRECT: 36

18. What is *Roe* versus *Wade*? [1973 Supreme Court ruling on abortion]
    CORRECT: 30
    INCORRECT: 28

19. Please name as many current U.S. Supreme Court justices as you can.
    9 CORRECT: 0
    8 CORRECT: 0
    7 CORRECT: 0
    6 CORRECT: 1
    5 CORRECT: 2
    4 CORRECT: 1
    3 CORRECT: 7
    2 CORRECT: 7
    1 CORRECT: 8
    NONE CORRECT: 35

20. What is McCain-Feingold? [campaign finance reform bill]
    CORRECT: 8
    INCORRECT: 50

21. Where did the planes crash on September 11, 2001? [New York City, the Pentagon, rural Pennsylvania]
    3 CORRECT: 33
    2 CORRECT: 10
    1 CORRECT: 15
    NONE CORRECT: 0

Bibliography

Abrahamson, David. *Magazine-Made America: The Cultural Transformation of the Postwar Periodical*. Creskill, NJ: Hampton Press, 1996.

Actors. Personal interviews, 7 May 2002.

Adweek.com. *Special Reports: Top 25 Magazines in Paid Circulation* [Web page]. 2002 [cited 27 February 2002]. Available from *http://www.adweek.com/adweek/features/magcharts.jsp*.

Alford, Andrea. Telephone interview, 14 April 2002.

Allen, Woody, and Marshall Brickman. *Annie Hall*. 1977.

Anderson, Benedict R. *Imagined Communities: Reflections on the Origin and Spread of Nationalism*. New York: Verso, 1992.

Arbitron Nationwide. Spring 1996–Spring 2001, Monday–Sunday, 6 A.M.–Midnight, NPR Stations. Data supplied by NPR, February 2002.

Aristotle. *Aristotle's Poetics*. Translated by S. H. Butcher. New York: Hill and Wang, 1961.

Asselin, Kristine C. Personal interview, 22 April 2002.

Author unknown. "The Empire Club Chief: Romantic Career of a Democratic Politician." *New York Times*, 14 January 1885, 2.

Bagdikian, Ben H. *The Media Monopoly*. 6th ed. Boston, MA: Beacon Press, 2000.

Baldwin, James. *Notes of a Native Son*. New York: Dial Press, 1963.

Barlow, John Perry. *A Declaration of the Independence of Cyberspace* [Web page]. 1999 [cited 19 December 2002]. Available from *http://www.eff.org/~barlow/Declaration-Final.html*.

Barnouw, Erik. *Tube of Plenty: The Evolution of American Television*. New York: Oxford University Press, 1975.

Barringer, Felicity. "Unresolved Clash of Cultures: At Knight Ridder, Good Journalism Vs. The Bottom Line." *New York Times*, 29 May 2001, sec. C1.

Barry, Dave. "Dave for President—Running on Empty." *Burlington Free Press*, 1 June 2003, sec. 2D.

Barthes, Roland. "Structure of the Fait-Divers." In *Critical Essays*. Evanston: Northwestern University Press, 1972.

Bellah, Robert N., Richard Madsen, William M. Sullivan, Ann Swidler, and Steven M. Tipton. *The Good Society*. New York: Alfred A. Knopf, 1991.

Belluck, Pam. "Jackson Says He Fathered Child in Affair with Aide." *New York Times*, 19 January 2001, sec. A21.

Bender, Thomas. *Community and Social Change in America*. New Brunswick, NJ: Rutgers University Press, 1978.

Bennett, William J. *First Lessons: A Report on Elementary Education in America*. Washington, DC: United States Department of Education, 1986.

Berkowitz, Dan. *Social Meanings of News: A Text-Reader*. Thousand Oaks, California: Sage, 1997.

Bernstein, Carl, and Bob Woodward. *All the President's Men*. New York: Simon and Schuster, 1974.

Bird, S. Elizabeth. *For Enquiring Minds: A Cultural Study of Supermarket Tabloids*. Knoxville: University of Tennessee Press, 1992.

Bishop Perry Middle School students. Personal interviews, 9 May 2002.

Biskupic, Joan. "Has the Court Lost Its Appeal? In Poll, 59% Can Name 3 'Stooges,' 17% Can Name 3 Justices." *Washington Post*, 12 October 1995, sec. A23.

Blendon, Robert J., Catherine M. DesRoches, John M. Benson, Melissa J. Herrmann, Kalahn Taylor-Clark, and Kathleen J. Weldon. *The Public and the Smallpox Threat* [Web-posted article]. The New England Journal of Medicine, 2003 [cited 23 December 2002]. Available from *www.nejm.org*.

Bogart, Leo. *Preserving the Press: How Daily Newspapers Mobilized to Keep Their Readers*. New York: Columbia University Press, 1991.

Boyce, George, James Curan, and Pauline Wingate. *Newspaper History: From the Seventeenth Century to the Present Day*. Beverly Hills: Sage, 1978.

Boyer, Peter J. "Under Fowler, F.C.C. Treated TV as Commerce." *New York Times*, 19 January 1987, sec. C15.

Bradlee, Benjamin C. *A Good Life: Newspapering and Other Adventures*. New York: Simon and Schuster, 1995.

Brandeis University students. Personal interviews, 22 April 2002.

Brinkley, David. *David Brinkley: 11 Presidents, 4 Wars, 22 Political Conventions, 1 Moon Landing, 3 Assassinations, 2,000 Weeks of News and Other Stuff on Television and 18 Years of Growing up in North Carolina*. New York: A. A. Knopf, 1995.

Brown, DeNeen L. "And the Winner Is . . . Chretien, First to Visit Bush." *Washington Post*, 4 February 2001, sec. A4.

Bumiller, Elisabeth. "Keepers of Bush Image Lift Stagecraft to New Heights." *New York Times*, 16 May 2003, sec. A1.

Carey, James W. "AEJ Presidential Address: A Plea for the University Tradition." *Journalism Quarterly* 55, no. 4 (1978): 846–55.

———. "The Communications Revolution and the Professional Communicator." *Sociological Review Monographs* 13 (1969): 23–38.

———. "Technology and Ideology: The Case of the Telegraph." *Prospects* 8 (1982): 302–25.

Carter, Bill. "The 2000 Campaign: The Ratings; Fewer Watched Last Debate Than Most Previous Ones." *New York Times*, 13 October 2000, sec. A25.

———. "Fox Mulls How to Exploit the Mojo of 'American Idol'." *New York Times*, 23 May 2003, sec. C1.

———. "Koppel Is the Odd Man out as ABC Woos Letterman." *New York Times*, 1 March 2002, sec. A1.

Carter, Bill, and Jim Rutenberg. "Letterman Offer Was News to Chief of ABC News." *New York Times*, 2 March 2002, sec. A1.

CBS. "CBS Evening News with Dan Rather (14 October)." 2003.

CBS News. "Television Coverage of the Democratic National Convention." 1968.

Cheers. *I'm Going to Get My Act Together and Stick It in Your Face (Episode 210)*, 1991. Television show.

Chideya, Farai. Phone interview, 10 November 2003.

CNN, Various dates. 2001–2004.

CNN.com. *Most Popular Links from CNN.com* [Web site]. 1 March 2002 [cited 1 March 2002]. Available from *http://www.cnn.com*.

————. *Most Popular Links from CNN.com* [Web Page]. 1 September 2001 [cited 1 September 2001]. Available from *http://www.cnn.com/*.

Cohen, Patricia Cline. *The Murder of Helen Jewett: The Life and Death of a Prostitute in Nineteenth-Century New York*. New York: Alfred A. Knopf, 1998.

Colbert, Ann. Telephone interview, 10 April 2002.

Colchester High School students. Personal interviews, 12 April 2002.

Cox, Liz. "Imagine: Sixty-Seven Young Journalists and the Newspaper of Their Dreams." *Columbia Journalism Review*, January/February 2003, 18–24.

Cozad, Kanon. Personal interview, 25 March 2002.

Cronkite, Walter. *A Reporter's Life*. New York: Random House in association with A. Knopf, 1996.

Crouthamel, James L. *Bennett's New York Herald and the Rise of the Popular Press*. Syracuse, NY: Syracuse University Press, 1989.

Cummings, Jonathon, Brian Butler, and Robert Kraut. *The Quality of Online Social Relationships* [Web page]. 16 October 2000 [cited 1 April 2002]. Available from *http://homenet.hcii.cs.cmu.edu/progress/research.html*.

Cummings, Jonathon, and Robert Kraut. *Domesticating Computers and the Internet* [Web page]. 4 May 2001 [cited 1 April 2002]. Available from *http://homenet.hcii.cs. cmu.edu/progress/research.html*.

Darnton, Robert. "Writing News and Telling Stories." *Daedalus* 104, no. 2 (1975): 175–94.

Davis, Allison, et al. Personal interview, 2 May 2002.

Davis, Richard, and Diana Marie Owen. *New Media and American Politics*. New York: Oxford University Press, 1998.

DDB Needham. *Life Style Survey, 1975–1998* [Web-posted data and report]. 2000 [cited 1 November 2001]. Available from *http://www.bowlingalone.com*.

Delli Carpini, Michael X., and Scott Keeter. *What Americans Know About Politics and Why It Matters*. New Haven, CT: Yale University Press, 1996.

Delli Carpini, Michael X., and Bruce A. Williams. "Let Us Infotain You: Politics in the New Media Environment." In *Mediated Politics: Communication in the Future of Democracy*, edited by W. Lance Bennett and Robert M. Entman. Cambridge, UK: Cambridge University Press, 2001.

Dewey, John. *The Public and Its Problems*. New York: H. Holt and Company, 1927.

Dionne, Jr., E. J. *Why Americans Hate Politics*. New York: Simon and Schuster, 1991.

Donley, John. Personal interview, 8 May 2002.

Doppelt, Jack C., and Ellen Shearer. *Nonvoters: America's No-Shows*. Thousand Oaks, CA: Sage Publications, 1999.

Downie Jr., Leonard, and Robert G. Kaiser. *The News About the News: American Journalism in Peril*. New York: Alfred A. Knopf, 2002.

Emery, Michael C., Edwin Emery, and Nancy L. Roberts. *The Press and America: An Interpretive History of the Mass Media*. 8th ed. Boston: Allyn and Bacon, 1996.

Entman, Robert M. *Democracy without Citizens: Media and the Decay of American Politics*. New York: Oxford University Press, 1989.

Evans, Harold, Gail Buckland, and Kevin Baker. *The American Century*. New York: Alfred A. Knopf, 1998.

Ferretti, Fred. "Nutritionist Says U.S. Study of TV Ads for Children Ignores Food." *New York Times*, 18 October 1970, 94.

Fitzmorris, John. Personal interview, 9 May 2002.

Fox. "American Idol (21 May)." 2003.

Frankel, Max. *The Times of My Life and My Life with the Times*. New York: Random House, 1999.

Franklin, John Hope, and Alfred A. Moss. *From Slavery to Freedom: A History of African Americans*. 7th ed. New York: McGraw-Hill, 1994.

Freedom Forum Pacific Coast Center. *Recapture Your Youth: How to Create a Newspaper for Future Generations*. Arlington: The Freedom Forum, 2001.

Friedland, Lewis A. "Communication, Community and Democracy: Toward a Theory of the Communicatively Integrated Community." *Communication Research* 28, no. 4 (2001): 358–91.

Friedman, Thomas L. *The Lexus and the Olive Tree*. New York: Anchor Books, 2000.

Galston, William A. *Does the Internet Strengthen Community?* [Web page]. 2001 [cited 15 August 2002]. Available from *http://www.puaf.umd.edu/IPPP/fall1999/internet_community.htm*.

Gannett. *Letter to Shareholders* [Web posted letter]. May 1997 [cited 15 May 2003]. Available from *http://www.gannett.com/annual/ann97/letter.htm*.

Genelius, Sandra M. E-mail correspondence, 19 May 2003.

Glassner, Barry. *The Culture of Fear: Why Americans Are Afraid of the Wrong Things*. New York: Basic Books, 1999.

Goldstein, Laurie. "The Christians: To Many Social Conservatives, an Ally." *New York Times*, 8 August 2000, sec. A23.

Grossman, Lawrence K. "Who Took the Body out of the Body Politic?" *Columbia Journalism Review*, January/February 2003, 49–50.

Habermas, Jürgen. *The Structural Transformation of the Public Sphere: An Inquiry into a Category of Bourgeois Society*. Trans. Thomas Burger, *Studies in Contemporary German Social Thought*. Cambridge, MA: MIT Press, 1989.

Halberstam, David. *The Powers That Be*. New York: Alfred A. Knopf, 1979.

Hallin, Daniel C. *The "Uncensored War": The Media and Vietnam*. New York: Oxford University Press, 1986.

Harper, Aaron. Personal interview, 7 May 2002.

Hickey, Neil. "Power Shift: As the FCC Prepares to Alter the Media Map, Battle Lines Are Drawn." *Columbia Journalism Review*, March/April 2003, 26–31.

Higher Education Research Institute. *The American Freshman: National Norms for Fall 2000* [Web page]. 22 January 2001 [cited 5 January 2003]. Available from *http:www.gseis.ucla.edu/heri/heri.html*.

———. *The American Freshman: National Norms for Fall 2001* [Web page]. 28 January 2002 [cited 5 January 2003]. Available from *http:www.gseis.ucla.edu/heri/heri.html*.

Horyn, Cathy. "Ah, Youth, but Does It Have Staying Power?" *New York Times*, 26 February 2002, sec. B10.

Huntzicker, William E. *The Popular Press, 1833–1865*. Westport, CT: Greenwood Press, 1999.

Johnson, Dirk. "Students Still Sweat, They Just Don't Shower." *New York Times*, 22 April 1996, sec. A1.

Johnson, Peter. "Trust of Media Keeps on Slipping." *USA Today*, 28 May 2003, sec. D1.

Johnstone, John Wallace Claire, William W. Bowman, and Edward J. Slawski. *The News People: A Sociological Portrait of American Journalists and Their Work*. Urbana: University of Illinois Press, 1976.

Jowett, Garth, and James M. Linton. *Movies as Mass Communication*. 2nd ed. Newbury Park, CA: Sage, 1989.

Koppel, Ted. "Network News Is Still Serious Business." *New York Times*, 5 March 2002, sec. A23.

Kovach, Bill, and Tom Rosenstiel. "All News Media Inc." *New York Times*, 7 January 2003, sec. A19.

————. *The Elements of Journalism: What Newspeople Should Know and the Public Should Expect.* New York: Crown Publishers, 2001.

Kraut, Robert, Sara Kiesler, Bonka Boneva, Jonathon Cummings, Vicki Helgeson, and Anne Crawford. "Internet Paradox Revisited." *Journal of Social Issues* 58, no. 1 (2002): 49–73.

Kraut, Robert, Vicki Lundmark, Michael Patterson, Sara Kiesler, Tridas Mukopadhyay, and William Scherlis. "Internet Paradox: A Social Technology That Reduces Social Involvement and Psychological Well-Being?" *American Psychologist* 53, no. 9 (1998): 1017–31.

Kurtz, Howard. "Grabbing the Headlines: The National Enquirer." *Washington Post,* 26 February 2001, sec. C1.

————. "Ted Koppel Takes on ABC in Op-Ed on Relevance of Nightline." *Washington Post,* 5 March 2002, sec. C1.

L. A. Pierce Junior College basketball players. Personal interviews, 6 May 2002.

Labaton, Stephen. "Deregulating the Media: The Overview; Regulators Ease Rules Governing Media Ownership." *New York Times,* 3 June 2003, sec. A1.

Layton, Charles, and Jennifer Dorroh. "The State of the American Newspaper: Sad State." *American Journalism Review,* June 2002, 18–33.

League of Women Voters of the Champlain Valley. "Citizenship Survey of Chittenden County High School Seniors." Vermont, 1998.

Lippmann, Walter. *Public Opinion.* New York: Free Press Paperbacks, 1949.

————. "Two Revolutions in the American Press." *The Yale Review* 20, no. 3 (1931): 433–41.

Long, Mike. Personal Interview, 12 April 2002.

Love, Robert. "The Kids Are All Right; Young People and the News: A Conversation." *Columbia Journalism Review,* January/February 2003, 27–29.

Lynch, Dianne, Howard Finberg, and Martha Stone. *Digital Journalism Credibility Study: What We Already Know; a Review of the Literature* [Web posted report]. Online News Association, 2002 [cited 14 May 2003]. Available from *http://www.onlinenewsassociation.org/programs/research.htm.*

Massing, Michael. "Does Democracy Avert Famine?" *New York Times,* 1 March 2003, sec. A19.

McFarland, Ruth. *Bacon's Newspaper Directory.* Hightstown, NJ: Primedia Information, Inc., 2000.

McLeod, Jack M., Dietram A. Scheufele, and Patricia Moy. "Community, Communication, and Participation: The Role of Mass Media and Interpersonal Discussion in Local Political Participation." *Political Communication* 16 (1999): 315 36.

McLuhan, Marshall. *Understanding Media: The Extensions of Man.* Cambridge, MA: MIT Press, 1995.

Mediamark. *Spring 2000 Median Age, Household Income and Individual Employment Income* [Web page]. 2001 [cited 25 February 2002]. Available from *http://www.mediamark.com/mri/techguide/tg_s00_age_hhi.htm.*

Melancon, Cory. Personal interview, 8 May 2002.

Meyer, Phillip. *The Newspaper Survival Book.* Bloomington: Indiana University Press, 1985.

Mifflin, Lawrie. "Media: Television; a Generation Gap in News Viewership Is Suddenly Wider." *New York Times,* 13 May 1996, sec. D7.

Milbank, Dana, and Claudia Deane. "Hussein Link to 9/11 Lingers in Many Minds." *Washington Post,* 6 September 2003, A1.

Mindich, David T. Z. *Just the Facts: How "Objectivity" Came to Define American Journalism.* New York: New York University Press, 1998.

Morris, John D. "Five Weeks of Hearings Strengthen F.T.C.'s Determination to Continue Aggressive Regulation of TV Ads." *New York Times*, 22 November 1971, 21.

MSNBC. "Countdown with Keith Olbermann (29 October)." 2003.

Mumford, Lewis. *The Culture of Cities*. New York: Harcourt Brace and Company, 1938.

Nakednews.com. *Naked News* [Web broadcast]. 14 October 2003 [cited 15 October 2003]. Available from *http://www.nakednews.com*.

Nashville Scene. *Grading the Daily* [Web site]. May 2001 [cited 15 May 2003]. Available from *http://www.nashvillescene.com/Grading_the_Daily/gannett1.html*.

National Honor Society. *Student Membership* [Web page]. 2003 [cited 17 May 2003]. Available from *http://www.nhs.us/membership/stud_mem.cfm*.

Negroponte, Nicholas. *Being Digital*. New York: Alfred A. Knopf, 1995.

New York Times. *Audience/Circulation* [Web sites]. May 2003 [cited 19 May 2003]. Available from *http://www.nytadvertising.nytimes.com/adonis/html/home.htm*.

New York Times. "Bob Franks for the Senate." *New York Times*, 25 October 2000, sec. A26.

———. "George Pataki for Governor." *New York Times*, 27 October 2002, sec. 4, 12.

———. "Television." *New York Times*, 27 February 1968, 87.

Newshour, the. *Searching for Youth* [Web page]. 6 June 2002 [cited 7 June 2002]. Available from *http://www.pbs.org/newshour/bb/media/jan-june02/youth_3-1.html*.

Nixon, Jackie. Telephone interview with author, 7 February 2002.

Norris, Pippa. *A Virtuous Circle: Political Communications in Postindustrial Societies*. Cambridge: Cambridge University Press, 2000.

Norris, Pippa, and David Jones. "Virtual Democracy." *Harvard International Journal of Press/Politics* 3, no. 2 (1998): 1–4.

O'Malley, Michael. *Keeping Watch: A History of American Time*. New York: Viking Penguin, 1990.

Overbeck, Wayne. *Major Principles of Media Law*. 2001 ed. Fort Worth, TX: Harcourt College Publishers, 2001.

Parton, James. *The Life of Horace Greeley, Editor of "The New-York Tribune," from His Birth to the Present Time*. Boston: Houghton, Mifflin and Company, 1889.

Patterson, Thomas E. "Doing Well and Doing Good: How Soft News and Critical Journalism Are Shrinking the News Audience and Weakening Democracy—and What News Outlets Can Do About It." 1–28: Joan Shorenstein Center on the Press, Politics, and Public Policy, 2000.

———. *The Vanishing Voter: Public Involvement in an Age of Uncertainty*. New York: Alfred A. Knopf, 2002.

Peiser, Wolfram. "Cohort Replacement and the Downward Trend in Newspaper Readership." *Newspaper Research Journal* 21, no. 2 (2000): 15–16.

Pew Internet in American Life Project. *Parents, Kids and the Internet* [Web page]. Princeton Survey Research Associates, 2001 [cited 21 August 2002]. Available from *http://www.pewinternet.org/*.

Pew Research Center for the People & the Press. *Americans Thinking About Iraq, but Focused on the Economy: Midterm Election Preview* [Web posted report and data]. 10 October 2002 [cited 4 November 2002]. Available from *http://www.people-press.org*.

———. *Audiences Fragmented and Skeptical: The Tough Job of Communicating with Voters* [Web-posted report and data]. 5 February 2000 [cited 1 December 2001]. Available from *http://www.people-press.org*.

———. *Domestic Concerns Will Vie with Terrorism in Fall: Criticisms of Bush and Congress as Job Worries Increase* [Web-posted report and data]. August 2002 [cited 20 August 2002]. Available from *http://www.people-press.org/*.

————. *Investors Now Go Online for Quotes, Advice: Internet Sapping Broadcast News Audience* [Web posted report and data]. 11 June 2000 [cited 1 December 2001]. Available from *http://www.people-press.org.*

————. *Ten Years of the Pew News Interest Index* [Web page]. Kimberly Parker and Claudia Deane, eds., 1997 [cited 15 November 2001]. Available from *http://www.people-press.org.*

————. *Terror Coverage Boosts News: But Military Censorship Backed* [Web posted report and data]. November 2001 [cited 5 December 2001]. Available from *http://www.people-press.org.*

————. *Youth Vote Influenced by Online Information: Internet Election News Audience Seeks Convenience, Familiar Names* [Web-posted report and data]. December 2000 [cited 5 December 2001]. Available from *http://www.people-press.org/.*

Pinckert, Kathy. Telephone Interview, 12 June 2001.

Plato. *Plato: Complete Works.* John M. Cooper. Indianapolis: Hackett, 1997.

Pollard, James Edward. *The Presidents and the Press.* New York: Macmillan, 1947.

Poniewozik, James. "The Nascar of News: Fox Goes from Upstart to Cable-News Ratings Leader with Punditry, Pizazz and a Little Populism." *Time,* 11 February 2002, 65.

Postman, Neil. *The End of Education: Redefining the Value of School.* New York: Alfred A. Knopf, 1995.

Program on International Policy Attitudes. *Misperceptions, the Media and the Iraq War* [Web-posted report]. 2 October 2003 [cited 22 November 2003]. Available from *http://www.pipa.org.*

Purdy, Matthew. "Live, Via Satellite, All the News That Fits Your Viewpoint." *New York Times,* 14 April 2002, sec. A29.

Putnam, Robert D. *Bowling Alone: The Collapse and Revival of American Community.* New York: Simon and Schuster, 2000.

Readership Institute. *Branding: From Consumer Insight to Implementation* [Web-posted report]. Northwestern University, April 2002 [cited 15 May 2003]. Available from *http://www.readership.org.*

————. *The Power to Grow Readership: Research from the Impact Study of Newspaper Readership* [Web-posted report]. Northwestern University, 2001. Available from *http://www.readership.org.*

Roper Center for Public Opinion Research. *General Social Survey 2003: NORC-GSS Cumulative Data File 1972–2003* (2003) [Computer File].

RoperASW. *National Geographic—RoperASW 2002 Global Geographic Literacy Survey* [Web-posted report]. November 2002 [cited 2 June 2003]. Available from *http://news.nationalgeographic.com/news/2002/11/1120_021120_GeoRoperSurvey.html.*

Rose, Chris. Personal interview, 8 May 2002.

Rosen, Jay. Telephone interview, 5 June 2003.

————. *What Are Journalists For?* New Haven, CT: Yale University Press, 1999.

Rosenberg, Howard, David Bartlett, Phyllis Kaniss, Jamie Malanowski, Ishmael Reed, Patricia Stevens, Todd Gitlin, Paul Steinle, Joseph C. Goulden, and Howard Kurtz. "Bad News." *American Journalism Review,* September 1993, 18–27.

Rosenfeld, Norman. Phone interview, June 2003.

Rosenstiel, Tom, Carl Gottlieb, and Lee Ann Brady. "Quality Brings Higher Ratings, but Enterprise Is Disappearing." *Columbia Journalism Review,* November/December 1999.

————. "Time of Peril for TV News: Quality Sells, but Commitment and Viewership Continue to Erode." *Columbia Journalism Review,* November/December 2000, 84–92.

Rowland, James, and George F. McCleary. Personal interview, 25 March 2002.

Rutenberg, Jim. "Audience for Cable News Grows." *New York Times*, 25 March 2002, sec. C8.

———. "CNN Aims at Young Viewers as It Revamps News Format." *New York Times*, 5 August 2001, sec. A1.

———. "Media: Hearts, Minds and Satellites." *New York Times*, 15 October 2001, sec. C1.

Rutenberg, Jim, and Micheline Maynard. "TV News That Looks Local, Even If It's Not." *New York Times*, 2 June 2003, sec. C1.

Salzfass, Lizzie. "Ms. Goes to College: Wesleyan University." *Ms.*, September 2001, 52–53.

———. Telephone interview, April 2002.

Schiller, Dan. *Objectivity and the News: The Public and the Rise of Commercial Journalism*. Philadelphia: University of Pennsylvania Press, 1981.

Schlesinger, Arthur Meier. *The Disuniting of America: Reflections on a Multicultural Society*. New York: Norton, 1992.

———. *Prelude to Independence: The Newspaper War on Britain, 1764–1776*. New York: Alfred A. Knopf, 1958.

Senesac, Joel. Personal interview, August 2001.

Seplow, Stephen. "G.A.S for the World." *American Journalism Review*, October/November 2003, 46–47.

Seregni, Jerry. Telephone interview with author's research assistant, Matthew Powers, 15 May 2003.

Services, Mercy Health. *The Woman's Doctor* [Web page]. 2002 [cited 21 October 2002]. Available from *http://www.mdmercy.com/womens/womens_doctor.html*.

Shah, Dhavan V., Jack M. McLeod, So-Hyang Yoon. "Communication, Context, and Community: An Exploration of Print, Broadcast, and Internet Influences." *Communication Research* 28, no. 4 (2001): 464–506.

Shah, Dhavan V., Nojin Kwak, and R. Lance Holbert. " 'Connecting' and 'Disconnecting' with Civic Life: Patterns of Internet Use and the Production of Social Capital." *Political Communication* 18 (2001): 141–62.

Shales, Tom. "The Pull of the Pullover; Rather Finds More Than Warmth in a Sweater; Rather's Sweater Tale." *Washington Post*, 8 February 1982, sec. C1.

Shapiro, Andrew L. *The Control Revolution: How the Internet Is Putting Individuals in Charge and Changing the World We Know*. New York: Public Affairs, 1999.

Shedden, David. *Media Credibility Bibliography* [Web page]. Poynter Online, 2 May 2003 [cited 17 May 2003]. Available from *http://poynteronline.org/content/content_view.asp?id=1205*.

Shenk, David. *The End of Patience: Cautionary Notes on the Information Revolution*. Bloomington: Indiana University Press, 1999.

Shepard, Alicia C. "Moguls' Millions." *American Journalism Review*, July/August 2001, 20.

Shilts, Randy. *And the Band Played On: Politics, People, and the AIDS Epidemic*. New York: Penguin Books, 1988.

Shribman, David. "The Anesthetic of the Masses." *Fortune*, 28 September 1998, 72.

Simon, Clea. "Music, Talk Stations Feel Impact." *Boston Globe*, 25 October 2001, sec. C16.

Smith, Jeffery Alan. *War & Press Freedom: The Problem of Prerogative Power*. New York: Oxford University Press, 1999.

Stanley, Alessandra. "How to Persuade the Young to Watch the News? Program It." *New York Times*, 19 January 2002, sec. C6.

Steinberg, Jacques. "The Grooming of an Anchor: Brian Who? NBC Works to Raise His Profile." *New York Times*, 9 February 2004, sec. C1.

Stephens, Mitchell. *A History of News*. Fort Worth, TX: Harcourt Brace College Publishers, 1997.

Stepp, Carl Sessions. "Of the People, by the People, Bore the People." *Washington Journalism Review*, March 1992, 22–26.

Stevens, Elizabeth Lesly. "Mouse Ke Fear." *Brill's Content*, December/January 1998/1999, 95–103.

Stoll, Clifford. *Silicon Snake Oil: Second Thoughts on the Information Highway*. New York: Doubleday, 1995.

Sunstein, Cass R. *Republic.Com*. Princeton, NJ: Princeton University Press, 2001.

The Onion. *A Shattered Nation Longs to Care About Stupid Bullshit Again* [Web page]. 3 October 2001 [cited 27 February 2002]. Available from *http://www.theonion.com/onion3735/a_shattered_nation.html*.

Times Mirror Center. *The Age of Indifference* [Web site]. 1990 [cited 1 August 2001]. Available from *http://www.people-press.org*.

Tocqueville, Alexis de. *Democracy in America*. Harvey C. Mansfield and Delba Winthrop. Chicago: University of Chicago Press, 2000.

Toner, Robin. "Trust in the Military Heightens among Baby Boomers' Children." *New York Times*, 27 May 2003, sec. A1.

Trumpeter Swan Society, The. *The Trumpeter Swan Society* [Web page]. Available from *http://www.taiga.net/swans/*.

Tucher, Andie. *Froth & Scum: Truth, Beauty, Goodness, and the Ax Murder in America's First Mass Medium*. Chapel Hill: University of North Carolina Press, 1994.

U.S. Census Bureau. *Historical Statistics of the United States, Colonial Times to 1970*. Bicentennial ed. Washington, DC: U.S. Dept. of Commerce Bureau of the Census, 1975.

———. *Voting and Registration* [Web posted dated and charts]. U.S. Census Bureau, 31 December 2002 [cited 14 May 2002]. Available from *http://www.census.gov/population/www/socdemo/voting.html*.

———. *Voting and Registration in the Election of November 2000* [Web posted data]. 27 Feburary 2002 [cited 12 May 2003]. Available from *http://www.census.gov/population/www/socdemo/voting/p20-542.html*.

U.S. Department of Education. *No Child Left Behind: Character Education* [Web site of the U.S. Department of Education]. 10 April 2003 [cited 22 May 2003]. Available from *http://www.nclb.gov/*.

United Missouri Bank workers. Personal interviews, 25 March 2002.

Updike, John. *Rabbit Redux*. New York: Alfred A. Knopf, 1971.

USA Today. "The Newspaper Readership Program: Excellence in Education." Waltham, MA: Report for Brandeis University, 2001.

Washington, George, and John H. Rhodehamel. *Writings*. New York: Library of America, 1997.

WBAL. *The WBAL Channel.Com* [Web page]. 17 October 2002 [cited 21 October 2002]. Available from *http://www.thewbalchannel.com/womansdoctor/*.

White, David M. "The "Gate Keeper": A Case Study in the Selection of News." *Journalism Quarterly* 27(1950):383–90.

Whitman, Walt. *Leaves of Grass*. New York: Aventine Press, 1931.

Wilkinson, Earl J. "A Special Report for the Newspaper Industry: Confronting the Newspaper Youth Readership Puzzle." Dallas, TX: International Newspaper Marketing Association, 2002.

Notes

Preface

1. Jim Rutenberg, "CNN Aims at Young Viewers as It Revamps News Format," *New York Times*, 5 August 2001, C8.

2. RoperASW, *National Geographic—RoperASW 2002 Global Geographic Literacy Survey* [Web-posted report] November 2002, available from http://news.nationalgeographic.com/news/2002/11/1120_021120_GeoRoperSurvey.html.

Chapter 1

1. Fox, "American Idol (21 May)," (2003).

2. Ibid. Bill Carter, "Fox Mulls How to Exploit the Mojo of 'American Idol'," *New York Times*, 23 May 2003, C1. The margin between the two American Idol finalists was 135,000.

3. Ibid. The *Times'* figure was 38 million for the show as a whole. However, numerous sources say that viewership peaked in the final half hour at around 40 million.

4. Bill Carter, "The 2000 Campaign: The Ratings; Fewer Watched Last Debate Than Most Previous Ones," *New York Times*, 13 October 2000, A25.

5. Pew Research Center for the People & the Press, *Audiences Fragmented and Skeptical: The Tough Job of Communicating with Voters* [Web-posted report and data] 5 February 2000, available from http://www.people-press.org. Author's analysis.

6. Wolfram Peiser, "Cohort Replacement and the Downward Trend in Newspaper Readership," *Newspaper Research Journal* 21, no. 2 (2000): 15.

7. The low end estimate comes from James Poniewozik, "The Nascar of News: Fox Goes from Upstart to Cable-News Ratings Leader with Punditry, Pizazz and a Little Populism," *Time*, 11 February 2002, 65. Fox News has been noted for its success in attracting younger viewers, but it too has a graying median audience: 56-years-old (Poniewozik). The higher estimate is from Rutenberg, "CNN Aims at Young Viewers as It Revamps News Format," A1.

8. Robert D. Putnam, *Bowling Alone: The Collapse and Revival of American Community* (New York: Simon & Schuster, 2000), 221. Jacques Steinberg, "The Grooming of an Anchor: Brian Who? NBC Works to Raise His Profile," *New York Times*, 9 February 2004.

9. Lawrie Mifflin, "Media: Television; a Generation Gap in News Viewership Is Suddenly Wider," *New York Times*, 13 May 1996, D7.

10. Times Mirror Center, *The Age of Indifference* [Web site] 1990, available from http://www.people-press.org.

11. Pew Research Center for the People & the Press, *Ten Years of the Pew News Interest Index* [Web page] Kimberly Parker and Claudia Deane, eds., 1997, available

from http://www.people-press.org. See chapter 2 of this book for a discussion of the news knowledge gap.

12.   A recent report by the industry, while an excellent overview of the problem is a case in point, concerned almost exclusively with the impact on the industry, not on democracy, a word that is completely absent from the report. The decline in readership, states the report, "is threatening the long-term viability of the medium as a daily franchise" (4). In contrast, my book sees the problem as mainly a societal one that must be addressed through journalism, education, politics, and government. Earl J. Wilkinson, "A Special Report for the Newspaper Industry: Confronting the Newspaper Youth Readership Puzzle," (Dallas: International Newspaper Marketing Association, 2002).

13.   William J. Bennett, *First Lessons: A Report on Elementary Education in America* (Washington, DC: United States Department of Education, 1986), especially 28–29 and 33–34. Bennett argued that "multiculturalism" was getting in the way of civics and American history (34). Arthur Schlesinger, Jr., coming from a different political slant, wrote about multiculturalism and how it tends to add to the balkanization of America. Arthur Meier Schlesinger, *The Disuniting of America: Reflections on a Multicultural Society* (New York: Norton, 1992). Postman wrote about the "privatizing of the mind . . . [making] the creation of a public mind quite impossible." Neil Postman, *The End of Education: Redefining the Value of School*, 1st ed. (New York: Knopf, 1995), 57.

14.   A case in point is the Bush Administration's education policy. See U.S. Department of Education, *No Child Left Behind: Character Education* [Web site of the U.S. Department of Education] 10 April 2003 available from http://www.nclb.gov/.

15.   Peter Johnson, "Trust of Media Keeps on Slipping," *USA Today*, 28 May 2003. Robin Toner, "Trust in the Military Heightens among Baby Boomers' Children," *New York Times*, 27 May 2003, A1.

16.   Plato, *Plato: Complete Works*, ed. John M. Cooper (Indianapolis: Hackett, 1997), 551–52. In this section of the Phaedrus, Socrates was recalling the argument of Thamus, the ancient king of Egypt.

17.   Michael X. Delli Carpini, and Scott Keeter, *What Americans Know About Politics and Why It Matters* (New Haven, CT: Yale University Press, 1996), 83–84. Only 44 percent knew that the Soviet Union was not part of NATO.

18.   In an interview with the *Columbia Journalism Review* in 2003, Jon Stewart, the host of the *Daily Show*, argued that young people are much smarter and more engaged than most people acknowledge. While they might not have all the facts (where Brazil is on the map, for example) they would still be able to understand concepts as well or better than their elders could (Brazil's history of colonialism, for example). Robert Love, "The Kids Are All Right; Young People and the News: A Conversation," *Columbia Journalism Review*, January/February 2003.

19.   Clea Simon, "Music, Talk Stations Feel Impact," *Boston Globe*, 25 October 2001, C16. Jim Rutenberg, "Media: Hearts, Minds and Satellites," *New York Times*, 15 October 2001, C1. Jim Rutenberg, "Audience for Cable News Grows," *New York Times*, 25 March 2002, C8. In March 2002, the gains of the three broadcast networks' evening newscasts were slight, only 3 percent over the previous year. Cable news saw much bigger advances (50% for CNN) although the audience size of CNN is less than 10 percent that of any of the networks'.

20.   E. J. Dionne, Jr. *Why Americans Hate Politics* (New York: Simon and Schuster, 1991), 10.

21.   Jeffery Alan Smith, *War & Press Freedom: The Problem of Prerogative Power* (New York: Oxford University Press, 1999), 10.

22.   David Shribman, "The Anesthetic of the Masses," *Fortune*, 28 September 1998, 72.

23. Bill Kovach and Tom Rosenstiel, *The Elements of Journalism: What News-people Should Know and the Public Should Expect.* (New York: Crown Publishers, 2001), 25. Delli Carpini and Keeter, *What Americans Know About Politics and Why It Matters*, 158–59.

24. Delli Carpini and Keeter, *What Americans Know About Politics and Why It Matters*, 19.

25. Freedom Forum Pacific Coast Center, *Recapture Your Youth: How to Create a Newspaper for Future Generations* (Arlington, MA: The Freedom Forum, 2001).

26. New York Times, "George Pataki for Governor," *New York Times*, 27 October 2002, Section 4, 12. See also the *Times'* endorsement of Bob Franks, a moderate Republican, in 2000: The New York Times, "Bob Franks for the Senate," *New York Times*, 25 October 2000, A26.

27. Putnam, *Bowling Alone*, 233.

28. Ibid., 222.

29. Richard Davis and Diana Marie Owen, *New Media and American Politics* (New York: Oxford University Press, 1998), 53.

30. Lewis Mumford, *The Culture of Cities* (New York,: Harcourt Brace and Company, 1938), 412. Another way suburbia affects newspapers is the "white flight" away from the newspapers' base, the cities. See Leo Bogart, *Preserving the Press: How Daily Newspapers Mobilized to Keep Their Readers* (New York: Columbia University Press, 1991), 42–43. Also see Kovach and Rosenstiel, *The Elements of Journalism*, 58.

31. Walter Lippmann, *Public Opinion* (New York: Free Press Paperbacks, 1949), 3.

32. Benedict R. Anderson, *Imagined Communities: Reflections on the Origin and Spread of Nationalism* (New York: Verso, 1992), 53.

33. Mitchell Stephens, *A History of News* (Fort Worth, TX: Harcourt Brace College Publishers, 1997), 53.

34. Ibid., 58–59.

35. Nicholas Negroponte, *Being Digital*, (New York: Alfred A. Knopf, 1995), 153.

36. Jürgen Habermas, *The Structural Transformation of the Public Sphere: An Inquiry into a Category of Bourgeois Society*, trans. Thomas Burger, *Studies in Contemporary German Social Thought* (Cambridge, MA: MIT Press, 1989), xi, 27.

37. Putnam, *Bowling Alone*, 223.

38. Jay Rosen, *What Are Journalists For?* (New Haven, CT: Yale University Press, 1999), 27–32.

39. Putnam, *Bowling Alone*, 223.

40. Davis and Owen, *New Media and American Politics*, 136.

41. Dhavan V. Shah, Nojin Kwak, and R. Lance Holbert, " 'Connecting' and 'Disconnecting' with Civic Life: Patterns of Internet Use and the Production of Social Capital," *Political Communication* 18 (2001): 154.

42. Leonard Downie Jr. and Robert G. Kaiser, *The News About the News: American Journalism in Peril* (New York: Alfred A. Knopf, 2002), 117.

43. Thomas L. Friedman, *The Lexus and the Olive Tree* (New York: Anchor Books, 2000), 44–45.

44. Stephens, *A History of News*, 38.

45. The distinction between community and society comes from Ferdinand Tönnies, whose distinction, in the original German, was between *Gemeinschaft* (community) and *Gessellschaft* (society). Thomas Bender, *Community and Social Change in America* (New Brunswick, NJ: Rutgers University Press, 1978), 17–18.

46. Lewis A. Friedland, "Communication, Community and Democracy: Toward a Theory of the Communicatively Integrated Community," *Communication Research* 28, no. 4 (2001): 385.

47.   William A. Galston, *Does the Internet Strengthen Community?* [Web page] 2001 available from http://www.puaf.umd.edu/IPPP/fall1999/internet_community.htm.

48.   For an excellent discussion of journalists' goals, see Kovach and Rosenstiel, *The Elements of Journalism*, 12–13.

49.   Cass R. Sunstein, *Republic.Com* (Princeton, NJ: Princeton University Press, 2001), 128. *A Declaration of the Independence of Cyberspace* has been published in numerous locations throughout the Web. John Perry Barlow, *A Declaration of the Independence of Cyberspace* [Web page] 1999, available from http://www.eff.org/~barlow/Declaration-Final.html.

50.   Wayne Overbeck, *Major Principles of Media Law* (Fort Worth, TX: Harcourt College Publishers, 2001), 167.

51.   Ibid., 166.

52.   John Dewey, *The Public and Its Problems* (New York: H. Holt and Company, 1927), 168.

53.   Sunstein, *Republic.Com*, 192, 8.

54.   Walter Cronkite, *A Reporter's Life* (New York: Random House, 1996), 257–58.

55.   Walt Whitman, *Leaves of Grass* (New York: Aventine Press, 1931), 42–44.

56.   For a discussion of lynching and the press, see David T. Z. Mindich, *Just the Facts: How "Objectivity" Came to Define American Journalism* (New York: New York University Press, 1998), chap. 5.

57.   James W. Carey, "AEJ Presidential Address: A Plea for the University Tradition," *Journalism Quarterly* 55, no. 4 (1978): 855.

58.   Laurie Goldstein, "The Christians: To Many Social Conservatives, an Ally," *New York Times*, 8 August 2000, A23.

59.   Putnam, *Bowling Alone*, 353–56.

Chapter 2

1.   CNN, news show, (2001).

2.   Times Mirror Center, *The Age of Indifference*.

3.   Newspaper circulation declined nationwide by 10 percent from 1990 to 2000 across the ages. Felicity Barringer, "Unresolved Clash of Cultures: At Knight Ridder, Good Journalism Vs. The Bottom Line," *New York Times*, 29 May 2001, C1. More important than declines in individual media, however, we must consider more generally how much young people are following the news. The data that follow in this chapter suggest that there has been no net gain in news knowledge or civic knowledge.

4.   Author's statistical analysis of DDB Needham, Life Style Survey, 1975–1998. Note, however, that the number of respondents is small: 487.

5.   Author's statistical analysis of Ibid.

6.   There was a slight rise to 30.1 percent in 2001. Because the 2001 test was given during the month surrounding the September 11 terrorist attacks, it is too early to detect a meaningful trend. Higher Education Research Institute, *The American Freshman: National Norms for Fall 2001* [Web page] 28 January 2002, available from http:www.gseis.ucla.edu/heri/heri.html. Higher Education Research Institute, *The American Freshman: National Norms for Fall 2000* [Web page] 22 January 2001, available from http:www.gseis.ucla.edu/heri/heri.html.

7.   Jackie Nixon, Director of Audience Research for National Public Radio sees the 35–44-year-old age cohort as relatively shallow in its news awareness. Jackie Nixon, Telephone interview with author, 7 February 2002.

8. U.S. Census Bureau, *Historical Statistics of the United States, Colonial Times to 1970*, Bicentennial ed. (Washington, DC: U.S. Dept. of Commerce Bureau of the Census, 1975), 1071–72. This source acknowledges, however, that race and citizenship complicated this data during the pre–civil rights era.

9. U.S. Census Bureau, *Voting and Registration*.

10. Grossman, "Who Took the Body out of the Body Politic?" 49.

11. Jack C. Doppelt and Ellen Shearer, *Nonvoters: America's No-Shows* (Thousand Oaks, CA: Sage Publications, 1999), 22. For a detailed analysis of nonvoters, including their media patterns, see Thomas E. Patterson, *The Vanishing Voter: Public Involvement in an Age of Uncertainty* (New York: Alfred A. Knopf, 2002).

12. Data supplied to the author by Michael Dimock, Research Director of the Pew Research Center for the People and the Press, 17 February 2004.

13. Times Mirror Center, *The Age of Indifference*.

14. Pew Research Center for the People & the Press, *Investors Now Go Online for Quotes, Advice: Internet Sapping Broadcast News Audience* [Web posted report and data] 11 June 2000 available from http://www.people-press.org. Author's analysis.

15. The Newshour, *Searching for Youth* [Web page] 6 June 2002, available from http://www.pbs.org/newshour/bb/media/jan-june02/youth_3-1.html.

16. Mike Long, Personal interview, 12 April 2002.

17. James Rowland and George F. McCleary, Personal interview, 25 March 2002.

18. Ann Colbert, Telephone interview, 10 April 2002.

19. Norman Rosenfeld, Phone interview, June 2003. Rosenfeld has been architect since 1961.

20. Cathy Horyn, "Ah, Youth, but Does It Have Staying Power?" *New York Times*, 26 February 2002, B10.

21. Putnam, *Bowling Alone*, 260.

22. Ibid., 220. Author's statistical analysis of DDB Needham, *Life Style Survey, 1975–1998*.

23. See also, Putnam, *Bowling Alone*, p. 219.

24. Roper Center for Public Opinion Research, *General Social Survey 2003: NORC-GSS Cumulative Data File 1972–2003* (2003) [Computer File].

25. Putnam, *Bowling Alone*, 220. Peiser, "Cohort Replacement and the Downward Trend in Newspaper Readership," 15–16. In 1985, Meyer looked at age cohorts over time, starting in 1967, and found that news habits didn't change much as people aged. This study predated Putnam's and Peiser's studies by 15 years. Phillip Meyer, *The Newspaper Survival Book* (Bloomington: Indiana University Press, 1985), 21.

26. Pippa Norris, *A Virtuous Circle: Political Communications in Postindustrial Societies* (Cambridge: Cambridge University Press, 2000), 74–79. Delli Carpini and Keeter also found that Germans were four times more likely than Americans to know the United Nations secretary general. Delli Carpini and Keeter, *What Americans Know About Politics and Why It Matters*, 90.

27. Pew Research Center for the People & the Press, *Investors Now Go Online for Quotes, Advice: Internet Sapping Broadcast News Audience*. Author's analysis. One caveat: the number of people polled was quite low: 749.

28. Downie Jr. and Kaiser, *The News About the News*, 65.

29. Elisabeth Bumiller, "Keepers of Bush Image Lift Stagecraft to New Heights," *New York Times*, 16 May 2003, A1.

30. Adweek.com, *Special Reports: Top 25 Magazines in Paid Circulation* [Web page] 2002 available from http://www.adweek.com/adweek/features/magcharts.jsp.

31.   Ibid. For an analysis of major changes in twentieth-century magazines, see David Abrahamson, *Magazine-Made America: The Cultural Transformation of the Postwar Periodical* (Creskill, NJ: Hampton Press, 1996).

32.   Adweek.com, *Special Reports: Top 25 Magazines in Paid Circulation. Time* and *Newsweek* each have a larger overall circulation than *Maxim* or *Cosmopolitan*. However, the median age of the news weeklies is about a decade older.

33.   I have included the magazines with a circulation greater than 1 million that increased revenue more than 40 percent, a list I compiled from Ibid. For the median ages of these magazines (except *Maxim* and ESPN, which I obtained from the publishers), go to Mediamark, *Spring 2000 Median Age, Household Income and Individual Employment Income* [Web page] 2001 available from http://www.mediamark.com/mri/techguide/tg_s00_age_hhi.htm. Some of these publications may have even younger median ages than the ones listed: In the case of *Teen People*, for example, the median age (30) may reflect some purchases by parents for their teenage children.

34.   Davis and Owen, *New Media and American Politics*, 53.

35.   Nixon.

36.   Nixon.

37.   Putnam, *Bowling Alone*, 221.

38.   Pew Research Center for the People & the Press, *Investors Now Go Online for Quotes, Advice: Internet Sapping Broadcast News Audience*. In an NPR study that asked people to rate CNN, NPR, PBS, and their favorite local and national network news sources, many respondents felt that they were not familiar enough with network news to rate it. "This is a big shift in terms of media consumption," said Jackie Nixon, the director of Audience Research for NPR [Author's interview, 7 February 2002].

39.   Alessandra Stanley, "How to Persuade the Young to Watch the News? Program It," *New York Times*, 19 January 2002, C6.

40.   Poniewozik, "The Nascar of News," 65. Rutenberg, "CNN Aims at Young Viewers as It Revamps News Format," A1.

41.   Putnam, *Bowling Alone*, 221.

Chapter 3

1.   Davis and Owen, *New Media and American Politics*, 127.

2.   Times Mirror Center, *The Age of Indifference*.

3.   Slightly more than one third of my respondents knew both of their United States senators. A similar rate of response could be found in a study of Vermont high school seniors. League of Women Voters of the Champlain Valley, "Citizenship Survey of Chittenden County High School Seniors," (Vermont: 1998).

4.   Lizzie Salzfass, "Ms. Goes to College: Wesleyan University," *Ms.*, September 2001, 52–53.

5.   Lizzie Salzfass, Telephone interview, April 2002.

6.   Ibid.

7.   Missouri was the 18th state of 50 on the scale. Putnam, *Bowling Alone*, 290–300.

8.   Kanon Cozad, Personal interview, 25 March 2002.

9.   Ibid.

10.   United Missouri Bank workers, Personal interviews, 25 March 2002.

11.   This list comes in part from Delli Carpini and Keeter, *What Americans Know About Politics and Why It Matters*, 101. Patrick Henry said "Give me liberty . . . " and

Bugs Bunny said, "What's up Doc?" Lenin was the father of the Soviet Revolution and Lennon was a Beatle.

12. Allison Davis, et al., Personal interview, 2 May 2002.

13. Ibid.

14. Cheers, *I'm Going to Get My Act Together and Stick It in Your Face (Episode 210)* (1991), Television show.

15. The exception to this was if only one copy was to be made. In that case, a scribe's rate was competitive with a printer's. But in 1483, a florin would buy you 20 pages of handwritten text from a scribe; for three florins you would get a thousand copies of 20 pages from a printer. Stephens, *A History of News*, 76.

16. Ibid., 93.

17. Ibid., 103–04.

18. Ibid., 122.

19. The earliest attempt at a newspaper was Benjamin Harris's *Publick Occurrences* in 1690. It was banned by the authorities for its sensationalism, including a disparagement of Native Americans aligned with the British and a rumor about the King of France.

20. Alexis de Tocqueville, *Democracy in America*, ed. Harvey C. Mansfield and Delba Winthrop (Chicago: University of Chicago Press, 2000), 177.

21. For the history of the *Sun* and other early nineteenth-century newspapers, the best source is William E. Huntzicker, *The Popular Press, 1833–1865* (Westport, CT: Greenwood Press, 1999). Also see Dan Schiller, *Objectivity and the News: The Public and the Rise of Commercial Journalism* (Philadelphia: University of Pennsylvania Press, 1981). For Bennett, see Mindich, *Just the Facts*, chaps. 1 and 2.

22. Stephens, *A History of News*, 239.

23. Andie Tucher, *Froth & Scum: Truth, Beauty, Goodness, and the Ax Murder in America's First Mass Medium* (Chapel Hill: University of North Carolina Press, 1994). Stephens, *A History of News*, 239. Patricia Cline Cohen, *The Murder of Helen Jewett: The Life and Death of a Prostitute in Nineteenth-Century New York* (New York: Alfred A. Knopf, 1998).

24. James L. Crouthamel, *Bennett's New York Herald and the Rise of the Popular Press*, (Syracuse, NY: Syracuse University Press, 1989).

25. For an account of Bennett's tangles with his editors, see Mindich, *Just the Facts*, chapter 1.

26. George Boyce, James Curan, and Pauline Wingate, *Newspaper History: From the Seventeenth Century to the Present Day* (Beverly Hills, CA: Sage, 1978), 180.

27. In *Public Opinion*, Walter Lippmann, wrote, "Somebody has said quite aptly that the newspaper editor has to be re-elected every day." Lippmann, *Public Opinion*, 321.

28. Harold Evans, Gail Buckland, and Kevin Baker, *The American Century* (New York: Alfred A. Knopf, 1998), 81.

29. Ben H. Bagdikian, *The Media Monopoly*, 6th ed. (Boston, MA: Beacon Press, 2000), 110–11.

30. Pam Belluck, "Jackson Says He Fathered Child in Affair with Aide," *New York Times*, 19 January 2001, A21. Howard Kurtz, "Grabbing the Headlines: The National Enquirer," *Washington Post*, 26 February 2001, C1.

31. S. Elizabeth Bird, *For Enquiring Minds: A Cultural Study of Supermarket Tabloids* (Knoxville: University of Tennessee Press, 1992), 49.

32. Downie and Kaiser of the *Washington Post* decided against publishing a report alleging a 1968 affair involving Bob Dole. The *National Enquirer* published the

story, which Downie and Kaiser called "strikingly accurate." Downie Jr. and Kaiser, *The News About the News*, 61.

33. Delli Carpini and Williams showed how "responsible journalists" downplayed the 1992 rumors about Clinton's affair with Gennifer Flowers. By 1998, responsible journalism "adapted to the new rules by increasingly mimicking the form and substance of its new media competitors." Michael X. Delli Carpini, and Bruce A. Williams, "Let Us Infotain You: Politics in the New Media Environment," in *Mediated Politics: Communication in the Future of Democracy*, ed. W. Lance Bennett and Robert M. Entman (Cambridge, UK: Cambridge University Press, 2001), 168, 76.

34. I am indebted to Mitchell Stephens for helping me develop this point. Also see Garth Jowett and James M. Linton, *Movies as Mass Communication*, 2nd ed. (Newbury Park, CA: Sage, 1989).

35. Brandeis University students, Personal interviews, 22 April 2002.

36. The professor was Michael Socolow. I am indebted to him for developing this point with his students.

37. Mindich, *Just the Facts*.

38. Farai Chideya, Phone interview, 10 November 2003.

39. Ibid.

40. Kovach and Rosenstiel, *The Elements of Journalism*, 152.

41. Thankfully, Andrea Thompson left CNN in 2002.

42. I'm not making this up. *Headline News*, 9 October 2001 ("for the boys") and 7? February 2002 ("Lay-ter").

43. In a 1950 study, David Manning White analyzed an editor, who he called "Mr. Gates." Gates, in charge of sifting through the wire stories, printed about 10 percent of the ones he received. While Gates tried to remain detached and free of prejudices, his decisions, of course, were based on his own views. His main reason for rejecting stories was that they were "not interesting." David M. White, "The "Gate Keeper": A Case Study in the Selection of News," *Journalism Quarterly* 27 (1950), 383–390.

44. New York Times, "Television," *New York Times*, 27 February 1968, 87.

45. For a good account of this, see Downie Jr. and Kaiser, *The News About the News*, 111–56.

46. Elizabeth Lesly Stevens, "Mouse Ke Fear," *Brill's Content*, December/January 1998/1999, 95.

46. Bill Carter, "Koppel Is the Odd Man out as ABC Woos Letterman," *New York Times*, 1 March 2002, A1.

48. Howard Kurtz, "Ted Koppel Takes on ABC in Op-Ed on Relevance of Nightline," *Washington Post*, 5 March 2002, C1.

49. Bill Carter and Jim Rutenberg, "Letterman Offer Was News to Chief of ABC News," *New York Times*, 2 March 2002, A1.

50. Ted Koppel, "Network News Is Still Serious Business," *New York Times*, 5 March 2002, A23.

51. Under Mark S. Fowler, the F.C.C. began to see television more as commerce. Television, said Fowler, is basically "a toaster with pictures." Peter J. Boyer, "Under Fowler, F.C.C. Treated TV as Commerce," *New York Times*, 19 January 1987, C15.

52. Nixon.

53. Chris Rose, Personal interview, 8 May 2002.

54. It is worth noting that the rise of sugary cereal correlated in the 1970s with the rise of entertainment television and advertising. See Fred Ferretti, "Nutritionist Says U.S. Study of TV Ads for Children Ignores Food," *New York Times*, 18 October 1970, 94. Also see John D. Morris, "Five Weeks of Hearings Strengthen F.T.C.'s Deter-

mination to Continue Aggressive Regulation of TV Ads," *New York Times*, 22 November 1971, 21.

55.   Robert M. Entman, *Democracy without Citizens: Media and the Decay of American Politics* (New York: Oxford University Press, 1989), 17.

56.   For tying editors' pay to profits, see Kovach and Rosenstiel, *The Elements of Journalism*, 50. For the *Salon* firings, see Freedom Forum Pacific Coast Center, *Recapture Your Youth*, 4.

57.   Tom Shales, "The Pull of the Pullover; Rather Finds More Than Warmth in a Sweater; Rather's Sweater Tale," *Washington Post*, 8 February 1982, C1.

58.   The Internet abounds with examples of how want trumps need. See David Shenk, *The End of Patience: Cautionary Notes on the Information Revolution* (Bloomington: Indiana University Press, 1999). Especially 27–29. Kathy Pinckert, Telephone interview, 12 June 2001. CBS, "CBS Evening News with Dan Rather (14 October)," (2003), Nakednews.com, *Naked News* [Web broadcast] 14 October 2003, available from http://www.nakednews.com. Calwell's show opened with the "International Report." Its top six stories, read by its two undressing anchors, Victoria Sinclair and Michelle Pantoliano, were 1. President Bush saying he was "in charge" of the U.S. policy towards Iraq; 2. the United Nation's vote to increase its Peacekeeping force; 3. an Israeli army battle in Gaza; 4. a Liberian leader returns to his country; 5. Iran's nuclear program; and 6. China's space program. On that day, CBS's lead stories had a more domestic slant: 1. the "Pledge of Allegiance" case before the Supreme Court ; 2. medical marijuana; 3. "The Battle for Iraq"; 4. Iran's nuclear program; 5. protests in Saudi Arabia; and 6. the transit strike in Los Angeles.

59.   Carey, "AEJ Presidential Address: A Plea for the University Tradition."

60.   Davis and Owen, *New Media and American Politics*, 5, 14.

61.   Pew Research Center for the People & the Press, *Ten Years of the Pew News Interest Index*.

62.   Pew Research Center for the People & the Press, *Audiences Fragmented and Skeptical: The Tough Job of Communicating with Voters*. For an interview with Jon Stewart about young people and the news, see Love, "The Kids Are All Right; Young People and the News: A Conversation."

63.   Dhavan V. Shah, Jack M. McLeod, So-Hyang Yoon, "Communication, Context, and Community: An Exploration of Print, Broadcast, and Internet Influences," *Communication Research* 28, no. 4 (2001).

64.   CNN.com, *Most Popular Links from CNN.Com* [Web Page] 1 September 2001 available from http://www.cnn.com/.

65.   The Onion, *A Shattered Nation Longs to Care About Stupid Bullshit Again* [Web page] 3 October 2001 available from http://www.theonion.com/onion3735/a_shattered_nation.html.

66.   CNN.com, *Most Popular Links from CNN.Com* [Web site] 1 March 2002 available from http://www.cnn.com.

67.   Max Frankel, *The Times of My Life and My Life with the Times* (New York: Random House, 1999), 437–38.

68.   Aristotle, *Aristotle's Poetics*, trans. S. H. Butcher (New York: Hill and Wang, 1961), 72.

69.   Roland Barthes, "Structure of the Fait-Divers," in *Critical Essays* (Evanston, IL: Northwestern University Press, 1972).

70.   Robert Darnton, "Writing News and Telling Stories," *Daedalus* 104, no. 2 (1975).

71.   Downie Jr. and Kaiser, *The News About the News*, 237.

72.   Shenk, *The End of Patience: Cautionary Notes on the Information Revolution*, 27–28.

73.   Actors, Personal interviews, 7 May 2002.

74.   L. A. Pierce Junior College basketball players, Personal interviews, 6 May 2002.

Chapter 4

1.   Ruth McFarland, *Bacon's Newspaper Directory* (Hightstown, NJ: Primedia Information, Inc., 2000), 84.

2.   Aaron Harper, Personal interview, 7 May 2002.

3.   Rosenfeld.

4.   Andrea Alford, Telephone interview, 14 April 2002.

5.   Actors.

6.   Stephens, *A History of News*, 10–11.

7.   Joel Senesac, Personal interview, August 2001.

8.   Rose.

9.   Brandeis University students.

10.   United Missouri Bank workers.

11.   Cory Melancon, Personal interview, 8 May 2002.

12.   L.A. Pierce Junior College basketball players.

13.   Putnam, *Bowling Alone*, 192–94.

14.   Ibid., 222.

15.   Robert Kraut et al., "Internet Paradox: A Social Technology That Reduces Social Involvement and Psychological Well-Being?" *American Psychologist* 53, no. 9 (1998).

16.   Salzfass.

17.   Colbert.

18.   Colchester High School students, Personal interviews, 12 April 2002.

19.   Long.

20.   Putnam, *Bowling Alone*, 192, 404.

21.   Cronkite, *A Reporter's Life*, 30–31.

22.   David Brinkley, *David Brinkley: 11 Presidents, 4 Wars, 22 Political Conventions, 1 Moon Landing, 3 Assassinations, 2,000 Weeks of News and Other Stuff on Television and 18 Years of Growing up in North Carolina* (New York: Alfred A. Knopf, 1995), 24–25.

23.   Frankel, *The Times of My Life and My Life with the Times*, 52, 64–67.

24.   Freedom Forum Pacific Coast Center, *Recapture Your Youth*, 56. This discussion is also available at http://slashdot.org/features/00/02/21/1125208.shtml.

25.   On April 12, 2002, I visited this civics class, taught by Jim Price, a history teacher.

26.   John Fitzmorris, Personal interview, 9 May 2002.

27.   Bishop Perry Middle School students, Personal interviews, 9 May 2002.

28.   Harper.

29.   In casual conversations, a few friends and acquaintances could name more than five. They were either older than 40, thus beyond the age range of this study, or lawyers.

30.   Cozad.

31.   Senesac.

32.   L.A. Pierce Junior College basketball players.

33.   USA Today, "The Newspaper Readership Program: Excellence in Education," (Waltham, MA: Report for Brandeis University, 2001). In 2002, About 230 newspapers were given away daily: 44 copies of *USA Today*, 88 copies of the *Boston Globe*, and 98

copies of the *New York Times*. While the free newspaper experiment appears to be a success, it still points to the gap between those who find reading "important" or "very important" and those who actually read. About 3000 undergraduates attend Brandeis. Kristine C. Asselin, Personal interview, 22 April 2002.

34. Salzfass.

35. Actors.

36. For the mass arrests, see Mindich, *Just the Facts*, chapter 3.

37. Cozad, Harper, Senesac.

38. Brandeis University students.

39. Whitman, *Leaves of Grass*. The phrase is from "Song of Myself" and refers to himself.

40. Pew Research Center for the People & the Press, *Domestic Concerns Will Vie with Terrorism in Fall: Criticisms of Bush and Congress as Job Worries Increase* [Web-posted report and data] August 2002 available from http://www.people-press.org/.

41. These data, from an Urban and Associates report, were supplied by Donley.

42. Jonathon Cummings and Robert Kraut, *Domesticating Computers and the Internet* [Web page] 4 May 2001 available from http://homenet.hcii.cs.cmu.edu/progress/research.html.

43. Pew Research Center for the People & the Press, *Youth Vote Influenced by Online Information: Internet Election News Audience Seeks Convenience, Familiar Names*.

44. In a recent poll, Pew found that the top six uses for the Internet among 12–17-year-olds were, in order: e-mail (92%); "no reason" or "fun" (84%); getting information about movies, TV shows, music, or sports stars (83%); instant messages (74%); hobbies (69%) and news (68%). Pew Internet in American Life Project, *Parents, Kids and the Internet* [Web page] Princeton Survey Research Associates, 2001 available from http://www.pewinternet.org/.

45. Many of the youngest students listed instant messaging as their primary activity on the Internet. Colchester High School students. Robert Kraut et al., "Internet Paradox Revisited," *Journal of Social Issues* 58, no. 1 (2002): 4, 8.

46. Cummings and Kraut, *Domesticating Computers and the Internet*.

47. Asselin. Data commissioned by Brandeis and supplied to author by Asselin.

48. Brandeis University students.

49. Kraut et al., "Internet Paradox."

50. Putnam, *Bowling Alone*, 170, 221.

51. Pippa Norris, and David Jones, "Virtual Democracy," *Harvard International Journal of Press/Politics* 3, no. 2 (1998): 1–4.

52. Shah, Kwak, and Holbert, " 'Connecting' and 'Disconnecting' with Civic Life," 154.

53. Kraut et al., "Internet Paradox Revisited."

54. Shah, Kwak, and Holbert, " 'Connecting' and 'Disconnecting' with Civic Life," 155.

55. Kraut et al., "Internet Paradox," 142.

56. Putnam, *Bowling Alone*, 179.

57. Marshall McLuhan, *Understanding Media: The Extensions of Man* (Cambridge, MA: MIT Press, 1995), 22–23.

58. Clifford Stoll, *Silicon Snake Oil: Second Thoughts on the Information Highway* (New York: Doubleday, 1995), 22.

59. For the trend in magazines, see Abrahamson, *Magazine-Made America: The Cultural Transformation of the Postwar Periodical*.

60. Donley.

61. The Trumpeter Swan Society, *The Trumpeter Swan Society* [Web page] 1 September 2002 available from http://www.taiga.net/swans/.

62. Colbert.

63. Kraut et al., "Internet Paradox."

64. Melancon.

65. Cozad.

66. Harper. The Internet Movie Database is at http://www.imdb.com. It is the most extensive public site on the Internet for movie information.

67. Mediamark, *Spring 2000 Median Age, Household Income and Individual Employment Income*. The figure for the *New York Times* was supplied to the author by the newspaper. For more details see New York Times, *Audience/Circulation* [Web sites] May 2003 available from http://www.nytadvertising.nytimes.com/adonis/html/home.htm.

68. The Readership Institute, at http://www.readership.org, has identified and quantified this core group of young readers.

Chapter 5

1. James Parton, *The Life of Horace Greeley, Editor of "the New-York Tribune,"* *from His Birth to the Present Time*. (Boston: Houghton, Mifflin and Company, 1889), 522.

2. Actors.

3. Cozad.

4. Harper.

5. Barry Glassner, *The Culture of Fear: Why Americans Are Afraid of the Wrong Things* (New York: Basic Books, 1999).

6. Howard Rosenberg et al., "Bad News," *American Journalism Review*, September 1993, 18–27.

7. Two recent credibility reports include bibliographies. A report by the Online News Association offered an overview of many credibility studies. See Dianne Lynch, Howard Finberg, and Martha Stone, *Digital Journalism Credibility Study: What We Already Know; a Review of the Literature* [Web posted report] Online News Association, 2002, available from http://www.onlinenewsassociation.org/programs/research.htm. The Poynter Institute included a detailed bibliography on its Web site: David Shedden, *Media Credibility Bibliography* [Web page] Poynter Online, 2 May 2003, available from http://poynteronline.org/content/content_view.asp?id=1205.

8. Downie Jr. and Kaiser, *The News About the News*, 245.

9. Ibid., 174–77, 244.

10. Mercy Health Services, *The Woman's Doctor* [Web page] 2002, available from http://www.mdmercy.com/womens/womens_doctor.html. Services, *The Woman's Doctor*. WBAL, *The WBAL Channel.Com* [Web page] 17 October 2002, available from http://www.thewbalchannel.com/womansdoctor/.

11. Downie Jr. and Kaiser, *The News About the News*, 127.

12. Jim Rutenberg and Micheline Maynard, "TV News That Looks Local, Even If It's Not," *New York Times*, 2 June 2003, C1.

13. Tom Rosenstiel, Carl Gottlieb, and Lee Ann Brady, "Quality Brings Higher Ratings, but Enterprise Is Disappearing," *Columbia Journalism Review*, November/December 1999.

14. Charles Layton and Jennifer Dorroh, "The State of the American Newspaper: Sad State," *American Journalism Review*, June 2002, 20–21. Between 2000 and 2002, the situation had slightly worsened.

15. Ibid.

16. Carl Sessions Stepp, "Of the People, by the People, Bore the People," *Washington Journalism Review*, March 1992, 22–26.

17. Downie Jr. and Kaiser, *The News About the News*, 171.

18. Pew Research Center for the People & the Press, *Audiences Fragmented and Skeptical: The Tough Job of Communicating with Voters.*

19. L.A. Pierce Junior College basketball players.

20. Pew Research Center for the People & the Press, *Investors Now Go Online for Quotes, Advice: Internet Sapping Broadcast News Audience.* Author's analysis.

21. Woody Allen and Marshall Brickman, "Annie Hall," (1977).

22. Mumford, *The Culture of Cities*, 412.

23. Putnam, *Bowling Alone*, 213.

24. Bogart, *Preserving the Press*, 42–43.

25. Norris, *A Virtuous Circle*, 69. Norris reports that this trend parallels trends in other developed countries as well, although the United States seems to have the dubious distinction of being a leader in this (73–79).

26. U.S. Census Bureau, *Voting and Registration in the Election of November 2000* [Web posted data] 27 Feburary 2002, available from http://www.census.gov/population/www/socdemo/voting/p20-542.html.

27. Putnam, *Bowling Alone*, 54–57.

28. Ibid. 28–32 (bowling), 114 (sports), 70–72 (church membership and attendance), 39 and 52 (political parties and associations), 101 (drinking), 186–187 (education), 105 (cards and casinos and dinners), 45 (list of declines in political involvement).

29. Dirk Johnson, "Students Still Sweat, They Just Don't Shower," *New York Times*, 22 April 1996, A1.

30. Erik Barnouw, *Tube of Plenty: The Evolution of American Television* (New York: Oxford University Press, 1975), 171.

31. Lippmann, *Public Opinion*, 138.

32. Downie Jr. and Kaiser, *The News About the News*, 124–25.

33. Putnam, *Bowling Alone*, 265.

34. Brandeis University students. This service requirement is outlined on the National Honor Society's Web page. National Honor Society, *Student Membership* [Web page] 2003 available from http://www.nhs.us/membership/stud_mem.cfm.

35. Delli Carpini and Keeter, *What Americans Know About Politics and Why It Matters*, 219–21.

36. Putnam, *Bowling Alone*, 354–55. One fascinating measure is that in 1937, only 46 percent of voters surveyed by Gallup said they would be willing to vote for a qualified Jewish candidate for president; in 1999, 92 percent said they would. Goldstein, "The Christians: To Many Social Conservatives, an Ally," A23.

37. Jack M. McLeod, Dietram A. Scheufele, and Patricia Moy, "Community, Communication, and Participation: The Role of Mass Media and Interpersonal Discussion in Local Political Participation," *Political Communication* 16 (1999). For the negative correlation, see Norris, *A Virtuous Circle*, 284–91.

38. McLeod, Scheufele, and Moy, "Community, Communication, and Participation: The Role of Mass Media and Interpersonal Discussion in Local Political Participation."

39. Shah, "Communication, Context, and Community," 480.

40. Putnam, *Bowling Alone*, 233.

41.	DDB Needham, *Life Style Survey, 1975–1998*. Author's analysis.

42.	de Tocqueville, *Democracy in America*, 500–05.

43.	James W. Carey, "The Communications Revolution and the Professional Communicator," *Sociological Review Monographs* 13 (1969): 29.

44.	Ibid.

45.	Shenk, *The End of Patience: Cautionary Notes on the Information Revolution*, 73.

46.	Pew Research Center for the People & the Press, *Americans Thinking About Iraq, but Focused on the Economy: Midterm Election Preview* [Web posted report and data] 10 October 2002 available from http://www.people-press.org.

47.	Stoll, *Silicon Snake Oil*, 219.

48.	McLuhan, *Understanding Media*, 86.

49.	Kraut et al., "Internet Paradox Revisited."

50.	Jonathon Cummings, Brian Butler, and Robert Kraut, *The Quality of Online Social Relationships* [Web page] 16 October 2000 available from http://homenet. hcii.cs.cmu.edu/progress/research.html.

51.	Friedman, *The Lexus and the Olive Tree*, 14, 358–59.

52.	Dewey, *The Public and Its Problems*.

53.	Rosen, *What Are Journalists For?*

54.	de Tocqueville, *Democracy in America*, 232.

55.	Sunstein, *Republic.Com*, 85, 192.

56.	Friedland, "Communication, Community and Democracy: Toward a Theory of the Communicatively Integrated Community," 385.

57.	Galston, *Does the Internet Strengthen Community?*

58.	Ibid.

59.	Bishop Perry Middle School students.

60.	Ibid.

61.	Fitzmorris.

62.	Bishop Perry Middle School students.

63.	Non-Hispanic blacks voted in the 2000 elections at a rate of 54.1 percent; non-Hispanic whites voted at a rate of 60.4 percent. Across most regions and most age groups, whites voted at a slightly higher rate than did blacks. U.S. Census Bureau, *Voting and Registration in the Election of November 2000*.

64.	Rose.

65.	During the last mayoral election, New Orleans had a 38 percent voter turnout, a higher rate than in comparable elections in Atlanta, Mobile, and New York City. Matthew Powers, my research assistant, culled these data from municipal records and local election officials.

66.	Sandra M. Genelius, E-mail correspondence, 19 May 2003. Jerry Seregni, Telephone interview with author's research assistant, Matthew Powers, 15 May 2003. Seregni noted that national and international events occasionally provoke a decline in the audience for their local coverage.

67.	Whitman, *Leaves of Grass*, 42–44.

Chapter 6

1.	David Halberstam, *The Powers That Be* (New York: Alfred A. Knopf, 1979), 490–91.

2.   Walter Lippmann, "Two Revolutions in the American Press," *The Yale Review* 20, no. 3 (1931): 435.

3.   Overbeck, *Major Principles of Media Law,* 38.

4.   See Mindich, *Just the Facts,* chapters 1 and 2.

5.   Bagdikian, *The Media Monopoly,* 46–47.

6.   Benjamin C. Bradlee, *A Good Life: Newspapering and Other Adventures* (New York: Simon and Schuster, 1995), 317.

7.   Carl Bernstein and Bob Woodward, *All the President's Men* (New York: Simon and Schuster, 1974), 247.

8.   Of course we can provide counter examples of this, too. In 1961 the Kennedy administration lobbied the *New York Times* to kill a story on its plans for the "Bay of Pigs" invasion of Cuba. Although the *Times* did not kill it, they downplayed it, leading to one of the great regrets of the newsroom. Kennedy told a *Times* editor something that would drive its thinking when it contemplated future questions of press freedom versus national security: "Maybe if you had printed more about the operation you would have saved us from a colossal mistake." Frankel, *The Times of My Life and My Life with the Times,* 209–11.

9. Lippmann, "Two Revolutions in the American Press."

10.   Dan Berkowitz, *Social Meanings of News: A Text-Reader* (Thousand Oaks, CA: Sage, 1997), 34.

11.   James Edward Pollard, *The Presidents and the Press* (New York,: Macmillan, 1947), 352–53.

12.   John Wallace Claire Johnstone, William W. Bowman, and Edward J. Slawski, *The News People: A Sociological Portrait of American Journalists and Their Work* (Urbana: University of Illinois Press, 1976), 226. More recent studies have echoed Johnstone et al.'s finding that journalists are typically moderate. When asked about their political leanings, a plurality of journalists say they are centrists. After that, the most popular response is a little left, then a little right, then left, then right. Even people who have left and right leanings can, and often do, achieve an ideological balance within their stories.

13.   Kovach and Rosenstiel, *The Elements of Journalism,* 99.

14.   Frankel, *The Times of My Life and My Life with the Times,* 515–16, 370.

15.   Daniel C. Hallin, *The "Uncensored War": The Media and Vietnam* (New York: Oxford University Press, 1986), 8.

16.   Robert N. Bellah et al., *The Good Society* (New York: Alfred A. Knopf, 1991), 254.

17.   Stephens, *A History of News,* 194. Crouthamel, *Bennett's New York Herald and the Rise of the Popular Press,* 21.

18.   Downie Jr. and Kaiser, *The News About the News,* 65.

19.   Ibid., 113.

20.   Ibid., 21.

21.   Ibid., 138.

22.   Frankel, *The Times of My Life and My Life with the Times,* 504.

23.   This is from the *American Journalism Review*'s 2001 study of the 13 biggest newspaper companies. Alicia C. Shepard, "Moguls' Millions," *American Journalism Review,* July/August 2001, 20.

24.   The quote from Gannett's annual report is from Gannett, *Letter to Shareholders* [Web posted letter] May 1997, available from http://www.gannett.com/annual/ann97/letter.htm. The figures are difficult to pin down, but estimates about Gan-

nett's operating margin for 1997, the last year I could find, range from 27.3 to 29.9 percent. According to an investigative report by the *Nashville Scene,* an alternative weekly, Gannett's 1997 operating profit margin for all its newspapers combined was 27.3 percent. According to the article, 36 of Gannett's newspapers had more than a 33.3 percent operating profit. The operating profit margins of all of the company's newspapers are listed on the *Scene's* Web site. Nashville Scene, *Grading the Daily* [Web site] May 2001, available from http://www.nashvillescene.com/Grading_the_Daily/gannett1.html.

25. Nashville Scene, *Grading the Daily.*

26. Frankel, *The Times of My Life and My Life with the Times,* 503 (profitable press), 370 (magazine).

27. Downie Jr. and Kaiser, *The News About the News,* 245.

28. Norris, *A Virtuous Circle,* 48–49, 87.

29. Ibid., 63.

30. Stephen Seplow, "G.A.S for the World," *American Journalism Review,* October/November 2003, 46–47.

31. Downie Jr. and Kaiser, *The News About the News,* 154–55.

32. Salzfass.

33. Barlow, *A Declaration of the Independence of Cyberspace.*

34. John Updike, *Rabbit Redux* (New York,: Alfred A. Knopf, 1971), 44.

35. Putnam, *Bowling Alone,* 92.

36. Downie Jr. and Kaiser, *The News About the News,* 127–28.

37. Jay Rosen, Telephone interview, 5 June 2003.

38. Anderson, *Imagined Communities,* 53.

39. Michael O'Malley, *Keeping Watch: A History of American Time* (New York: Viking Penguin, 1990), 55, 94–109.

40. James W. Carey, "Technology and Ideology: The Case of the Telegraph," *Prospects* 8 (1982): 315–21.

41. John Hope Franklin and Alfred A. Moss, *From Slavery to Freedom: A History of African Americans,* 7th ed. (New York: McGraw-Hill, 1994), 178.

42. Mindich, *Just the Facts,* 61–62, 158–59.

43. Author unknown, "The Empire Club Chief: Romantic Career of a Democratic Politician," *New York Times,* 14 January 1885.

44. Overbeck, *Major Principles of Media Law,* 35.

45. Habermas, *The Structural Transformation of the Public Sphere,* 26–27. Habermas wrote that the concept of this "public sphere" emerged in the mid-eighteenth century.

46. Matthew Purdy, "Live, Via Satellite, All the News That Fits Your Viewpoint," *New York Times,* 29 April 2002, A29.

47. Friedman, *The Lexus and the Olive Tree,* 8–19.

48. Ibid., 14.

49. Robert J. Blendon et al., *The Public and the Smallpox Threat* [Web-posted article] The New England Journal of Medicine, 2003, available from www.nejm.org.

50. Dana Milbank and Claudia Deane, "Hussein Link to 9/11 Lingers in Many Minds," *Washington Post,* 6 September 2003, A1.

51. DeNeen L. Brown, "And the Winner Is . . . Chretien, First to Visit Bush," *Washington Post,* 4 February 2001, A4.

52. From an unpublished part of Marc Gunther's interview with Jay Leno from 15 January 2004. Sent from Gunther to the author via e-mail, 8 February 2004.

53. The number 537 is, of course, only the official count; I will not wade into the discussion of the various ways the ballots were recounted, or should have been.

54. Thomas E. Patterson, "Doing Well and Doing Good: How Soft News and Critical Journalism Are Shrinking the News Audience and Weakening Democracy—and What News Outlets Can Do About It," (Joan Shorenstein Center on the Press, Politics, and Public Policy, 2000), 5.

55. Whitman, *Leaves of Grass*, 507.

56. James Baldwin, *Notes of a Native Son* (New York: Dial Press, 1963), 86–87.

57. I have discussed the issues of balance and inclusion elsewhere. Mindich, *Just the Facts*, chapter 2. It is, of course, an impossible task to find a true balance. I once met a rightwing Christian journalist who regularly balanced stories between rightwing views. In the case of abortion, for example, he would balance the views of two people: one who would ban all abortions and one who would make an exception for health reasons. Finding the right balance often involves exploring how you and your readers place the fulcrum and define the boundaries of the debate.

58. Michael C. Emery, Edwin Emery, and Nancy L. Roberts, *The Press and America: An Interpretive History of the Mass Media*, 8th ed. (Boston: Allyn and Bacon, 1996), 127.

59. Arthur Meier Schlesinger, *Prelude to Independence: The Newspaper War on Britain, 1764–1776* (New York: Alfred A. Knopf, 1958), 179. Schlesinger's book, while old, is still an excellent introduction to the press's role in the American Revolution.

60. Ibid., 73.

61. George Washington and John H. Rhodehamel, *Writings, The Library of America* (New York: Library of America, 1997), 1026.

62. Kovach and Rosenstiel, *The Elements of Journalism*, 28–29, 189.

Chapter 7 (Conclusion)

1. Downie Jr. and Kaiser, *The News About the News*, 266.

2. Wilkinson, "Confronting the Newspaper Youth Readership Puzzle," 2.

3. Readership Institute, *The Power to Grow Readership: Research from the Impact Study of Newspaper Readership* [Web-posted report] Northwestern University, 2001, available from http://www.readership.org.

4. Freedom Forum Pacific Coast Center, *Recapture Your Youth*.

5. The most probable solutions I've seen come from young reporters who gave their ideas to the *Columbia Journalism Review*. However, these solutions were, in the words of the article "fairly grounded" in existing practices. See Liz Cox, "Imagine: Sixty-Seven Young Journalists and the Newspaper of Their Dreams," *Columbia Journalism Review*, January/February 2003.

6. Carey, "AEJ Presidential Address: A Plea for the University Tradition," 855.

7. Putnam, *Bowling Alone*, 410.

8. New York Times, "Television," 87.

9. Under Mark S. Fowler, the F.C.C. began to see television more as commerce. Television, said Fowler, is basically "a toaster with pictures." Boyer, "Under Fowler, F.C.C. Treated TV as Commerce."

10. The two-and-a-half minute show ran from 1971 to 1979, eight times every Saturday morning. That's a total of 20 minutes every Saturday. Genelius.

11.   For a better model of news for kids, see *Time For Kids*, at http://www.time-forkids.com/TFK/. It does contain a lot of fluff, and it is a bit too heavy on the stuff kids crave—animals, dinosaurs, and space—but its news section offers kids a decent amount of political detail, too. *Junior Scholastic* and the *New York Times UPFRONT* are two other decent models.

12.   Sunstein, *Republic.Com*, 147–48.

13.   Bill Kovach and Tom Rosenstiel, "All News Media Inc.," *New York Times*, 7 January 2003, A19. Neil Hickey, "Power Shift: As the FCC Prepares to Alter the Media Map, Battle Lines Are Drawn," *Columbia Journalism Review*, March/April 2003, 26–31. Stephen Labaton, "Deregulating the Media: The Overview; Regulators Ease Rules Governing Media Ownership," *New York Times*, 3 June 2003, A1.

14.   Bagdikian, *The Media Monopoly*, 223–37. Bagdikian correctly noted that regulation is legally much easier in broadcasting rather than print. The former, Bagdikian wrote, is owned by us; the latter is not.

15.   Sunstein, *Republic.Com*, 181. Andrew L. Shapiro, *The Control Revolution: How the Internet Is Putting Individuals in Charge and Changing the World We Know* (New York: PublicAffairs, 1999), 205–06.

16.   Senesac.

17.   Brandeis University students.

18.   Alford.

19.   Stephens, *A History of News*, 10–11.

20.   U.S. Department of Education, *No Child Left Behind: Character Education*. The "No Child Left Behind" agenda emphasizes "standards," particularly reading, math, and to a lesser extent, science. One of the goals is "character," which includes "citizenship," but this is not a standard to which schools will be held accountable. See http://www.nclb.gov/Newsletter/20030215.html. The civics class in Colchester was taught by Jim Price.

21.   CBS News, "Television Coverage of the Democratic National Convention," (1968).

22.   Dave Barry, "Dave for President—Running on Empty," *Burlington Free Press*, 1 June 2003, 20.

23.   For a great discussion of nonvoters, see Doppelt and Shearer, *Nonvoters*, 22.

24.   Dionne, *Why Americans Hate Politics*, 311.

25.   Norris, *A Virtuous Circle*, 153.

26.   Putnam, *Bowling Alone*, 414.

27.   Dewey, *The Public and Its Problems*. Lippmann, *Public Opinion*.

28.   Downie Jr. and Kaiser, *The News About the News*, 226.

29.   Kovach and Rosenstiel, *The Elements of Journalism*, 60, 29.

30.   Tom Rosenstiel, Carl Gottlieb, and Lee Ann Brady, "Time of Peril for TV News: Quality Sells, but Commitment and Viewership Continue to Erode," *Columbia Journalism Review*, November/December 2000, 84–85.

31.   Readership Institute, *Branding: From Consumer Insight to Implementation* [Web-posted report] Northwestern University, April 2002 available from http://www.readership.org.

32.   Frankel, *The Times of My Life and My Life with the Times*, 425.

33.   Program on International Policy Attitudes, *Misperceptions, the Media and the Iraq War* [Web-posted report] 2 October 2003, available from http://www.pipa.org.

34.   MSNBC, "Countdown with Keith Olbermann (29 October)," (2003).

35. Chideya.

36. Cronkite, *A Reporter's Life*, 3.

37. Sunstein, *Republic.Com*, 88–89. Michael Massing, "Does Democracy Avert Famine?" *New York Times*, 1 March 2003, A19.

38. Friedman, *The Lexus and the Olive Tree*, 163.

Index

Page numbers in italics refer to figures.

A

A Tale of Two Cities. See Dickens, Charles
ABC News, 7, 51–53
Abdul, Paula, 2
Accessibility, in journalism, 122–23
Actors, interviews in Los Angeles. *See* Interviews
Adams, Samuel, 110
Afghanistan War, 18–19, 50, 68
Age of Indifference, 34
AIDS, seen by the media as a "gay" disease, 109
Aiken, Clay, 2
Alford, Andrea, 62–63, 118
All in the Family, 15
Allen, Woody, 83
American Idol, 1–3, *3*, 5

Anderson, Benedict, 9–12, 103–9
Antique cookie cutter, 59
AOL Instant Messenger, 71, 77, 89
AOL Time Warner, 50
Apathy, 6
Aristotle, 58
Ashcroft, John, ix, 35, 37, 66
Axis of evil, 35, 37

B

Bagdikian, Benjamin, 116
Baldwin, James, 109
Barlow, John Perry, 15, 102
Barnes & Noble, 123–24
Barry, Dave, 120
Barthes, Ronald, 58
Bartlett, Dan, 30

Index

Bauer, Gary, 23–24

Beecher, Henry Ward, 121

Bellah, Robert, 98

Bender, Thomas, 14

Bennett, James Gordon 45, 96, 99

Bennett, William, 4

Berelson, Bernard, 63, 118

Bishop Perry Middle School, 67, 92–94. *See also* Interviews with young people, New Orleans

Blair, Selma, 61

Boston Tea Party, 110

Bowling Alone. See Putnam, Robert D.

Bowling, 84

Brandeis University, 13, 71. *See also* Interviews with young people, Waltham, Mass. (Brandeis)

Brandeis, Louis D., 15

Brinkley, David, 66

Brokaw, Tom, 14, 99, 101

Buchanan, Patrick, 23–24

Burlington Free Press, 100, 102

Burlington, Vt. interviews. *See* Interviews, Burlington, Vt.

Bush, George, H. W., 122

Bush, George W., 11, 37, 46, 91, 122; criticized by the news media, 7, 98; election against Gore in 2000, 1; extrajudicial arrests, 122; public's knowledge of candidate in 2000, 23–24; public relations of his administration, 29; vaccinated for smallpox, 105–6

C

Cam Ne, village of, 95

Campaign finance reform, 121. *See also* McCain-Feingold

Carey, James W., 16, 88–89, 104, 105

Cartoon Network, 14, 73, 116

CBS News, 26, 33, 94, 120; children's news programming, 115–16;
kills story about big tobacco, 7; Morley Safer's Cam Ne story and Lyndon Johnson's response, 95

CD-ROMs, marketing newspapers with, 113

Celebrities, knowledge of, 4

Central Casting practice of centralized programming on "local" radio, 81

Cheers, 34, 41–42

Chicago Sun-Times, 113–14

Chicago Tribune, 113–14, *114*

Chideya, Farai, 48, *49*, 90, 125

Childhood habits, 66–68

Children's programming, 115–16

Chretien, Jean, 106

Christie, Agatha, 9

Church attendance, 84

Cicero, 10

Citizen Kane, 101

Civic involvement, 69, 84, 87; and media use, 72–74. *See also* Social capital

Civil rights era, coverage of, 109

Clark, Wesley, 25, 126

Clear Channel Communications, 80–81

Clinton, Bill, 11, 46, 78, 126; criticized by the news media, 7, 98; on MTV, 126; public relations of his administration, 29; Whitewater, 122

Clinton, Hillary, 37

Clubs and organizations, 84

CNBC, 32

CNN, 14, 42, 99; author's appearance on, 18–19; median viewer age, x, 3, 32; network's style, 48; top stories, as selected by viewers, 57–58; viewers as more informed than those of Fox news, 124–25

Cohort replacement, 28–29. *See also* Newspaper readership

Colbert, Ann, 66, 75
Colchester, Vt. interviews. *See*
     Interviews, Colchester, Vt.
Cold media. *See* Hot and cold media
College admissions, and news
     consumption, 118
Columbus (Georgia) *Ledger-Enquirer*,
     11, 99
Commute time. *See* Suburbia
Competition, 49–59
Complacency, 6
Congressional elections, 2, 22. Election
     of 1998, 2
Conversation, and news consumption,
     63–66, 118
Cosby, William, 96
Cosmopolitan, 30, 59
Countdown with Keith Olbermann, 125
Cowell, Simon, 2
Cozad, Kanon, 35, 37–39, *38*, 76, 90;
     followed local news closely,
     78; inspired by September 11 to
     deepen news knowledge, 69
Credibility. *See* Media credibility
Cronkite, Walter, 85; childhood
     influences, 66; report from
     Vietnam in 1968, 15, 51–52
C-SAT, a proposal for a college
     entrance exam, 119
Cummings, Jonathon, 71
Cynicism, 40–41

D

Daily Show, 57, 125
Darnton, Robert, 58
Daschle, Tom, 35, 59, 61, 113
Dateline, 59
Davis, Allison, 40
DDB Needham polls, 19–21, 87
Dean, Howard, 91
Debates, U.S. presidential, 120–21
*Declaration of Independence in
     Cyberspace*, 15, 102

Delli Carpini, Michael X., 21, 24, 25,
     86–88
Democratic national convention, 1968,
     119–20
Demographics, television news, x, 3
     See Television news viewership;
     Newspaper readership and
     reading habits
Depth in the news, 29–30
Dewey, John, 15, 90, 121–22
Diana, Princess of Wales, 122
Dickens, Charles, 41–42
Dionne, E. J., Jr., 6, 120
Diplomatic License, 42
Disney, 7, 51–53, 97, 115
Disturbed causality, 58
Dole, Bob, 56
Dominion Post (West Virginia),
     81–82
Donley, Jon, 74–75
Douglass, Frederick, 104
Downie, Len Jr., 80, 85–86, 112
Ducks Unlimited, 62–63, 118

E

Economist, 38
Editor and Publisher, 79–80
Edwards, John, 113
Eisner, Michael, 52, 115
Elections. *See* Presidential Elections,
     Congressional Elections, Voting
E-mail, 71, 77
Entertainment, 13–14, 39–59, 118
Entman, Robert, 54, 78
ER, 57
ESPN, 14, 25, 113, 125
ESPN (Magazine), 30

F

F Troop, 51
Far Side, 107, *107*

FCC (Federal Communications
        Commission), 52, 80, 101, 103,
        115–16
FEC (Federal Election Commission), 120
Federal Matching Funds, 120–21
Fisher, Amy, 56–57
Fishkin, James, 116
Food Network, 14
Forbes, Steve, 23–24
Fourth Estate, 96
Fox News, 14, 32, 54–55, 124–25
Frankel, Max, 58, 66–67, 98–100, 123
Frasier's dilemma, 41–43
Free newspapers aimed at youth,
        113–15
Friedland, Lewis, 14, 91
Friedman, Thomas, 14, 89, 105
Friends, 47–48

G

Galston, William A., 91
Gannett, 100
Garrison, William L., 104
Gatekeeper function of the press, 50–51
General Social Survey, 28–29
Ginsburg, Ruth B., 68
Gitlin, Todd, 97
Google News, 117, *117*
Gore, Al, 1
Graham, Katherine, 97
Greatest democracy for the greatest
        numbers, test, 123
Greeley, Horace, 77–79, 97–98
Greenhouse, Linda, 98
Gulf War (1991), 6
Gunther, Marc, 107
Gutenberg, Johannes, 43

H

Habermas, Jürgen, 11
Halbert, R. Lance, 72

Hallin, Daniel, 98
Hapathy, 6
Harper, Aaron, 59–63, *62*, 68, 76, 79, 90
Hatch, Orrin, 23–24
Hear it Now, 85
Hearst, William R., 45, 101
Heyward, Andrew, 26
Homelessness, 49
Hot and cold media, 73
Hudson, Rock, 109
Humanity in the news, 47–48, 125
Hustler (online), 33

I

I Love Lucy, 15, 51
Imagined communities. *See* Anderson,
        Benedict
In the News, 115–16
Independent journalism, 96–101
Independent voters, 23
Instant messenger. *See* AOL Instant
        Messenger
InStyle, 30
Intellectual arbitrage, 103–5
Internet, 32–33, 38, 70–76; making
        choices on, 73–76; online
        communities and real ones,
        compared and contrasted,
        89–94; rising popularity of, 70,
        89; tuning in on the 'net, 76
Interviews with young people:
        Burlington, Vt., 40–42;
        Colchester, Vt., 66–68, 119;
        Kansas City, 37–39, 61, 65, 68,
        78–79; Los Angeles, 59–63, 65,
        68–69, 78–79, 82; New Orleans,
        35, 65, 67–70, *67*, 74, 82, 92–93,
        117; Waltham, Mass. (Brandeis
        University), 47–48, 65, 69, 71,
        86, 118, 124; *See also* Alford,
        Andrea; Davis, Allison;
        Melancon, Cory; Salzfass,
        Lizzie; Senesac, Joel; Rose, Chris

Iraq War, 106, 124; misperceptions
  about, 124
Iverson, Allen, 59, 61

J

Jackass. See MTV
Jackson, Jesse, 46
Jackson, Michael, 44, 122
Jackson, Randy, 2
James, Clive, 45
Jefferson, Thomas, 6
Jennings, Peter, 14, 47–48, 51, 53
Johnson, Lyndon B., 95
Jones, David, 72

K

Kaelin, Kato, 60
Kaiser, Robert G., 80, 85–86, 112
Kaniss, Phyllis, 79
Kansas City interviews. *See* Interviews,
  Kansas City
Katz, Jon, 67
Keeter, Scott, 21, 24, 25, 86–88
Kennedy, John F. Jr., 122
Kerry, John F., 91
Keyes, Alan, 23–24
Keys, Alicia, 39, 59, 61
King, Larry, 48
Knowledge of political facts. *See* News
  knowledge
Koppel, Ted, 51–52, 97
Kovach, 110, 122
Kraut, Robert, 65, 71, 72, 75, 89
Kuralt, Charles, 89
Kwak, Nojin, 72

L

L. A. Pierce Junior College, 60, 68
Larson, Gary, 107

Late Show with David Letterman, 56
Late-night comedians as news source,
  57
Law and Order, 57
Lay, Kenneth, 50
Lenin, Vladimir I., 40
Lennon, John, 40
Leno, Jay, 107
Letterman, David, 52, 56, 97
Lewinsky, Monica, 46, 48
Liberator, 104
Limbaugh, Rush, 14, 31, 55
Lincoln, Abraham, 97–98
Lincoln-Douglas debates, 56
Lippmann, Walter, 85; debate with
  Dewey, 121–22; stages of press
  history, 96–97; story about
  Pacific island, 9–11
Literacy, 5
Livingston, John, 110
Local news, 77–94; decline in local and
  statewide political coverage,
  81–82; declines in viewership,
  83; and ethical lapses, 79–81;
  and its poor business practices
  and coverage, 79–83; and
  violence, 81
London plan, 45
Long Island Lolita / Slobodan
  Milosevic inverse correlative,
  56–57
Long, Mike, 66
Los Angeles Times, 7, 54, 79–80,
  100
Lynching, 16

M

Maher, Bill, 125
Marketplace of ideas, 103–5
Martin, Ricky, 47
Mass public and mass private, birth
  of, 74

Massification, 88–89

Maxim, 30, 59

McCain, John, 2, 23–25, 33

McCain-Feingold, 24–25, 37

McLeod, Jack M., 87

McLuhan, Marshall, 73

Media consumption by media type, 27–33

Media credibility, 4, 7

Melancon, Cory, 75–76, *75*

Mercer, Rick, 106

Mercy Hospital, 80

Milosevic, Slobodan, 56–57

Milton, John, 104–5

Moyers, Bill, 125

Ms., 35–37, *36*

MSNBC, 32

MTV, 4, 14; Clinton appears on MTV and answers "boxers or briefs?" question, 126; network's show, *Jackass*, 33, 53; network's show, *Real World*, 53; Powell appears on MTV, 56

Mumford, Lewis, 9

Murrow, Edward R., 85, *85*

N

Nader, Ralph, 102

Nakednews.com, 14, 55–56, *56*

National Enquirer, 30, 43, 46

National Honor Society, 86, 118

National Public Radio (NPR), 30–31, 38, 48, 53, 124

NBC News, 58–59

Need v. want, 41–47

Negroponte, Nicholas, 11

New Orleans interviews. *See* Interviews, New Orleans

New Orleans Times-Picayune, 53, 70, 93–94

New Orleans, 70, 92–94; as a model of diversity and community, 92–94

New York Herald, 45, 96

New York Sun, 45

New York Times, 7, 33, 37, 52, 62; as a beautiful reflection of democracy, 94; independence of, 46, 97–98, 100; median reader age, 76; newspaper's appeal to readers' tastes, 46–47, 124; as part of a large media universe, 33; read by New Orleans middle school students, 68; readers' tendency to remain on the front page, 58

New York World, 96–97

New Yorker, 30

News ballads, 43, *44*

News interest, by age, 20–21; by income, 20; by gender; 20, by race, 20

News knowledge, 12, 23–25, 35–41. Knowledge of political facts during 2000 campaign, 23–25

News magazines, 30

Newspaper readership and reading habits, ix, 3, 28–30, 76; in Germany, 29

Newspaper strike of 1945, 63

Newsroom (Los Angeles), 60

Newsweek, 30, 49, *50*

Nick News, 116

Nightline, 51–52, 65

Nixon, Jackie, 31, 53

Nixon, Richard M., 35, 97, 122

Nola.com, 70, 74–76

Nonpartisanship, 7, 96–101

Nonvoters, 21–23

Norris, Pippa, 72, 101

Nostalgia, 5

Now with Bill Moyers, 125

NPR. *See* National Public Radio

O

O'Brien, Miles, 18–19

Olbermann, Keith, 125

Onion, 57
Organizations. *See* clubs and
     organizations
Osbourne, Ozzy, 33

P

Paine, Thomas, 110
Parent Teacher Association. *See* PTA
Party affiliation, 22–23
Pataki, George, 7
Patterson, Thomas, 108
PBS. *See* Public Broadcasting
     Service
Peiser, Wolfram, 28–29
Penny Press, 45
Pentagon papers, 97
People, 49, 50
Personal digital assistant, programming
     news on, 38
Pew Research Center for the People &
     the Press; polls revealing
     knowledge of candidates and
     issues, 24–25; poll revealing late
     night comedians as a source for
     news, 57; poll revealing news
     interest, by age, 18; poll
     revealing party affiliation, by
     age, 23; poll revealing
     percentage of Americans who
     understood the federal budget,
     11; revealing declines in local
     news consumption, 83; time
     studies, 29, 32
Pindell, James, 81
Plato, 5
Playboy Channel, 14
Political engagement, 26
Political power, the news as a check on,
     29–30, 96–98, 126–27
Poutine, "Prime Minister," 106
Powell, Colin, ix, 56
Power Rangers, 106
Presidential elections 1–2, 11, 22–25;
     accessing election news in 2000,

70; compared with American
     Idol, 1–2; election of 2000, 102,
     108; election of 2004: 11, 25, 91;
     knowledge of candidates and
     issues, 23–24
Printing Press, 43
Profits, 98–103
Progressive differentiation, 88–89
Project for Excellence in Journalism,
     123
Prolonged adolescence, 65–66
PTA, 8, 83
Public Broadcasting Service, 124
Public journalism, 11, 121, 126
Public trust expectation. *See* FCC
Pulitzer, Joseph, 45, 96, 100
Putnam, Robert D., 39, 65–66, 87; civic
     involvement and trust, 69;
     decline of social capital, 7,
     83–84; Internet, news
     consumption, and civic
     involvement, 71–73; news
     media consumers as generalists,
     31–32; newspaper readership,
     28–29; offers solutions to
     excessive media consumption,
     115; plan to rebuild social
     capital, 121–22

Q

Quality journalism, promoting, 122–24
Quayle, Dan, 23–24
Question time, 121

R

Radio news, 30
Rather, Dan, 14, 48, 53, 80; compared
     with Victoria Sinclair of
     Nakednews.com, 54–56; median
     viewer age of his news show, 3;
     punched during the 1968

Rather, Dan, (*Continued*)
    Democratic national
    convention, 120; *See also*
    CBS News
Readership Institute, 113
Reagan, Ronald, 29, 122
Real Time with Bill Maher, 125
Real World. See MTV
Red Streak, 113
RedEye, 113–115, *114,* 124
Rehnquist, William, 40, 68
Revolutionary War, 109–10
Richmond, Barbara, 42
Rivers, Joan, 47
Rock, Chris, 47–48
Roe v. Wade, 37
Roosevelt, Theodore, 46
Roper ASW, 33
Rose, Chris, 53–54, 64, 93
Rosen, Jay, 11, 90, 103
Rosenfeld, Norman, 26, 61–62
Rosenstiel, Tom, 50–51, 110, 122
Rosenthal, Abe, 98
Roth, Richard, 42
Rumsfeld, Donald, 68
Rynders, Isaiah, 104

S

Safer, Morley, 95
Salant, Jonathan, 82
Salon, 54
Salzfass, Lizzie, 35–39, *36,* 41, 65, 69;
    discusses the "college bubble,
    65; protests contrasted with
    online communities, 90;
    tolerance of, 101–2
SAT, 5, 119
Scalia, Antonin, 68
Schumer, Chuck, 37
Schwarzenegger, Arnold, 47; 2003
    California race, 82
Seacrest, Ryan 1, 48

Seditious libel, 96
See it Now, 85, *85*
Seinfeld, 15
Sen, Amartya, 127
Senesac, Joel, 63, *64,* 69, 90, 118
Sensationalism, 43–47
September 11, 2001, 17, 30, 110;
    high news consumption on
    that date and in the days
    following, 18; misconceptions
    surrounding the attacks, 106;
    the need for good journalism
    following the changes wrought
    by the event, 55
Shah, Dhavan, 12, 57, 72, 87
Shapiro, Andrew, 116
Shawn, William, 46
Shenk, David, 59
Simpson, O. J., 79, 122
Simpsons, 65
Sinclair Broadcast Group, 81
Sinclair, Victoria, 55–56, *56*
Six Feet Under, 57
Smallpox, 105
So Hyang Yoon, 87
Soap operas, 113
Social capital, 39; decline of, 7–12,
    84. *See also* Civic
    involvement
Socrates, 5
Solutions, 112–27; existing, 112–15
Soren, Tabitha, 4
Spears, Britney, 47–48, 53, 64, 124;
    compared with William
    Rehnquist, 40; how newspapers
    use the pop star to attract
    readers, 113
Sports, knowledge of, 4
Sportscenter. See ESPN
Stanton, Frank, 95
Staples Center fiasco. *See Los Angeles
    Times*
Stephens, Mitchell, 10, 14, 43
Stewart, Jon, 57, 125
Studdard, Ruben, 1–2

Suburbia, 9, 83
Sunstein, Cass, 15, 116
Super-empowered individuals, 105
Supreme Court, U.S., ix, 2, 39, 61, 68.
    See also names of individual
    justices
Survivor, 40, 53. *See also* Interviews,
    Burlington, Vt.

U

U.S. News and World Report, 30, *50*
United Missouri Bank (UMB), 37–39,
    68. *See also* Interviews with
    young people, Kansas City
Universal white manhood suffrage, 21,
    26
Updike, John, 102

T

Teen People, 30
Telegraph, 103–5
Television and social capital, 8–9
Television news viewership, x, 3,
    31–32; local news, 83
Television viewership, 1, 3, 12, 15,
    31–32
Television, technical changes in, 49–51
Temptation Island, 53
Thin citizenship, 21–25
Thomas, Clarence, 68
Thomas, Isaiah, 110
Time, 30, 49, *50*
Times Mirror Center for The People &
    The Press, 19, 25, 34, 56–57
Times Mirror, 100. *See also Los
    Angeles Times*
Tocqueville, Alexis de, 13, 45, 88, 90
Tolerance, 16–17, 86–87, 101–2
Tonight Show, 107
Tönnies, Ferdinand, 145 n. 45
Torricelli, Robert, 98
Trends in news consumption, 19–21,
    26–27
Trumpet of the Swan, 74
Trumpeter Swan Society, 74, *74*
Trust, 87–88; in government, 4, 7, 69.
    See also Media credibility
Tuned in young people. *See* Alford,
    Andrea; Cozad, Kanon; Harper,
    Aaron; and Senesac, Joel
Tuning back in. *See* Solutions

V

Values of young people, 27
Vietnam War, 51, 95, 109
Viewership. *See also* television
    viewership and television news
    viewership
Volunteerism, 86, 118
Voting, 2, 21–23; and race, 92

W

Wall Street Journal, 7, 48, 97–98,
    124
Wallace, Mike, 120
Walters, Barbara, 48
Wars. *See* Afghanistan War, Gulf War,
    Iraq War, Revolutionary War,
    Vietnam War
Washington Post, 7, 58–59, 97, 118
Washington, George, 110
Watergate, 95, 122
WBAL (Baltimore), 80
WCBS (New York City), 80
Weaver, Sigourney, 47
Webb, James Watson, 45, 96
Wells, Ida B., 16
West Wing, 57
Westin, David, 52
White, Byron, 37
White, E. B., 27, 74

Whitman, Walt, 16, 94, 108–9
Willes, Mark, 100
Williams, Brian, 14
Williams, Jody, 90
Windsurfing, 73
Woods, Tiger, 53
Workplace influence on news
    consumption, 61–62
WWL (New Orleans), 94

X

YAHOO! Internet Life, 30
Yahoo! News, 117

Z

Zenger, John Peter, 96